BARRY KĀTZ was born in 1950 in Chicago, Illinois. He studied the history of social and political thought at McGill University, Montreal, and went on to do postgraduate research at the London School of Economics and then at the University of California, Santa Cruz, where he received his PhD in 1980. Barry Kātz currently teaches in the Program in Values, Culture and Technology at Stanford University, California, and is editor of the forthcoming *Decision: An Anthology of Free Culture*.

Barry Kātz

Verso

Herbert Marcuse and the Art of Liberation

An Intellectual Biography

An early version of chapter 1 appeared as 'New Sources of
Marcuse's Aesthetics' in *New German Critique*, 17, spring 1979.

First published 1982

© Barry Martin Kātz 1982

Verso Editions and NLB
15 Greek Street, London W1

Filmset in Baskerville by
Wayside Graphics, Clevedon, Bristol

Printed and bound in Great Britain by
Thetford Press, Norfolk

British Library
Cataloguing in Publication Data

Kātz, Barry
    Herbert Marcuse and the art of liberation
    1. Marcuse, Herbert
    I. Title
    193   B33035.M/

    ISBN 0-86091-050-4
    ISBN 0-86091-750-9 Pbk

CONTENTS

To the Kātz family
To the memory of Herbert Marcuse

We must do something about this immediately!

HERBERT MARCUSE

ACKNOWLEDGEMENTS

From 1976 to 1979 I held intensive discussions with Herbert Marcuse on biographical and theoretical aspects of this work. I believe I have honoured the agreements that existed between us, but he did not live to see this study in a complete or finished form, and it must therefore be regarded as my personal interpretation and appreciation.

Many friends and relatives of Herbert Marcuse assisted me with interviews, correspondence, or informal discussion which I hope I have used in a responsible way. I wish to thank Dr and Mrs Eric Marcuse, Mrs Else Dannen, Erica Sherover-Marcuse, Mrs Harriet Henze, Mr Osha Neumann, Professors Leo Löwenthal, H. Stuart Hughes, Bernard Morris, Jürgen Habermas, Carl Schorske, Gabriel Almond, and Victoria Bonnell.

A number of friends and scholars, including Drs Thomas Bass, Jonathan Beecher, Josef Chytry, Martin Jay, Conrad Johnson, Francis Mulhern, and Hayden White have been generous with their time and uncompromising in their criticism. To thank them at this point may be superfluous, but I am happy to do so once again.

Professor Norman O. Brown – a model, for me, of a certain kind of teacher and intellectual – pronounced a severe judgement upon what I naively believed to be a final draft. I recognize that the extensive revisions and corrections that followed only begin to meet his objections, and that to do so fully a different book would be required; I hope he writes it.

Finally, I wish to thank the various agencies of the University of California at Santa Cruz that provided me with the institutional and financial support that enabled me to complete this project: the Board of Studies in the History of Consciousness and especially my friend Billie Harris who must by now be aware of my admiration and appreciation, Provost Joe Silverman and the staff and fellows of Stevenson College, Mrs Joan Hodgson and her Inter-Library Loan staff, and my friend Sharon Báez who performed so heroically at the typewriter.

INTRODUCTION

Herbert Marcuse died in Starnberg, near Munich, as the conclusion of this biography was being prepared. In the course of winning his cooperation in this project, an exchange took place in his living-room that may reflect him as precisely as anything written here. I had made the mistake of quoting Marcuse to himself in order to combat his reticence: 'Historical Materialism has never denied the individual as a historical force.' (1929) He raised his eyebrows and gave me what I deserved: 'Aber *ich* bin keine "geschichtliche Kraft!".' In the following study of the course of his life and thought I suggest that Marcuse was mistaken in his modest but undialectical claim, and I regret that I have not been able to confront him with my final conclusions.

It is gratifying to find examples where the turning points of a century – their given character, but also their historical constitution and future potentialities – are so precisely reflected in the evolution of an intellectual career: the decline of the pre-1914 imperial bourgeoisie, two world wars, the betrayal of both European liberalism and Soviet Marxism, and the present period of apparent stabilization – but also the insistent presence of a radical opposition, the militant fellowship of intellectual comrades-in-arms, and the perpetual flowering of a defiant avant-garde. Is it really so unlikely, then, that his work should have become a 'historical force' in the world of politics and ideas?

Parallel to this historical argument runs a philosophical interpretation which proposes that the work of the Marxist Herbert Marcuse can best be understood as an attempt to articulate a dimension of life and a corresponding domain of consciousness in which a frankly transcendent standard is operative. This suggests not a metaphysical quest, however, but a political one, for the practical function of this theoretical construct has been to provide a standard of criticism against which the prevailing reality may be judged and condemned in terms of its own potentialities. The *praxis* of political revolution, then, is always mediated by the *poiesis* of the aesthetic imagination, and the truth, for Marcuse, lay in the tension between the two. Indeed, although philosophical and psychoanalytical categories provide the vehicle for his quest at important stages of his career, the clearest access to this dimension has been through the work of art; consequently, the primacy of aesthetics in the evolution of his thought will prove to be central to this interpretation.

Herbert Marcuse was neither systematic nor always explicit in his view of the integration of the political and the poetical transformation of the world. As a result, it has not been possible to confine this presentation to an explication of a body of published books and essays, and support has been drawn from unpublished writings, personal interviews, declassified government documents, as well as from the historical contours of the life itself. If Marcuse derived the poetic standard from the timeless and unchanging reaches of aesthetic Form, the practical imperatives were imposed by the events of the twentieth century, and these will enter the discussion in so far as they entered his philosophical work. Similarly, there are periods in which Marcuse's personal circumstances provide a necessary backdrop to an understanding of his intellectual work, and these will also be recorded where appropriate. It may be added, however, that parallel to his advocacy of a political life was his abiding concern over the erosion of the private sphere in the advanced industrial societies, and this theoretical and practical concern has been respected. Those who are interested in knowing more about 'what kind of a man he was' can really do no better than read his books.

PART ONE

ORIGINS
(1898~1920)

'A Berlin Childhood Around 1900'

At the end of 1879, in the first of a celebrated series of articles, the distinguished historian Heinrich von Treitschke sounded an alarm to the German nation: 'Year after year there pours over our Eastern frontier . . . from the inexhaustible Polish cradle, a host of ambitious, trouser-selling youths, whose children and children's children are one day to dominate Germany's stock exchanges and newspapers . . .'. If Treitschke had included radical leftist politics in the spheres of modern Prussian life to be dominated by the descendents of those 'ambitious, trouser-selling' Jewish youths, his prophecy would have been complete, and he would have accounted for the ancestry of Herbert Marcuse.

Carl Marcuse was born in 1864, into a prosperous family of horse-traders in the Pomeranian village of Greifenhagen; there is some evidence to suggest that his ancestors had drifted north following the expulsion of Jews from Spain at the end of the fifteenth century. This was the beginning of a period of mass internal migration from the eastern provinces of the empire to the urban centres, and true to Treitschke's formula, he and his two brothers became part of the continuous shift to the capital which had swollen the Jewish population of Berlin to nearly five per cent by the turn of the century. Although his gradually acquired 'Junker habitus' hardly fitted the pervasive stereotype of the typical trouser-selling Eastern Jew – a photograph shows a huge equestrian in a commanding pose, manoeuvring his horse through the Grünewald – he did indeed enter the expanding German textile trade. He started young, but advanced steadily to a full partnership in his firm, and was already a successful Berlin businessman when, in 1895 or 1896, he married Gertrud Kreslawsky. She was a talented and literate woman whose family (originally from East Prussia) owned a paper factory that specialized in gilded book edges, and thus owed its fortune to an affluent and increasingly cultivated German bourgeoisie. The first of their three children – Herbert – was born on 19 July 1898; a sister, Else, followed in 1902, and a brother, Erich, in 1907.

The children were raised in a period of general economic prosperity that especially favoured the expanding industrial and commercial middle class. With the reversal, beginning in 1896, of two decades of economic depression, a temporary, deceptive ebbing of the wave of anti-semitism that had welled up in the 1880s and 1890s lent a further sense of security to a conspicuous part of that class.[1] The circumstances of the Marcuse family in particular were quite comfortable, for Carl Marcuse was an enterprising individual, far-sighted and versatile. He had begun his business career, moreover, in circumstances that were excellent from a commercial point of view. The peace terms of the Franco-Prussian War, out of which the German Reich had emerged in 1871, provided for the annexation of the territories of Alsace-Lorraine, and with them Germany inherited a mature network of weaving and spinning mills. Interrupted only by a decade of economic liberalism in the Caprivi era, the German textile industry was to flourish, under the benevolence of a system of state protectionism and moderate tariffs.[2]

The personal fortunes of Carl Marcuse ran parallel to those of the industry generally, but with success came boredom. After the birth of their third child, he shifted his business interests into real estate – building and property development – and the resultant firm of 'Friedenthal und Marcuse' brought an architect and a businessman into mutually profitable alliance. Herbert Marcuse, then, like Horkheimer, Lukács, and a significant number of other radical social critics of his generation, grew up in an extremely comfortable household that extended to him the material offerings of the capitalist system. It is significant that his later challenge to the bourgeois social order was to be directed against its moral and

1. Sources for this period include Peter Pulzer, *The Rise of Political Anti-Semitism in Germany and Austria,* New York 1964, pp. 75–126, and Werner Angress, 'Prussia's Army and the Jewish Reserve Officer Controversy Before WWI', James Sheehan, ed., *Imperial Germany,* New York 1976, pp. 93–115. (Much of the material presented in part 1 is drawn from interviews and correspondence with Herbert Marcuse and members of his family over the years 1976–79.)

2. Cf. J. H. Clapham, *Economic Development of France and Germany, 1815–1914,* Cambridge 1966, ch. 11; Gustav Stolper, *German Economy 1870–1940. Issues and Trends,* New York 1940, part 2, chs. 2, 6.

cultural foundations, presupposing at least the possibility of a substantial measure of economic well-being.

There is, however, little in this 'Berlin childhood around 1900' that appears directly to prefigure the directions he would later follow – indeed, in its broad outlines his early biography corresponds closely to the social history of the ascending industrial-commercial bourgeoisie of the late empire.[3] The family was solidly patriarchal, dominated by a strict and imposing father against whom Frau Marcuse served as 'a softer counterweight'. Together, the parents fitted well enough into the cultural stereotype of 'typical Jewish liberals', well-to-do and comfortably assimilated into the German upper middle class: they attended synagogue twice annually on the Jewish High Holidays, expressed a fashionable and probably self-conscious distaste for the conspicuous wave of *Ostjuden* that followed them to Berlin, and celebrated Christmas for its prominent, pagan *'Natursymbol'*.

In the political sphere, their electoral allegiance ultimately came to rest – predictably enough – with the prestigious German Democratic Party, created out of the shambles of post-war German political life. Prior to the First World War, Carl Marcuse's liberal principles may have occasioned some sympathy for the Progressives, the left wing of middle-class opinion, but the Progressive Party drew little support from the industrial and commercial bourgeoisie, and the class identification of the family was clearly with the protectionist, expansionist, and anti-socialist National Liberal establishment. For the elders of the Marcuse family, disdain for the Social Democratic Party was more a matter of class snobbery toward the *Arbeiterpartei*, 'the party of the working class', than of politics.

At the age of six, Herbert Marcuse was enrolled in a Berlin *Vorschule* or preparatory school, already a fact not without significance in Wilhelmine Germany where the educational system was a consciously and conspicuously organized facet of a hierarchical society confronting modernization. Unlike the eight-year *Volksschule*, which the vast majority of German school children attended in the course of being fashioned into the industrious producers, obedient soldiers, and loyal subjects of the Reich, the exclusive *Vorschulen*

---

3. Walter Benjamin's highly personal memoirs – 'Berliner Kindheit um Neunzehnhundert' (*Gesammelte Schriften*, IV, i, Frankfurt 1972) and *Berliner Chronik*, Gershom Scholem, ed., Frankfurt 1970, capture some of the social and domestic ambience of their generation.

provided a three-year course of instruction designed to prepare the children of parents who could afford it for admission to a Gymnasium at the age of nine or ten. In 1907, on schedule, the nine-year-old Marcuse entered Berlin's Mommsen Gymnasium, named after the only prominent 'mandarin' academician to rise publicly against the nationalist and anti-semitic excesses of Treitschke.

Throughout the nineteenth century, the classical German Gymnasium had been the route to the universities, and then to the higher ranks of civil service, most professions, and the host of special privileges and offices open to the proportionately small educated or 'cultivated' elite. In the traditional social order, this was a highly functional hierarchy in which an academically trained elite was groomed for careers of power, status, and influence, while the Latin secondary schools, the *Realschulen*, trained young people for technical and clerical positions in commerce and industry.

Viewed against the rapidly shifting class structure of Imperial Germany, the content of primary and secondary education, as well as the very organization of the school system, 'served as a brake upon social mobility and tended to freeze the existing social system'.[4] In a period of widespread accommodation to norms increasingly set by industry and technology, however, the classical Gymnasium education, structured around Greek and Latin and devoted to traditional humanistic ideals of self-cultivation, no longer guaranteed access to the highest economic and political positions. If prominent members of the entrepreneurial classes began to allow their sons to pursue the classical, humanistic course of higher education, this would have to be regarded as a luxury item of secondary practical value, a link with old elites at the level of status. Carl Marcuse, *nouveau riche* and himself with no more than a Gymnasium education, seems to have had a strong sense of the limits of mere wealth in a society – even a changing society – that had traditionally conferred distinct status privileges upon its

---

4. Gordon Craig, *Germany, 1866–1945,* Oxford 1978, p. 189; cf. also Fritz K. Ringer, *The Decline of the German Mandarins,* Cambridge 1969, pp. 42–61; Thomas Alexander, *The Prussian Elementary Schools,* New York 1918, ch. 3; and R. H. Samuel and R. H. Thomas, *Education and Society in Modern Germany,* London 1949, chs. 1–2. On the accommodation between new and old classes, cf. James Sheehan, 'Conflict and Cohesion among German Elites in the Nineteenth Century', in Sheehan, ed., *Imperial Germany,* New York 1976, pp. 62–92.

academically educated citizens, for this was the course chosen for his eldest son at an early age.

Marcuse's conscious immersion in the tradition of Western intellectual and aesthetic culture really began, then, at the Kaiserin Augusta Gymnasium in the fashionably modern suburb of Charlottenburg – in 1911 the family and household staff had moved from the crowded central district into a luxurious ten-room apartment in the building in the Bismarckstrasse designed and built by the firm of 'Friedenthal und Marcuse'.[5] Berlin had been transformed, almost literally within the space of a generation, from an austere and regimented imperial *Residenz* into an industrial capital and the political and economic hub of the most advanced nation in continental Europe. After the turn of the century its cultural evolution began to keep pace with the commercial and administrative importance of the city in ways that would have been plainly felt by an alert secondary school student. Indeed, it was the feeling of Stefan Zweig, who has left a richly textured (if politically naive) description of Berlin in these years, that with its generously endowed museums, theatrical productions, and musical offerings, it held out tremendous promises precisely to the young, for 'just because there was no real tradition, no century-old culture, youth was tempted to try its hand'.[6]

From the very beginning, it was this 'high culture' to which Herbert Marcuse was drawn. Indeed, by way of contrast, it was only for a very brief and not especially memorable period in his early adolescence that he participated in one of the great movements of 'popular culture' of Imperial Germany. By joining a group of boys in a hiking club he became part of the sizeable and controversial social movement known in its first phase (until 1919) as the *Wandervogel*, which swept the urban, middle-class youth of his generation. However diverse, unsystematic, or overtly apolitical its proclamations may have been, the camaraderie and rebellious idealism of the *Wandervogel* themselves suggested an alternative to the mundane bonds of bourgeois existence: 'Nature', 'Eros', 'the *Volk*' were celebrated as the basis of genuine community. The fact, however, that in his teens Marcuse evinced only the most short-lived

5. Christopher Isherwood leaves some illuminating descriptions of this district in his *Berlin Stories* (1935).
6. Stefan Zweig, *The World of Yesterday*, New York 1964, p. 112; cf. also Gerhard Masur, *Imperial Berlin*, New York 1970, chs. 3–5.

and half-hearted interest in the German Youth Movement – with its characteristic *Volksgemeinschaft* rhetoric and profoundly bad artistic taste – strongly suggests that his cultural orientations were already developing in the direction of an elitism of a quite different sort.[7]

Though the status of the 'Jewish *Volk*' within the *Wandervogel* movement was always problematic, this uncertainty did not dampen the enthusiasm of numerous Prussian-Jewish schoolboys of Herbert's age and background, and it was surely not this feature of its ill-defined *Weltanschauung* that drove him from its ranks. Indeed, he was at this time not much more attentive to 'the Jewish Question' than his parents, for, like a conspicuous number of his later colleagues, he was born into a well-assimilated Berlin household against which he felt little inclination to assert a distinct Jewish identity. In general, the family felt itself to be solidly German: Carl Marcuse's gentile associations were numerous – mostly arising out of his passionate devotion to his riding club – and no noteworthy incidences of anti-semitism disrupted the complacent routine of their lives.

The three children, in their turn, attended synagogue indifferently, resistantly, and only under the moral compulsion of their (maternal) grandparents. Herbert in particular, in addition to his regular course of Gymnasium studies, did attend weekly religious instruction, but brought to it such an evident lack of seriousness that the presiding rabbi felt moved to assure him that it was most doubtful whether he would ever become a useful participant in society. Unshaken by this admittedly ambiguous prophecy, Marcuse concluded his religious studies with his Bar Mitzvah in 1911, and it reflects further upon his milieu that the gifts he received (and continued to value) were mostly secular books. The fine sets of Schiller, Grillparzer, and Shakespeare in the Schlegel translation that lined the walls of his living-room in Southern California surely represented a most tenuous link with his Jewish ancestry.

The Bar Mitzvah, then, like the sporadic and ceremonial participation in the Jewish community of Berlin generally, had more the character of a bourgeois than of a specifically Jewish

---

7. On the *Wandervogel* movement, cf. Walter Laqueur, *Young Germany*, New York 1962, esp. chs. 5 and 9; George Mosse, *The Crisis of German Ideology*, New York 1964, pp. 171–89. Gustav Wyneken's group, to which Walter Benjamin had belonged, advocated political liberalism, religious toleration, and artistic experimentation, but was definitely a minority faction.

experience, a realization that served to persuade him that being Jewish was a mere historical accident, a matter of relative unimportance both to himself and to the surrounding social and cultural environment. Even when this widely held indifference was brutally corrected by the events of the 1930s, Marcuse revised not the 'subjective' side of his estimation of the importance of being Jewish, but only his view of its objective significance in modern European society: if his Jewish ancestry became a conscious factor at all in his identity, it was because he was so defined, rather than due to any internal motivation.

It was rather his secular studies that engaged Marcuse in this period, although intellectual stimulation could not come from many points in the still rigidly structured curriculum and disciplined environment of the Gymnasium. History was still the official *Regierungsgeschichte*, classical languages still constituted the focal point of instruction, and the prevailing social and political conventions of Imperial Germany were filtered down to students in such a way as to discourage the formation of critical perspectives: 'It sought to instil not so much the concept of the rights of the citizen but the duties of the subject.'[8] The life of the Gymnasium student could be so effectively insulated from the realities of political life that the young Marcuse was not particularly aware of the rising political tensions within the European political system during those years. Even the outbreak of the war, two weeks after his sixteenth birthday, caused no serious disruption in the routine of his life: seized neither by the prevailing war fever, nor by youthful sentiments of opposition, he recalled viewing it all as 'a damned nuisance'.

This is surely an exaggeration, however, for there clearly were, in those critical years, strong influences coming from the Gymnasium environment – not from the official curriculum, to be sure, but from the 'underground' fellowship of certain among his schoolfriends. He was already reading constantly, if not compulsively, but, little attracted by the absurdly virtuous Nordic supermen of the popular *Wandervogel* novels, he was drawn almost instinctively to the great works of every period and culture. At the same time, however, he and his friends were also reading theories of modern architecture and following the course of the Viennese *Sezession*, and had begun to explore sophisticated movements of literary modernism: in his years

---

8.   Paul Kosok, *Modern Germany: A Study of Conflicting Loyalties*, Chicago 1933, p. 164.

as a Gymnasium student Marcuse came to know the writers of the French avant-garde, especially Gide, the esoteric critical, historical, and poetic works of Stefan George and members of his circle, and also the early novels and short stories of Thomas and especially Heinrich Mann. And admittedly, even his classical studies were not sheer drudgery, for he was given a lasting sense of the vitality of Greek thought, above all through a course on Plato's *Apologia* taught by the director of the school.

It was, then, a secure and comfortable Berlin childhood, sheltered by a close-knit nuclear family, money, spacious homes, servants, European holidays, and summer excursions to the country, but also exposed both to the traditional monuments of the European cultural inheritance and to modernist experimentation. Freedom from pressing material concerns helped to distance the young Marcuse from the practical, social and political issues created by the expanding empire, and rather opened up for him the transcendental realm of art and ideas. The illusory serenity of the bourgeois way of life had already sustained heavy losses by 1914, however, and was completely shattered by the war that had broken over Europe in August. In the spring of 1916, the seventeen-year-old Herbert Marcuse was forced to conclude his Gymnasium studies with the emergency wartime *Notabitur* as he was conscripted into the Imperial German Reichswehr.

ii
'BERLIN ALEXANDERPLATZ'

In the last months of the war, the twenty-year-old narrator of Remarque's *All Quiet on the Western Front* summed up the shock and dislocation felt by a whole generation: 'Had we returned home in 1916, out of the suffering and the strength of our experiences we might have unleashed a storm. Now if we go back we will be weary, broken, burnt out, rootless, and without hope. We will not be able to find our way any more.' The experience of the war was decisive for Herbert Marcuse as well. He entered as a bookish high-school student from a comfortable upper-class suburb; two years later his role was that of a young revolutionary and militant assigned to stand in the Berlin Alexanderplatz with a rifle and return sniper fire.

Although the war had been raging for nearly two years by the time of Marcuse's conscription, its full impact had thus far been felt only on the front lines and in informed military and industrial circles. Fought on foreign soil, and filtered back to Germany in an indirect and distorted way, it still seemed remote to the civilian population. Wages dropped and prices rose, but the increasing subjection of civilian life to military control was not yet apparent: 'The belief was firmly held in Germany that the war would be fought by the military forces alone. It would leave civilians to continue their peaceful trades or professions . . .'.[1]

To a certain extent, then, it is understandable that in its earlier stages the war did not figure more prominently in the life and thoughts of the young Gymnasium student. Germany's war aims were presented in a chain of contradictory, ambiguous, and duplicitous official statements, and the war itself was being prose-

1. Albrecht Mendelssohn-Bartholdi, *The War and German Society. The Testament of a Liberal*, New Haven 1927, reissued 1971, p. 215.

cuted under a cloak of propaganda, censorship, suppression of public debate, and outright deception that extended to the highest levels of civilian life. It is telling that, after a year of desperate fighting on two fronts, the press in Germany was preoccupied with the extent of the territorial concessions to be demanded of France and Russia.

Herbert Marcuse was drafted into military service in the middle of 1916, one of the most disastrous years of the war for Germany, and was sent for training to Darmstadt, near Frankfurt, where he joined an army reserve unit, *Train-Ersatz-Abteilung 18*. By this time the prospects of military victory had come to look uncertain at best, as each of the three active fronts began to show serious signs of strain: in the West, early departure from the Schlieffen Plan had resulted in Germany's becoming stalemated in a protracted confrontation with more-than-equal enemy forces; this had prevented a decisive victory over the Russian armies on the Eastern front, despite the brilliant military manoeuvres of Hindenburg and Ludendorff; and on the domestic 'front' the *Burgfrieden* or 'Civil Truce' with which the Kaiser had lured the parliamentary parties into unanimous support of the war effort, had begun to break apart as the war dragged on and confidence in the Military High Command and the Imperial Government began to vanish among sections of all classes of the population. On the left, the hitherto dormant socialist opposition was finally stirred into activity, as dissident factions began to crystallize out of the ranks of the SPD around prominent critics of the war such as Eduard Bernstein, Karl Kautsky, and the militant radicals Karl Liebknecht and Rosa Luxemburg.

In August 1916, amid food riots, the first important political strikes, and the heightening of tensions between labour, industry, the bureaucracy and the military, the gradual militarization of broad spheres of civilian life became official with the accession of Hindenburg and Ludendorff to the Supreme Army Command, the latter's *de facto* seizure of absolute political power. From that point the course that Germany was to follow for the duration of the war was set.

Marcuse was fortunate, however, for his late-night readings of the European avant-garde now paid off handsomely: he had ruined his eyesight, and had to remain throughout the war in Germany. After his initial period of military training in Darmstadt he was transferred back to Berlin early in 1918, and he spent the duration of the war in the comparative safety of the *Luftschiffe-Ersatz-Abteilung 1* – the Zeppelin Reserves – in Potsdam. These airships had scored some devastating tactical successes against London and other British targets in the first half of the war, but as they began to succumb to new anti-aircraft defence systems, their military effectiveness was drastically reduced and only four bombing raids were carried out in the last year of the war. Accordingly, the military regimen of the soldiers connected with the Zeppelins became considerably relaxed, and Marcuse was even able to gain permission to attend lectures at Berlin University on an irregular basis. As long as he was not transferred, he enjoyed the wartime luxury of being able to concern himself with matters other than bare survival.

Even if he took every occasion to affirm his fittedness for the life of a scholar over that of a soldier, Marcuse could not and did not remain unaffected by his military environment. The reserve battalions, especially those garrisoned on German soil and virtually inactive throughout the war (as were, most significantly, the crews of the great battleships of the High Seas Fleet moored in Kiel and Hamburg), were the scene of some of the first challenges to the traditional military-feudal authorities, which were charged with the responsibility for bringing about and prolonging the increasingly unpopular war. Just as the contrast between general hardship and flagrant war profiteering, exploitation of labour, and political persecution was serving to exacerbate the civilian class tensions under the harsh conditions of war, dangerous antagonisms were also beginning to be felt within the Army and Navy, where the system of privileges enjoyed by the officers seemed insupportable. The excesses of the elite officer corps were especially obvious among the military units stationed at home, where no common danger mitigated the rigid military hierarchy, and the boredom and drudgery of endless, pointless drilling fuelled popular resentment and provoked a marked rebelliousness.[2]

As the promised six-week war entered its third year, confidence in the Imperial Government began to turn into outright hostility among still small but growing sectors of the German civilian

2. This characteristic pattern was confirmed in conversation as the experience of Marcuse. For background, cf. Arthur Rosenberg, *Imperial Germany. The Birth of the German Republic*, Boston 1964, ch. 3; A. J. Ryder, *The German Revolution of 1918*, Cambridge 1967, passim.

population, and there were likewise signs of radicalization among certain domestic military reserve units. It was in these circumstances that Herbert Marcuse, stationed in the political centre of the country, began to develop political consciousness. More mystified than outraged by the senselessness of the violence, he began to follow the debates being carried on within the opposition parties in the Reichstag, and increasingly to engage in political discussion himself. In 1917 he joined the Social Democratic Party, his first and last formal party affiliation.

The decisive factor in his radicalization was the war, which had brought the whole structure of German politics and society to the point of crisis, and had left him with powerful but inarticulate feelings of revulsion. In these critical years the search for alternatives was understandably widespread within his generation, and as the future of the German Empire was being threatened from without by military defeat, joining the SPD meant challenging its legitimacy from within. It was a fitting response from a hitherto apolitical young man of the middle class, and can be seen as a radical break with his past, even if membership involved little active participation, and even if the SPD was by this time a most uncertain heir to its revolutionary ancestry. Indeed, although it had frequently served as a powerful opposition party during peacetime, it was only in the year Marcuse joined that German Social Democracy was finally shaken into opposition to the war – at the heavy cost of socialist unity.

The SPD leadership had been lured into support for the war policy of the Imperial government by the promise of political and social reforms that would repay the German workers for their patriotic service to the national cause, and its members were bound to unanimity by the time-honoured principle of socialist *Fraktionsdis-ziplin.* There was, in addition, the spectre of the defeat of the nation that had engendered the most powerful and best-organized working-class movement in Europe, at the hands of Tsarist absolutism. As both the promises and threats bound up with the war effort came increasingly into question, however, so too did the party discipline that had imposed a fragile truce upon opposed factions and personalities within the party. Debate was reopened, not just around the issue of the proper socialist attitude toward the war, but on the very goals and tactics of the socialist movement itself. Although the roots of disunity reached far back into the history of the SPD, by the time of Marcuse's affiliation the break-up of German socialism was complete and involvement meant a choice among at least three political options.[3]

The SPD was guided by the moderate reformism of the Second International, and its position on the war was summed up by the slogan 'peace without annexations', reflecting the belief that Germany was engaged in a war of national defence against British and French imperialism in league with Russian absolutism. As early as December 1914, however, this official party line had been challenged by the lone dissenting voice of Karl Liebknecht in the Reichstag debate on the renewal of war credits, and by the spring of the following year a broad opposition group had begun to take shape. Dominated by such politically diverse figures as left-radical party leaders Haase and Ledebour, the centrist theoretician Karl Kautsky, and Eduard Bernstein on the right, this group, which came to be formally constituted in April 1917, as the Independent Social Democratic Party (USPD), embodied many of the same internal conflicts as the socialist movement as a whole.

Still, the greater part of the USPD membership stood decidedly to the left of the so-called 'Majority Socialists' of the SPD, irreconcilably opposed to the war and poised between the alternatives of parliamentary democracy and revolutionary proletarian dictatorship. This latter position was upheld by the revolutionary *Spartakusbund,* or Spartacus League, a militantly anti-war and internationalist group that had come to operate semi-autonomously within the USPD since July 1916. Though the following of the Spartacus League was never large, the sophistication of its political analysis and the commanding presence of its leadership – Liebknecht and Rosa Luxemburg – made it a conspicuous force in 1917, and one to be reckoned with by socialists.

None of the socialist parties presented a powerful and united opposition – the Independents were weakened by the attempt to contain widely divergent positions on the war and on socialism generally, and the Spartacists suffered from a hopelessly small base within the German working class – and the Majority Socialists remained the party most closely associated with the established

---

3. On 'the development of the great schism' within the SPD, cf. Carl Schorske, *German Social Democracy,* New York 1965; also Georges Haupt, *Socialism and the Great War,* Oxford 1972, for international ramifications.

government and its policies. For Marcuse to have joined the SPD at a time when its platform was being openly attacked and the hegemony of its leadership over German socialism publicly challenged cannot, therefore, have been entirely fortuitous.

Nor was this an unlikely identification for him at this time, for he was young, inexperienced, and came from a solidly middle-class background in which politics did not figure at all prominently. Like so many others of his generation, Marcuse's political education was acquired abruptly, imposed upon him by circumstances. At this juncture, the contradictions of the Wilhelmine political order had been exposed by the war, but it can hardly be said, even in retrospect, that the lines of a realistic socialist alternative were obvious. Nor can it be assumed that at this early point in his political career Marcuse felt that he had no stake whatsoever in certain of the economic and cultural institutions of the society in which he had been so comfortably raised. Accordingly, it is not surprising that his involvement in the SPD during the final years of the war was not that of a party activist, and involved little more than paying dues and reading *Vorwärts*.

However cautious his commitment may have been, this was nonetheless the period of Marcuse's political initiation: he remained a Social Democrat until the end of the war, and although he never became a party activist, he recalled that it was at this time that he began to explore the theoretical underpinnings of the socialist opposition in the writings of Marx. By the last months of the war, when military defeat had finally settled the fate of the Second German Empire, Marcuse was again called into action – not in the service of the Reich this time, but in the defence of the revolution.

Marcuse's situation was typical, in the months that saw the collapse of Germany in war and revolution. By the end of 1917, the threat to the socialist working class represented by Tsarist absolutism had been permanently removed, and together with the rapidly deteriorating conditions in the German cities, the argument for peace and reform seemed plain. It was the Berlin working class, behind the revolutionary shop stewards movement, that staged the first challenge to the virtual military dictatorship, launching a massive general strike at the end of January 1918. The Imperial Government held fast, however, and the socialist working class opposition, like the new leadership of Soviet Russia, was compelled to submit to the will of the General Staff. All was quiet now, except on the Western Front, as Quartermaster-General Ludendorff prepared to mount his final offensive in the spring of 1918.

The account of what followed belongs to the annals of military history, for it was the reversal of the great offensives in northern France that were to cost Germany the war, and it was the military defeat that made social revolution a possible, if not inescapable, course. On 29 September the Supreme Command, no longer able to guarantee a German victory, issued the famous demand for an armistice, and began to make arrangements for the reform of the Prussian suffrage, revision of the Bismarckian constitution, and the return of political power to the Reichstag – the democratization of the political system which the German middle class had abandoned after 1848. Despite the initiation of the process of reform, the Reichstag had lost touch with the nation and the masses had lost confidence in the Reichstag, which was unable to stem the rising tide of popular discontent. The revolution finally reached Berlin, via Kiel and Munich, on Saturday, 9 November, 'the day on which it was just impossible to carry on any longer'.[4]

Herbert Marcuse was still in Berlin, fortunate in not having been called to the front in the late months of the war when the American presence shifted the balance of fighting forces decisively in favour of the Allies. In the first week of November, once the sailors revolt had broken out in Kiel, army reservists whose discipline had already been in a state of the utmost fragility joined the revolutionaries, and the military revolt spread rapidly from Hamburg across Germany. Workers and Soldiers Councils were formed everywhere, and in a northern working-class suburb of Berlin, where understanding was low but excitement high, Marcuse was elected to the Reinickendorf *Soldatenrat.* Thus he found himself, as a soldier, a socialist, and an elected delegate of a Soldiers Council in Berlin, in the political storm-centre of the country.[5]

---

4. Philip Scheidemann, *Der Zusammenbruch,* p. 210. For the German revolution generally, cf. A. J. Ryder, *The German Revolution of 1918,* Cambridge 1967; D. W. Morgan, *The Socialist Left and the German Revolution,* Ithaca 1975; G. Ritter and S. Miller, *Die deutsche Revolution 1918–1919. Dokuments,* Hamburg 1975, and the highly informative *Illustrierte Geschichte der deutschen Revolution,* Berlin 1929.

5. Conversations with Marcuse (HM). The typical character of his experience is confirmed by Heinz Oeckel, *Die revolutionäre Volkswehr, 1918–19,* Berlin 1968, pp. 75–140, and Ulrich Kluge, *Soldatenräte und Revolution,* Göttingen 1975, chs. I.5 and II.2,3; cf. also the review of Kluge by David Morgan, *Central European History,* X, 3, September 1977, for more on political attitudes among the soldiers.

In the last months of the war, Marcuse's politics had evolved beyond those of the Spd, which was solidly a part of the government and its policies and devoid of a creative socialist vision. Although most of his comrades from the *Soldatenrat* were inexperienced political moderates, largely without ideological preconceptions and still prepared to endorse the Majority Socialist call for a constitutional republic, this course was becoming increasingly problematical for Marcuse. At the other political extreme, the Spartacus League saw the events of the first week of November as signalling not the conclusion, but the beginning of the revolutionary process, which must now be pursued through the dictatorship of the proletariat in alliance with international socialism. In the following weeks, Marcuse was to attend meetings at which Liebknecht and Rosa Luxemburg spoke, but he did not in fact ally himself with the Spartacists because, as he later claimed, their intransigent revolutionary aspirations were still remote from the reality of German working-class consciousness. Although the theory of an objectively possible class consciousness which could be rationally ascribed or 'imputed' (*zugerechnet*) to the working class was to be formulated for the first time only two years later,[6] if Marcuse's retrospective evaluation is accurate, he was already applying a standard that would theoretically justify his distance both from the reified consciousness of the 'empirical' proletariat, and from those socialists who identified themselves with it uncritically.

Poised between the demand for an early return to a national constituent assembly and for the expansion of the revolutionary council structure, the Independent Socialists were now showing signs of the very schism that had splintered the socialist movement during the war. Although Marcuse was already approaching the categorical refusal to compromise with a 'bad reality' that was to become associated with his name, his attraction to one revolutionary scenario enacted by the Uspd should be recorded: in Munich, an Independent Socialist faction headed by the visionary poet and idealist Kurt Eisner stepped into a momentary political vacuum and proclaimed a Bavarian Socialist Republic. Eisner, who was eulogized after his assassination as 'a *Schwärmer*, and at the same time a tireless

---

6. By Georg Lukács in his essay, 'Class Consciousness' (March 1920), published in his *Geschichte und Klassenbewusstsein* (1923); trans. Rodney Livingstone, *History and Class Consciousness*, London 1968, pp. 46–81, esp. p. 51f.

student of reality', attracted a following that included the idealistic poets and playwrights Ernst Toller, Erich Mühsam, and Gustav Landauer, and other young philosophers, artists, and littérateurs. Their attempt to transform revolutionary politics into an ethic and an aesthetic ended in murder, prison, and ridicule, but Marcuse nevertheless regarded the specifically 'aesthetic' dimension of Eisner's political movement with admiration, and always considered it to have represented one of the most progressive tendencies of the German revolution.[7]

The last weeks of 1918 were decisive – for the revolution, for Germany, and for Marcuse. He continued to attend political meetings, rallies, and street demonstrations, and, as part of the *Sicherheitswehren*, the civilian security force mobilized to defend against counter-revolution and reluctantly supported by the *Soldatenräte*, he was sent to the Alexanderplatz, detailed to return the fire of snipers. Such duties hardly found him in his proper element: he was frankly relieved by his discharge in December, and later confessed to his brother, 'I must have been crazy!'

The fledgling German Socialist Republic was also under fire during those weeks, maintaining a precarious existence amid heightening violence and internecine strife. Towards the end of December the three Independent People's Commissars resigned from the compromise coalition government whose foundations had been laid only six weeks earlier, and shortly thereafter the new year was ushered in on a wave of strikes, demonstrations, and street actions in Berlin. The conservative SPD leadership now turned vigorously to the consolidation and defence of its own position, not against the threat from the right, but against the radical challenge of the Independents and Spartacists (now constituted as the German Communist Party), and the ultra-militant revolutionary shop stewards movement. The fatal alliance between the ruling socialists and the deposed military command was struck during those critical days, which climaxed on 13 January with the abduction and murder of Karl Liebknecht and Rosa Luxemburg.

Thus the ultra-nationalists – in the form of the reactionary

7. Conversations with HM, in which he compared Eisner's impulses with those that surfaced in Paris in 1968. On the Bavarian revolution of 1918–19, cf. Allan Mitchell, *Revolution in Bavaria: The Eisner Regime and the Soviet Republic,* Princeton 1965, and the article by Falk Wiesemann in Karl Bosl, ed., *Bayern in Umbruch,* Munich and Vienna 1969.

Freikorps assembled by the Socialist Defence Minister Noske – were drawn into the service of the socialist government.[8] Four days later the issue of the revolutionary councils was closed, as national elections charged the SPD with the task of forming a constitutional government in coalition with the Democratic Party and the Catholic Centre, and the final, desperate rising of the radical opposition in early March left 1,200 dead in the streets of Berlin. The first battle of the German revolution, or, as Max Weber put it, of 'the enormous collapse which is customarily called the Revolution', was over.[9]

Of course, possibilities for organized political action on the left remained, but the prospects of success came to look only more distant. Marcuse had already withdrawn from the SPD in reaction to the assassinations of Luxemburg and Liebknecht, for which he held the party leadership accountable. His perception of the growing rigidification of the Independents, and of the incipient submission of the new KPD to Soviet influence, only added to his discouragement. Now, with the apparent closure of the political system and the collapse of the leftist opposition, he allowed the question of the link between theory and practice to lapse and prepared to resume his studies.

Marcuse entered the Humboldt University in Berlin where he studied *Germanistik* for the four regular semesters of 1919 and 1920, continuing the humanistic education of his Gymnasium years. This was obviously his first love, but at a deeper, still unreflective level, this decision clearly anticipates his later theoretical position that the intellectual and aesthetic ideals of bourgeois culture can themselves serve simultaneously as a point of retreat and resistance in the face of bourgeois society.

His studies were not confined to the deeply traditional and hierarchical university setting in the post-revolutionary period, for he also met frequently in those months with a dozen friends in a left-radical literary group. His regular comrades included Walter Benjamin, the expressionist playwright Walter Hasenclaver, and the poet Adrian Turel – all to become major figures of the literary

8. Cf. Robert G. L. Waite, *Vanguard of Nazism: The Free Corps Movement in Postwar Germany, 1918–1923,* New York 1969, ch. III.
9. Max Weber, 'Politik als Beruf' (lecture, Munich 1918), in C. W. Mills and H. H. Gerth, eds., *From Max Weber,* London 1948, p. 113.

avant-garde themselves – and they were joined on his occasional visits to Berlin by Georg Lukács, who had recently become a Communist, and had by that time already embarked on the writing of *History and Class Consciousness*. Marcuse evidently came into contact with Lukács's thought at this point, but it must be recalled that he was still barely twenty, and only beginning to explore the dimensions of cultural and political radicalism that were opening up to him. He declared himself an 'existentialist' in those days, one for whom the experiences of life in Berlin could be appropriated not merely as events, but as comprehensive world-views: poetry '*als Weltanschauung*', drunkenness '*als Weltanschauung*', sex '*als Weltanschauung*'. He and his literary accomplices met through 1919, when this little-known stage in the prehistory of the Frankfurt School ended abruptly with the unexpected return of his father in the midst of one of their 'existential evenings' in the Marcuse living-room.

The Humboldt University was even less receptive than Carl Marcuse to intellectual and existential experimentation. Its political ambience in the first years of the Weimar Republic is reflected in the fact that when the ultra-rightist Erhardt Brigade marched through the Brandenburg Gate on 12 March 1920, under the leadership of Ludendorff, Lüttwitz, and Dr Wolfgang Kapp, and declared the republican government deposed, their attempted putsch was publicly applauded by the Rector on behalf of a large part of the university professors, and the reactionary rebels enjoyed the further support of a majority of the students.[10]

Nor was the intellectual environment congenial to Marcuse, although he did attend lectures by the great and controversial theologian Ernst Troeltsch, as well as those of Carl Stumpf, one of the commanding figures in the prehistory of the phenomenological movement and also of Gestalt psychology. Nonetheless, much of the university's nineteenth-century eminence in the intellectual-humanist tradition had by this time faded, and it was more in the physical sciences than in literary or humanistic studies that new directions in thinking were welcomed.

The Albert-Ludwig University of Freiburg-im-Breisgau contrasted sharply with the austerity of Berlin, and was emerging as a new

10. Heinrich Ströbel, *The German Revolution and After,* London 1923; cf. also Jürgen Schwarz, *Studenten in der Weimarer Republik. Die deutsche Studentenschaft in der Zeit 1918 bis 1923 und ihre Stellung zur Politik,* Berlin 1971.

centre of experimentation in the humanistic disciplines. It thus offered a more congenial environment for a student whose ties to the prevailing bourgeois order were wearing increasingly thin, and it was to Freiburg that Marcuse transferred for the following academic year.

PART TWO

FOUNDATIONS
(1920~1941)

1
THE AESTHETIC DIMENSION
(1920–1928)

The departure of the 22-year-old Herbert Marcuse from revolutionary Berlin to the serene university town on the edge of the Black
Forest was more than a merely geographical retreat from the
turbulence of German political life. Indeed, nothing in his move, or
in his activities in Freiburg, suggests that there was any direct
political continuity between the brief episode of militancy during
the revolution and his subsequent period of university study. The
opposite appears rather to have been the case, and consequently,
such continuity as exists must be sought at a deeper level; only in
retrospect is it possible to appreciate the full significance of the
Freiburg period for his later political and intellectual career.

In contrast to a syndrome especially well documented among
upper-middle-class youth of Marcuse's generation, his own flirtation
with radical politics and departure from the already tenuous
religious identification of his parents did not create bitter generational antagonisms within the Marcuse family, such as those that
characterized the early years of his later colleagues Max Horkheimer and Walter Benjamin.[1] Marcuse tended to be somewhat
intimidated by his domineering father, and avoided confrontations
– indeed, at an early age he had headed almost instinctively for a
realm over which his father could exercise no authority. Carl
Marcuse in turn (and notwithstanding the fact that his name grows
out of the same genealogical roots as that of Karl Marx!) found

1. On Benjamin, see Hannah Arendt's introductory essay to his *Illuminations,* New
York and London 1969; Horkheimer's passing domestic difficulties are recorded
in Helmut Gumnior and Rudolf Ringguth, *Max Horkheimer in Selbstzeugnissen und
Bilddokumenten,* Hamburg 1973.

himself unable to extend much influence over his two radical sons (it was unquestionably the younger Erich who was the real activist in the family) and his strong-willed daughter. But even when the patriotic elder volunteered for the citizen *Bürgerwehr* to defend the newly-born Republic against leftists like his sons, relations between them never became so strained as to leave him disinclined to support their university studies.

Carl Marcuse was both willing and eminently able to do so, for long before this time he had transferred the bulk of his business activities from manufacturing to real estate. The wisdom of this decision now became manifest, for the textile industries, subject to wartime unemployment, emergency legislation, and deprived by the blockade of essential raw materials, were among the hardest hit by the war.[2] Nor did the end of the war signal recovery, for under the terms imposed by the Versailles Treaty, the textile mills of the Alsace region suddenly ceased to be one of the most profitable parts of the German textile manufacturing industry and became instead its chief competitor. Deficit spending and the massive destruction of capital during the war years, and the domestic turmoil that followed its conclusion, were already creating a dangerously inflationary situation,[3] and in such conditions, investment in fixed capital – real estate – was one of the few guarantees of relative financial security. Those who, like Carl Marcuse, had been able to afford the initial investment were able to recover well enough from the severe privations of the great inflation.

As little as financial security had been an issue for Herbert Marcuse was it interesting to him: supported by a regular stipend from home, he occupied himself at Freiburg with subjects far removed from the practical world of business and administration. At the Albert-Ludwig University he did shift his studies to a more contemporary course than that which he had followed at Berlin, where the curriculum in German studies (*Germanistik*) had been oriented toward the classics of the intellectual and cultural tradition. Although these works provided a lasting foundation for his thought (if subject to radical reinterpretation), he now undertook a some-what less orthodox course of studies in which modern German

2. Gerald D. Feldman, *Army, Industry, and Labor in Germany, 1914–1918,* Princeton 1968, part 1.

3. Fritz K. Ringer, *The German Inflation,* Oxford 1969, pp. 44–7.

literature constituted his main field, supplemented by lectures in philosophy and political economy (*Nationalökonomie*). Reflecting his lack of interest in concrete political analysis at this time, his work within the social sciences was minimal – probably no more than necessary to meet the requirements of a minor field of study.[4]

Indeed, although the philosophical implications of his research into modern European literary history were considerable, and he drew widely from classical as well as modern writings on aesthetics in establishing the foundations of his work, even his formal studies of philosophy remained secondary to his main interests. The fact of Marcuse's immersion in literary studies even in the years in which the philosophical faculty was dominated by Edmund Husserl seems already to call attention to the dichotomy between art and philosophy that was to stimulate some of the most radical conceptions of his later career.[5]

Husserl was by this time at an advanced stage of his career, and phenomenology already constituted a systematic philosophical method, having reached a mature formulation in the first volume of his *Ideas* (1913). Marcuse attended Husserl's lectures (as did, for a semester, Max Horkheimer[6]), as well as those of the prominent neo-Kantian Alois Riehl, the influential neo-Thomist Josef Geyser, and a number of less eminent philosophers, but there are no resonances whatever of Husserl's radical new directions in phenomenological analysis in his own writings at this stage. To the contrary, it will be seen that the essential philosophical authority for Marcuse in his early Freiburg years was already Hegel, then only beginning to attract renewed attention as a possible key to the neo-Kantian deadlock that had dominated German intellectual life in the years before the war, and never a serious influence upon the

---

4. This is surely a fair assumption, judging from the professors whose lectures he heard: Hermann Schumacher was an entrepreneurial economist whose work was consistent with the line of the conservative, anti-Socialist DVP; Paul Mombert was a more critical thinker, but still solidly within the mainstream of bourgeois economics, as was Rudolf Eberstadt. Only Karl Diehl, a Proudhon scholar, addressed topics in radical economic theory which might have engaged Marcuse in the light of his recent political initiation, although Marcuse himself would never admit to any youthful anarchist sympathies.

5. Husserl replaced the neo-Kantian Heinrich Rickert who had moved to Heidelberg in 1916, leaving his younger colleague Jonas Cohn, a philosopher of culture whose lectures Marcuse attended, and whose *Allgemeine Aesthetik* (1901) contributed theoretical support to his dissertation.

6. Noted in Gumnior and Ringguth, p. 22.

development of Husserl's own 'phenomenology'.[7]

It was rather in the study of modern German literature that Marcuse found his most congenial home, and within this faculty he prepared his doctoral dissertation on the German *Künstlerroman* under the direction of Professor Philipp Witkop. Witkop (1880–1942) was a relatively unorthodox literary modernist in his sympathies, with leanings toward the poetic and critical (and avowedly anti-political) esoterism of the Stefan George circle, to which Marcuse had himself been attracted since his later Gymnasium years. He also had a considerable body of publications to his credit, however, covering nearly the whole tradition of German lyric poetry, and was thus able to serve as a stimulating critic to the young scholar. The dissertation in the history of modern German literature was successfully defended against the faculty – including Husserl – and Marcuse was awarded the PhD *magna cum laude* in October 1922.

The dissertation itself dealt with an important but fairly conventional topic within German literary studies, the *Künstlerroman*.[8] A sub-type of the German *Bildungsroman*, the novel of 'education' or 'inner development' wherein a central character passes from innocence to mature self-consciousness as the story unfolds, the *Künstlerroman* defines the hero to be an artist. Accordingly, the complex of situations and events represented generally refers to the development of a specifically artistic self-consciousness and mode of life, and the attendant tension with the surrounding world. However traditional a subject matter for an academic dissertation, Marcuse's work, simply entitled *Der deutsche Künstlerroman*, contains embryonic formulations of so many of the themes of his later intellectual projects that it is necessary to examine it – his first piece of sustained writing – in some depth.[9]

---

7. Husserl followed his own teacher Brentano in regarding Hegel as a case of the 'extreme degeneration of human thought', an estimation revised slightly upward late in his career; cf. Herbert Spiegelberg, *History of the Phenomenological Movement*, The Hague 1969, vol. 1, pp. 13–14.

8. The *Künstlerroman* (literally: 'artist-novel') is a characteristic genre of many of the great European literatures, but the *Künstlerroman* outside of Germany was drawn into Marcuse's discussion only 'in so far as it brought new, decisive formulations and changes of the problem' (p. 333). Since it is considered only from within the context of the German literary tradition, and there is in any case no equivalent English term, it will be left untranslated here (similarly *Künstlernovelle*, its short-story form).

Marcuse established the problematic of the *Künstlerroman* in terms of the sought-after accommodation between *Künstlertum* and *Menschentum*, the artistic existence and the fully human existence. This dualism carries with it the implication that a genre of fiction in which the artist assumes the central role is a possibility only in a society that has developed lines of differentiation and stratification that permit the 'artist' to be identified as a specific social type: 'the dissolution and tearing asunder of a unitary life-form, the opposition of art and life, the separation of the artist from the surrounding world, is the presupposition of the *Künstlerroman*, and its problem, the suffering and longing of the artist, his struggle for a new community.' (332) The artist thus appears set against a non-artistic environment and its modes of life, which are themselves alien and antagonistic to the artistic experience: the goal of the artist's life (and consequently, the characteristic theme of the *Künstlerroman* in its historical manifestations) becomes the solution or resolution of this alienation.

In the forceful and at times almost rhapsodic prose of his theoretical introduction, Marcuse examines the significance of a work of fiction in which a distinct social type or mode of life – that of the artist – is depicted in its uniquely characteristic outlooks, conflicts and aspirations. The very fact of this distinctiveness presupposes that the life of the artist, indeed, the essence of the artistic existence as such, is somehow at variance with the subjective and objective realities of the surrounding culture. In contrast to the great national epic, which reflects in verse the collective life of a whole people and out of which the novel emerges, the *Künstlerroman* becomes possible 'only when the artist represents a specific life-form [*Lebensform*], when the life-forms of the totality no longer correspond to his own essence, that is, if art is no longer immanent in life'.(10)

The artist thus represents 'a life-form which does not fundamentally coincide with the surrounding world', (12) a social and human type whose essence it is to stand outside of the limits of the established society, estranged from it in ecstasy, anger, or despair: the substance of this life is beauty, but the life-*form* is alienation and

9. Herbert Marcuse, '*Der deutsche Künstlerroman*', Phil. Diss., University of Freiburg-im-Breisgau, October 1922, 454 pages. Page numbers (in parentheses) refer to the text recently published by Suhrkamp as Volume I of Marcuse's *Schriften* (Frankfurt 1978); all translations are my own, and are based on the original typescript, obtained through the courtesy of the Universitätsbibliothek Freiburg.

the impossibility of integration. The struggle to overcome this debilitating schism is activated by the conception of a primordial state of harmony in which no opposition exists between artistic subjectivity and the life-forms of the surrounding world, indeed, between subject and object, Idea and reality, art and life; where, in Nietzsche's classic evocation, 'man is no longer an artist, he has become a work of art'.[10] Invoking a candidly mythic view of history, Marcuse identified the pre-Socratic Greek culture of the time of epic poetry, 'where life was itself art, and mythology life', (10) and – at the origins of the Germanic *Geist* – the tightly integrated culture of the Vikings, wherein 'the perfect unity of art and life' spoke through the ancient bard. (11) In such heroic epochs the world itself appeared as the embodiment of art, and the artistic mode of life merged undistinguished into the collective life of the people.

The dialectical method of his argument necessarily presses on to a darker picture of that originary unity torn asunder, of a long 'historical' epoch of division and difference, with inner life and outer world cast into glaring opposition. This is the European world of the repressive Church and the bourgeois city, an environment contin- uous with our own, in which the subject, like Grimmelshausen's Simplizissimus, confronts a world 'utterly devalued, impoverished, brutal, and hostile, offering no fulfilment'. (14) With the reception of the dogmas and institutions of Christianity and the consequent 'flight of the gods', life gradually ceased to provide in itself the material and the form of aesthetic fulfilment: 'devoid of art and distant from the Idea, it became a "problem" '. (13) As the age of chivalry was closed, however, a new group of figures emerged, in the form of a counter-culture made up of a restless 'travelling communi- ty of musicians and mimes, but in particular, young clerics and students . . . whose assault shatters the stability of the established and ecclesiastical restrictions . . . They are totally outcast, perman- ently excluded; for them there is no place in the life-forms of the surrounding world. Too arrogant, too wild in their ecstatic pursuit of freedom to seek compromise or conciliation, their lives vanish into the mists of restless wandering, of dissolute vagrancy.' (13) On the shadowy margins of pre-modern society, irreconcilable opposition was being raised to a life-principle. The dignitaries of Church and

10. Friedrich Nietzsche, *The Birth of Tragedy* (1872), trans. Walter Kaufmann, New York 1967, p. 37.

State were supplanted by the dignity of the free spirit, and the prevailing orthodoxies of ideology and authority rejected in favour of rebellious images of eroticism and play. From within this migrant underground fellowship of the medieval period, the poet steps forth to give voice to this new attitude toward life, and thereby becomes 'perhaps the first self-conscious artist, in whom artistic necessity stresses the life of wandering, the state of opposition to the surrounding world'. (13)

There is, then, a third component that comes into view, through which the resolution of this condition of alienation is prefigured, though not accomplished: even in a time of universal suffering and oppression, the lost values of a world at one with itself, of the immediate unity of the artistic life and the fully human life, are preserved – if in attenuated form – in the shape of artistic subjectivity. With its evocation of the fully developed artistic self-consciousness, the *Künstlerroman* thus represents both a symptom of the devaluation of the world, of a reality estranged from its own potentialities, and a concrete anticipation of the negation and transcendence of this estrangement. The alienation of the artist from an artless world, which is embodied in the '*Zwischen-zwei-Weltenstehen*' of literary characters from Werther to Tonio Kröger, is the guarantee of a refuge of transcendent ideals against a deficient reality. Of the suffering of the artist we may say, as Hegel said of Schiller, that 'in this respect he only paid the debt of his times'.[11]

In this account, Marcuse reveals the first sign of the sensitivity to the 'underside' of the respectable tradition of European thought and culture which was to become one of the central motifs of his later thought. His analysis describes the artistic existence being carved out of the opposing forces of an expanding bourgeois world and the unrestrained protest against that world in spiritual and mystical lyricism. The true artist emerges for the first time as a specific human type, an embodiment of negation, straining against the oppressive restraints of the established society: 'He finds no fulfilment in the narrow confines of the life-forms of the surrounding world; his nature and his longings do not merge into them or unfold within them, and he stands alone, over and against reality.' (16) With the progressive articulation of an artistic self-con-

---

11. G. W. F. Hegel, *Aesthetics. Lectures on Fine Art* (1823–29), trans. T. Knox, Oxford 1975, vol. 1, p. 61.

sciousness and a faintly outlined aesthetic dimension of life, the conditions finally exist for the emergence of the *Künstlerroman*. Inevitably, it will represent the antagonism between the artist and a contemptuous or uncomprehending world, and will express the desperate striving to create a new resolution of this unendurable alienation: 'The artist must break out of this division: he must strive to achieve a life-form which binds the inner disunity into a new wholeness, resolves the opposition between spirit and sensuality, art and life, the artistic existence and the surrounding world.' (16)

On the basis of this formulation, Marcuse proceeds to examine exemplars in the evolution of the nineteenth-century *Künstlerroman*, disclosing the range of possibilities through which they confront the contradiction between the artistic life and the totality of mundane social life-forms. The two forms of the 'resolution' lie at the opposite poles of the century-and-a-half tradition of the *Künstlerroman*: the triumphant integration of Wilhelm Meister and the disintegration of Gustav von Aschenbach represent the two outcomes of the sought-after accommodation of the artist and society, the reconciliation of *Künstlertum* and *Bürgerlichkeit*, the artistic existence and the bourgeois way of life. Detailed textual studies of works from the sorrows and strivings of Goethe's artists to the *Künstlernovellen* of Thomas Mann make up the body of the dissertation.

Historically, the rise of the *Künstlerroman* is inseparable from the liberation of subjectivity forged out of the opposing forces of pietism and enlightenment rationalism: it is prefigured philosophically in the thought of Hamann, Rousseau, and Herder, and in the 'longing for the unlived life' (Novalis) associated with the literary currents of the *Sturm und Drang* period. Though the writers of *Sturm und Drang* (notably Wilhelm Heinse and Karl Philipp Moritz) failed to grasp the essential problematic of the dualism between art (the artistic existence) and the prevailing cultural and material realities, Marcuse nevertheless regards their efforts with unmistakable sympathy, for they represent 'the first attempts of the liberated artistic existence to press forward to a new life-form'. (40) In particular, their writings contained concrete anticipations of the fulfilment of the artistic quest in their characteristic 'feeling for Nature' and 'the experience of Love': 'Only in two spheres did reality itself make a bid to lay hold of the Idea: in *Naturgefühl* and in the *Liebeserlebnis*. In the complete surrender to nature the *Stürmer und Dränger* experienced the Soul of the World [*die Seele des Alls*], the radiance of divine beauty, the purity and immediacy of the cosmic force . . . And indeed, so is the case with the experience of love.' (42) At these two points, the artist grasps at a 'separate reality' (*die Einzel-Wirklichkeit*) within the finite and human world. In the writings of the young Goethe this drive attains its first mature formulation, and there the *Künstlerroman* historically begins.

In the special studies that follow, Marcuse examines the two-dimensionality of the *Künstlerroman* by tracing the attitudes and actions through which this dichotomy between the real and the ideal has been either sustained or overcome. The 'rhythm' of his argument is in fact determined by the two polar conceptions of the artistic experience which appear in the *Künstlerroman* of each literary period: the 'subjectivistic and realistic, romantic and epic, the artistic life which flees the world and that which penetrates it'. (332) These alternative orientations, which correspond to very broadly conceived historical categories, translate into two literary-philosophical modes: the first would submit the world to an ultimate aesthetic standard that can never be concretely realized, as in the transcendental rejection of reality by the early Romantics (Tieck, Schlegel, Novalis) or the aesthetes of *l'art pour l'art*, who create in their work 'a poeticized reality, a dream-like world which is in the final sense no longer a "problem" to the artist'. (104) The second mode of response is developed in the novels of the later Romantics (Brentano, Hoffman, Eichendorff) or the politicized writers of Young Germany (Theodor Mundt, Heinrich Laube, Karl Gutzkow), in whose partisan novels 'the demand for the radical restructuring of life-forms came to be formulated in practical terms as demands for social and political reform'. (180) Here the artist is rooted in the deficient world as it actually exists, but is committed to its practical transformation.

Once Marcuse had established the theory and method of 'the German *Künstlerroman*' in this manner, the inherently critical categories that guided his interpretation could emerge plainly and powerfully. Modern society was characterized in its agony as '*die entgötterte Welt*' (14), a world within which the magical powers of gods and heroes can no longer be exercised and whose enchantment finds refuge in an underground counter-culture of spiritualism, mysticism, and the occult; he suggestively raised an 'essential' standard of truth, transcending the objectively posited facts of the material world, and visible in the surrender to Nature and the embrace of Love; and almost as if he were delimiting in advance the competing claims that were to define the remainder of his career, he identified two tactics for realizing it: the practical and the poetic transformation of the prosaic reality of everyday life.

Clearly, Marcuse's doctoral dissertation cannot be regarded as purely linear survey, assembling and ordering material in a simple internal chronology. There is rather a continual movement between two poles, the subjectivistic and the realistic, through which the historical, dialectical progression of a literary genre is developed. Nor is the course of the argument arbitrary: however much some of his formulations may suggest the liberties of a youthful romanticist fancy, his work is grounded in the aesthetics of Hegel, 'the most serious of all serious philosophers'.[12]

The turn to Hegel was one of the most outstanding features of the reorientation of German intellectual life in the early decades of this century.[13] The first major contribution to this revival 'in which the findings of the Hegelian philosophy were concretely applied to aesthetic problems,' had appeared in 1916 when the *Zeitschrift für Aesthetik und Allgemeine Kunstwissenschaft*, a journal under the editorial direction of Marcuse's former professor, the Berlin aesthetician Max Dessoir, published Georg Lukács's pioneering study *The Theory of the Novel*.[14]

Marcuse had studied Lukács's elegant, pre-Marxist writings on literature – *The Theory of the Novel* and the earlier *Soul and Form* (1911) – and it was through Lukács that he came to work with the Hegelian principle of the historicization of the categories of aesthetics and the dialectic between genres of literature in 'integrated' *(geschlossen)* and 'problematic' *(problematik)* civilizations. This distinction stipulates the existence of a unified society, a homogeneous world in which 'essence' is manifest in the concrete forms of social life and individual action, and in which 'art' did not exist as a separate category, since the ideals and aspirations of the artist stood realized in the closed circle of existence. Lukács characterized the Homeric world of the Greeks as such an age, contrasting it with the

12. The phrase appears in an extraordinary disputation with Norman O. Brown in the summer of 1967 (reprinted in Marcuse's *Negations*, p. 229).
13. Cf. Heinrich Levy, 'Die Hegel-Renaissance in der deutschen Philosophie', in *Philosophische Vorträge*, Charlottenburg 1927.
14. Georg Lukács, *Theorie des Romans,* first published in book form in 1920; reissued in 1962 with a new Preface by the author from which this quote is taken (trans. Anna Bostock, Cambridge 1971, p. 15).

modern age of the differentiation of social functions and the fragmentation of social roles, a world whose 'very disintegration and inadequacy . . . is the precondition for the existence of art and its becoming conscious'.[15] It is evident that Marcuse had taken over Lukács's neo-Hegelian framework, adapting it to the problematic of modernity as represented in the *Künstlerroman*.[16]

It had been Hegel's great insight that genres of art, like modes of thought, stand in an internal dialectical relation to one another as well as to the external historical conditions within which they are produced. In Lukács's adaptation, the art form most expressive of integrated cultures is the great national epic in which the world at large appears as a true home for the human spirit; where the relation of culture and society has become 'problematic', and the world has lost its all-embracing mythic aspect, art turns inward and the modern novel ultimately takes shape, giving expression to a 'transcendental homelessness'. In a passage in which Marcuse himself found a concise formulation from which to begin his own study, Lukács wrote: 'The epic and the novel . . . differ from one another not by their authors' fundamental intentions, but by the given historico-philosophical realities with which the authors were confronted. The novel is the epic of an age in which the extensive totality of life is no longer directly given, in which the immanence of meaning in life has become a problem yet which still thinks in terms of totality.'[17]

In their respective works, Lukács and the younger Marcuse both incorporate the Hegelian dialectic of the literatures of the modern age, and both share Hegel's metaphysical disdain for the 'abstract-

15. Ibid., p. 38.
16. In fact, the 'Hegelian framework' had been substantially modified by Lukács, whom the young Marcuse seems to have followed rather uncritically, apparently having no independent conception of Hegel's treatment of art in Greek culture. There is no evidence – nor any reason to believe – that Marcuse was at this time familiar with the most important of Hegel's writings on this subject, namely the basic treatment of the Hellenic *Kunstreligion* in the section of the *Phenomenology of Mind* entitled 'Religion in the Form of Art' (trans. Baillie, pp. 709–49) which receives no mention; nor do the much later *Lectures on the Philosophy of History* where the 'aesthetic state' is characterized as the 'political work of art' (trans. Sibree, pp. 250–74). In both cases, and in the Hegelian philosophy generally, it is not Homeric Greece but the radical democracy of the classical Athenian *polis* (for Hegel, 492–431 BC) in which free individuality is reflected in the free collectivity, whose basis was uniquely expressed in art (cf. also Charles Taylor, *Hegel*, Cambridge 1977, pp. 200–6).
17. Lukács, p. 56 (quoted in part by Marcuse in '*Der deutsche Künstlerroman*', p. 2).

ness' of the real world – abstracted, that is, from its Idea in a situation rendered problematic by the work of art: 'Fallen gods, and gods whose kingdom is not yet, become demons; their power is alive, but no longer penetrates the world, or does not yet do so . . . The demons' power remains effective because it cannot be overthrown . . . The novel is the epic of a world that has been abandoned by God.'[18] Though the metaphorical brilliance of the expression itself argues against an overly literal reading, the remoteness of the two young critics from their later Marxian formulations is nonetheless clear. At most, one can interpret the 'abandonment of God' as the flight of intelligibility from the modern, bourgeois world, but surely this was a stance shared by such evidently non-Marxist cultural critics as Nietzsche, Spengler, and Weber: the passage to Marx remained possible but was, at this point, by no means necessary.

In the last analysis, then, it is Hegel's *Aesthetics* (1823–29), as adapted and 'applied' by Lukács, that provides the theoretical underpinning of Marcuse's *Künstlerroman* thesis. He drew especially heavily upon Hegel's discussion of 'epic poetry' in the last section of the *Aesthetics*, where it is contrasted with the modern condition in which 'the spirit of the artist is different from that through which the actual life and deeds of the nation described acquired their existence' – a disunity which Hegel, like Marcuse after him, finds 'inappropriate and disturbing'.[19]

The unique character of the heroic age of epic poetry, in Hegel's presentation, and that which proved so compelling to the young Marcuse, is that 'epic' refers not simply to one of the genres of poetry, but simultaneously to the 'poetically ordered world' that it depicts and within which it necessarily and exclusively exists. It is, in other words, not solely an art form, but a *historical* category describing the constitutive principle of the world that it reflects and within which it is possible: the epic world of poetic embodiment demands 'a new domain, a new ground on which we can tread only after forsaking the prose of the theory and practice of our ordinary

18. Ibid., pp. 86–8.
19. G. W. F. Hegel, *Vorlesungen über die Aesthetik;* trans. T. M. Knox, *Aesthetics, Lectures on Fine Art,* Oxford 1975, vol. 2, p. 1047 (some translations will be slightly altered where Marcuse has misquoted Hegel). Again, Marcuse does not explicitly acknowledge his departure from Hegel, for whom epic poetry was clearly a deficient mode of art, corresponding to a deficient reality – deficient because the individual was at that stage still in a state of undifferentiated 'immediacy', still predestined to his role.

life and way of thinking'.[20] It is thus contrasted throughout with the more familiar historical world of actuality, accuracy, and accident, of the narrowly circumstantial 'prose of commonplace thinking out of which art struggles on its way to truth'.[21]

The epic world is one in which a national spirit has awakened and begun to be objectified in the collective life of a people, and the life of the individual is not yet fragmented by the conflicting claims of private rights and public duties, feeling and will, heart and mind. This 'immediately poetic existence' binds all aspects of life together within an integrated social ethic under shared and universal principles, and stands prior to the 'prosaic' articulation of separate spheres of religion, civil and moral law, and political constitution which impose substantive obligations as a necessity external to the individual. In this community of freely willed thought and action, portrayed most perfectly in the Homeric poems, we find for the first time, 'a world hovering beautifully between the universal foundations of life in the ethical order of family, state, and religious belief and the individual, personal character; between spirit and nature in their beautiful equipoise, between intended action and external outcome, between the national ground of undertakings and the intentions and deeds of individuals'. Marcuse himself adds, referring again to Hegel, that this is evidence of 'a reality akin and friendly to art'.[23]

The organic whole of the epic world as interpreted by Marcuse, governed and transformed by art, indeed sets a standard of individual and collective life against which the modern world of machines and factories, of politics and law, appears pathetically impoverished. 'For the whole state of the world today', Hegel concludes, 'has assumed a form diametrically opposed in its prosaic organization to the requirements which we found to be irremissible for genuine epic'.[24] Accordingly, since epic poetry is the natural expression of an entire world outlook, with the passing of this world the original poetic inspiration passes into new forms of art, which Hegel is able to trace through the beginnings of the novel in his own time: against a decidedly 'prosaic' reality, 'romance, the modern popular epic . . . regains for poetry the right it had lost'.[25]

20. Hegel, *Aesthetics,* vol. 2, pp. 1011–2.
21. Ibid., p. 968.
22. Ibid., pp. 1098–9.
23. Marcuse (p. 17), quoting Hegel, *Aesthetics,* vol. 2, pp. 1092–3.

There is a sense in which the youthful Marcuse, writing almost exactly a century later, was continuing the investigation of the dialectic of literary genres begun by Hegel: indeed, he picked up the theme of the world-historical significance of the novel with Goethe, precisely where Hegel had laid it to rest. It was 'Georg von Lukács', however, who was his guide through Hegel, and it is consequently not surprising that Lukács's retrospective evaluation of his own work relative to Hegel should apply equally to Marcuse: although Hegel had focused upon the fractured unity of art and life, he had been concerned with the 'prosaic' character of reality only in so far as it had rendered art problematic – not as problematic in itself. Lukács regarded his own work as having represented a critical advance over Hegel by accepting the general Hegelian method but substantively inverting it: the problem of the novel-form became 'the mirror-image of a world gone out of joint . . . a symptom, among many others, of the fact that reality no longer constitutes a favourable soil for art'.[26] Both the *Theory of the Novel* and 'The German *Künstlerroman*' are critical works, more explicitly so than Hegel's and subversive of the prevailing orthodoxies of the bourgeois world of prose, not just the aesthetic form which corresponds to it.

Indeed, although the author of 'The German *Künstlerroman*' generally recedes far into the background of the text, his voice can be heard in an unmistakable sympathy with the plight of art and the self-conscious artist confined by a narrowly materialistic society, a sympathy whose standard is the poetic world of the beautiful, but which extends to 'the struggle of the German people for a new community'. (333) The last chapter of the thesis offers a penetrating account of the final stage in the development of the *Künstlerroman* in the form of an analysis of Thomas Mann's resolution of the artist into bourgeois society, both in his own literary career and in that of Gustav von Aschenbach, the semi-autobiographical 'master craftsman' of *Death in Venice* (1911). The earlier novellas – especially *Tonio Kröger* (1903) – had depicted the artist 'suspended between two worlds' (*Zwischen-zwei-Weltenstehen*), aspiring to the ordered permanence of the bourgeois way of life, but remaining foreign to it. To this

24. Hegel, *Aesthetics*, vol. 2, p. 1109.
25. Ibid., p. 1092.
26. Lukács, p. 17.

outsider condemned to a life of human impoverishment, '*Bürgerlich-keit* assumes ever more of the splendour of a distant longing', (307) and his art itself seeks out the narrow measure of a bourgeois profession in order to secure 'a sphere where a certain kind of communion can exist, a sphere where the eternal loneliness stops'.[27]

With Aschenbach ' – or von Aschenbach, as he had been known officially since his fiftieth birthday – '[28] the problematic of the *Künstlerroman* would appear objectively to have been resolved: 'The artist is no longer poised between two worlds, he is no longer an outsider, excluded and stigmatized: *Bürgerlichkeit* had taken him up and established him, his art had entered into its values and become an ethical calling'. (326) It is precisely Aschenbach's achievement, however, that betrays the hopelessness of the artistic quest for accommodation with the bourgeois world which had been the generic theme of the *Künstlerroman*. For all his honours and acclaim, for all the heroic determination that enabled him to regulate his art by the bourgeois standard of an ethical calling, the artist Aschen-bach served drives that were darker, deeper, and demonic: 'he belonged to a different order of humanity, to a different world, and in the face of the Dionysian forces which have their roots in that humanity and that world, no heroism or determination could protect him . . . if they break through only once, they demolish the bourgeois existence, shatter all harmony, bring to ruin all stability and order.' (326) Beneath the superficial forms of bourgeois respectability, the artist is powered by elemental forces that the bourgeois way of life cannot contain and which take precedence over it: the striving for the pure Eros of aesthetic form.

'The German *Künstlerroman*' thus carries within its concepts and categories a distinct, if evasive, denunciation of contemporary European society. It is nevertheless the case that the implicit critique of *Bürgerlichkeit* is a long way from an explicit critique of the

27. Lukács's insight into the bourgeois professionalism of the writer Theodor Storm was another important source for Marcuse: '*Bürgerlichkeit und l'art pour l'art*' (1909) in Georg Lukács, *Die Seele und die Formen* (1911); *Soul and Form,* trans. Anna Bostock, Cambridge 1974, p. 57.

28. Thomas Mann, *Death in Venice and Other Stories,* trans. H. T. Lowe-Porter, New York 1954, p. 57. Marcuse verified a further autobiographical reference in *Death in Venice* when he sent his final chapter to its author. Thomas Mann, like Gustav von Aschenbach, replied in a prompt, cordial note of appreciation – identical to all the others sent out in gracious but perfunctory response to 'a daily post heavy with tributes from his own and foreign countries'. (p. 9)

capitalist mode of production that sustains it. Marcuse's aesthetic analysis remains abstract, and is conducted on a philosophico-literary plane far removed from concrete socio-historical institutions. Even when he is not flirting audaciously with the mythological, his historical categories are of an extremely general, if not impressionistic character – for example, the pre-1830 period of 'absolute power and orthodox intolerance' (174) or the post-1848 climate of 'advancing technology and increased alienation' (232) – intended more to set a thematic context than to provide any sort of social history of the novel.[29]

Neither does the author of 'The German *Künstlerroman*' assume a partisan stance of his own on the politics of the novel, even where his own recent experiences in the streets of revolutionary Berlin might have found an easy parallel with the German artists who, during the uprisings of 1848, 'entered on the side of the revolutionary *Volkes*, shared in their strivings and sufferings, took part in their attack against the old life-forms'. (195) Marcuse, like the artists of Germany's earlier '*verfehlte Revolution*', had discovered that a direct alliance with the revolutionary masses was not conducive to his own manner of political *praxis*. In the end, neither the political nor the poetical restructuring of the world was explicitly called for, and he looks toward the future with a mixture of anticipation and resignation: 'For the German *Künstlerroman*', he concludes, 'community is not something given, but rather something given up'.[30]

Marcuse's thesis is by no means a conservative work; its elements are, however, unselfconsciously fused, and it was only fifty years later that the critical, subversive implications of its concepts were fully assessed and their profoundly radical content rendered explicit. At this juncture, it can only be noted that he has programmatically outlined a principle of life – *Künstlertum*, the artistic-aesthetic mode

29. Again, the veiled politics of Marcuse's early aesthetics appear to correspond closely with Lukács's repudiation of the war and bourgeois society at the time of the *Theory of the Novel* (1914–15): assuming the downfall of the three empires, he asked 'who was to save us from Western civilization?' (*Theory of the Novel*, p. 11.) Ferenc Feher, in his essay 'Is the Novel Problematic?' writes that Lukács's study 'transforms the defence of progress through contradictions into an overtly romantic anti-capitalism that nevertheless also contains a specifically revolutionary viewpoint' (*Telos*, 15, spring 1973, p. 47).

30. '*Für den deutschen Künstlerroman ist die Gemeinsamkeit nichts Gegebenes, sondern ein Aufgegebenes*', (333). '*Aufgegebenes*', has a double meaning here, suggesting 'something given up' as well as 'something to strive for', 'a task to be carried out'.

of existence – that is in its essence irreconcilably opposed to the prevailing society. He has implicitly put forward the notion that an abstract concept and its embodiment in a concrete social type can express a persistent critical standard, immune to the integrative forces of the status quo – of *any* status quo. Thus, while he has plainly concerned himself only marginally with the material realities of society and history, he has provided himself with the conceptual armament for a socio-historical critique which extends far beyond the scope of any conventional materialist analysis.

Marcuse returned to Berlin toward the end of 1922, a time of desperation for many sectors of the German population, and had his father's holdings been elsewhere than in real estate, the period of the great inflation might have had a more lasting impact upon him. As it was, the state of emergency that prevailed throughout 1923 passed, leaving in its wake only a dangerous conjuncture of events whose long-range implications were not yet obvious: the ruin of much of the middle class, the inflammatory French-Belgian occupation of the Ruhr, waves of political assassinations, Hitler's first bid for power in Bavaria, abortive uprisings in Saxony and Thuringia, and the physical collapse of Lenin, incapacitated by his third stroke on 9 March.

It was in this critical period that Marcuse undertook his really systematic study of Marx. In Berlin he began to follow Lukács's path out of Hegelian literary criticism to Marxist political criticism, but unlike Lukács, who had entered the Communist Party in 1918, Marcuse retained his political independence. He and his friends read sympathetically the *Internationale Presskorrespondenz*, the news bulletin of the International, but his perceptions of Soviet penetration of German socialism left him with deep misgivings, which were only compounded by Stalin's first major purges of 1926–27.[31]

In general, there appears to have been a gradual intellectual radicalization during the years Marcuse stayed in Berlin, but there is no evidence of any overtly political involvement. Indeed, the respective political careers of Lukács and Marcuse diverged radically after their early, pre-Marxist writings on aesthetics, and have

31. Conversations with HM; on the Soviet intervention into the affairs of the German KPD, cf. Louis Fischer, *Russia's Road from Peace to War*, New York 1969, ch. 11; and E. H. Carr, *The Interregnum*, Harmondsworth 1954, ch. 7.

come to represent alternative paradigms of leftist politics in the twentieth century: Lukács was to maintain with increasing determination that disciplined allegiance to the only organized arm of the revolutionary proletariat, even entailing obligatory intellectual and political obeisances to Stalin, was a tactical necessity, 'an entry ticket to all further partisan warfare',[32] while Marcuse was already in the *überparteiliche* stance of the 'homeless left' which was to become virtually emblematic of later phases of his career.[33] Confronted with the submission of the German KPD to the dictates of the embattled Soviet state, and the Social Democrats' 'alliance with reactionary, destructive, and repressive forces',[34] he refused to make an impossible choice – a refusal whose political implications were distinctly prefigured in the estranged figure of the artist in the *Künstlerroman* thesis, though still to be developed into a consistent theoretical principle.

The *Künstlerroman* thesis, especially where it had touched on Goethe's *Wilhelm Meister*, had also hinted at the theatre as offering an image of liberation, and living in Berlin in the twenties Marcuse had almost unimaginable opportunities to test this conjecture. He was, in fact, more actively engaged in the luminous cultural life of the Weimar Republic than in its darker political course, becoming a *habitué* of an avant-garde theatre dominated by the personalities of Max Reinhardt, Erwin Piscator and Brecht, and although he personally had neither instruction nor talent, he further pursued the aesthetic dimension into the now-legendary opera houses and concert halls of the city.

Marcuse was not entirely relegated to the audience of the Berlin avant-garde, however, for he even collaborated in a memorable, if short-lived, publishing venture: *Das Dreieck*, a Berlin monthly with an expressionist slant which he edited with his friend Walter Gutkelch. Its first issue provocatively appearing in a triangular format (yet printed in the Gothic *Altschrift* as if to heighten the

32. Georg Lukács, *History and Class Consciousness*, trans. Rodney Livingstone, London 1971, p. xxxviii, from the 1967 Preface.
33. On 'The Search for a "Third Force" in Pre-Nazi Germany' cf. George L. Mosse, *Germans and Jews*, New York 1970, pp. 3–33 and 171–225; also Istvan Deak's fine study of the shades of left-wing non-partisanship among the Weltbühne circle: *Weimar Germany's Left-Wing Intellectuals*, Berkeley and Los Angeles 1968.
34. Marcuse's statement in the course of lectures given at the Free University in Berlin in 1967, published in *Five Lectures*, p. 103.

tension between the avant-garde and the old culture), *Das Dreieck* was an eclectic review that ranged freely between cultural and political criticism, original mythopoeic verse and prose, and polemical reviews and commentaries. 'Why Triangle?', its first number demanded rhetorically – for publicity, to be sure, but also to assert an annoyingly visible presence against bourgeois conventionality. But this was obvious, it continued, 'for the answer, of course, stares out of the question itself: The Triangle is the face of the Trinity – a tragic Trinity, that is, which finds expression in Philosophy, Poetry, and Criticism . . . the three stages of the retrograde march of spirit towards the intellect.'[35]

Although its editors asserted the principle of '*methodische Physiognomielosigkeit*' (which might best be rendered as 'methodical featurelessness'), the anti-bourgeois, oppositional character of *Das Dreieck* gave it a clearly left-wing aspect, and Marcuse's (pseudonymous) editorial involvement brought him into contact with the work and also the persons of its many well-known contributors: his good friend the critic and publicist Siegfried Jacobsohn, the novelist Alfred Döblin and playwright Carl Zuckmayer, Leo Lania (who had been Piscator's early theatrical collaborator), the prominent expressionist writers Ernst Toller and Kurt Pinthus, and Egon Erwin Kisch, one of Europe's most feared and respected investigative journalists. Though Marxists and other radical political writers were represented in the columns of *Das Dreieck* during the brief period of its appearance, Marcuse was, perhaps more significantly, presented to people who conceived of themselves as revolutionaries in a sense that was not confined (and perhaps did not extend) to the political.[36]

The distorted universe of expressionism and post-expressionism was not the one through which Marcuse habitually travelled during the Weimar years, however. He was in fact living a more settled existence, installed in a lower floor of the family's apartment

---

35. *Das Dreieck. Monatzeitschrift für Philosophie, Dichtung, und Kritik* (lit. The Triangle. Monthly Journal for Philosophy, Poetry, and Reviews), hrsg. Walter Gutkelch, Berlin, April 1924 – March 1925; seven issues appeared (obtained courtesy of Schiller-Nationalmuseum, Marbach a.N.). All translations are my own.

36. On the cultural politics of the independent intellectual left and the attempt 'to bridge the gap between *Geist* and political power' in this period, cf. Lewis D. Wurgaft's study, 'The Activists: Kurt Hiller and the Politics of Action on the German Left, 1914–1933', *Transactions of the American Philosophical Society*, December 1977.

building in Charlottenburg with his wife Sophie, a former student of mathematics and statistics at Freiburg, whom he had married in 1924. Their flat soon became a sort of revolutionary *salon*, with the younger Erich often slipping down the back stairs to attend spirited discussions of Marxian theory, Gestalt psychology, abstract painting, and fashionable currents of contemporary German philosophy. His father had meanwhile helped him to buy a partnership in the firm of the publisher and antiquarian book dealer S. Martin Fraenkel, where he worked primarily as a catalogue researcher and bookseller. Despite his ongoing studies of Marx and his turn toward a more rigorous brand of philosophy than that which had formed the apex of *Das Dreieck*, it is not surprising that his own first publication should have taken the form of an assignment in the *Antiquariat*: a scholarly revision of the Trömel bibliography of the writings of Schiller.[37]

The *Schiller-Bibliographie* was the first comprehensive record in sixty years of the numerous editions of Schiller's poetry and prose, and while it is fully annotated, the notes are of a purely technical and organizational nature and reveal nothing of the personality or priorities of the editor. Still, Marcuse's immersion in the works of Schiller – the poet who had declared *beauty* to be a standard of judgement transcending the narrowly political demands of the revolutionaries in eighteenth-century Paris, and who raised the banner of the *aesthetischer Staat* high above that of the French *tricouleur* – cannot be overlooked. Schiller's influence would reappear, explicit and acknowledged, in Marcuse's later works, conveying a critical sensibility that would be central to his own attempts to devise an 'aesthetic education of man'. But in fact, it is not necessary to anticipate, for the strains of aesthetic idealism can be detected in his thought from the very outset.

The strains in the political life of the Republic are less easy to identify in Marcuse's development. At the end of February 1925 the Social Democrat Friedrich Ebert had died, and in the close-run elections held two months later the presidency passed to Hindenburg. Marcuse cast his vote for the KPD candidate (Thaelmann), as

---

37. Herbert Marcuse (hrsg.), *Schiller-Bibliographie. Unter Benutzung der Trömelschen Schiller-Bibliothek,* Berlin 1925, in three parts: I. Collected Works to 1840 II. Single Works to 1805 III. Important Editions since Schiller's Death. Marcuse's senior partner, Fraenkel, ended his career in prison following a conviction for fraud and shady business dealings.

was his custom when he voted at all, but without much conviction.[38] Despite the return of the aged general to power, however, the middle twenties in Germany were a period of relative political stability, diplomatic initiative, economic recovery, and cultural efflorescence. An event that caused a far greater disruption in Marcuse's life was the publication in 1927 of Heidegger's *Being and Time*. Marcuse studied it with his closest friend of that period, the similarly-inclined Alfred Seidemann, and where other German students found a *völkische Lebensphilosophie*, they saw what they thought was the missing dimension of Marxism.[39] Marcuse resolved to return to Freiburg and resume his academic career in philosophy.

38. Marcuse's recollection, in conversation. Buck-Morss confirms the widespread sympathies of non-affiliated Berlin intellectuals for the KPD (p. 207, n. 195), as does Mosse.
39. On Heidegger's reputation among Marcuse's generation at that time, cf. Hannah Arendt, 'Martin Heidegger at Eighty', trans. Albert Hofstadter, *New York Review of Books,* vol. XVII, 6, 21 October 1971.

2

HEIDEGGER AND CONCRETE PHILOSOPHY (1928–1932)

The year in which Marcuse returned to Freiburg to study with Heidegger was one of the most hopeful in the life of the Weimar Republic. Under the diplomatic leadership of Stresemann, Germany's post-war status in European politics had been negotiated dramatically upward, culminating in the Kellogg-Briand pact of August of that year which promised a new era of peaceful international relations; huge American loans artificially buoyed production and employment, and for the first time since 1914 the masses of Germany enjoyed a measure of political security and material well-being. The electoral results of 1928 reflected the enhanced confidence of the population: at the expense of nearly every one of the non-socialist parties, the SPD and the Communists registered impressive gains.[1] Shortly after the Social Democrats re-entered the government, reviving the Great Coalition with the Catholic Centre and Stresemann's People's Party, the new Chancellor could declare with confidence that 'the foundations of the Republic stand firm and unshakable'.[2]

Other foundations had been laid in that year as well. In 1928, Carl Marcuse fulfilled an ancient dream when he and his family moved into a palatial modern mansion in suburban Dahlem – custom built, needless to note, by the architectural firm of 'Friedenthal und Marcuse'. The luxuriously fitted home, with its five reception rooms, elegant English fireplace, and accommodation for a household staff of two housemaids, a cook, a pair of laundry

---

1. Erich Eyck, *History of the Weimar Republic,* New York 1962, vol. 2, p. 155. The year 1928 was also one of the worst for the political fortunes of the National Socialists.
2. SPD Chancellor Hermann Mueller, quoted in S. William Halperin, *Germany Tried Democracy,* New York 1965, p. 361.

maids, and the driver of the family Packard, epitomized the self-assurance of the wealthy Republican bourgeoisie. Their new residence also reflected the precarious situation of the German Jews, however, for from his upstairs bedroom – bedecked with posters of Marx and Lenin – Herbert's brother Erich could look onto the house of their next-door neighbour, an unemployed provincial schoolmaster named Bernhard Rust, soon to become the powerful Nazi Minister of Science, Education and Popular Culture.

Less visible were the subterranean forces that were already undermining the foundations of prosperity and security: the unimpaired autonomy of the army, the concentration of the mass media and certain heavy industries in the hands of wealthy industrialists with links to splinter parties of the extreme right, and Germany's vulnerability to fluctuations of the American economy. In fact, the forces were now being consolidated that would soon push the Republic into its final phase.[3]

At that time, however, Marcuse was still more preoccupied with the consolidation of his own intellectual forces. He had, in his ongoing private studies since his university years, surveyed much of the landscape of contemporary European thought, touching down in such areas as art criticism and Gestalt psychology, though always remaining at a theoretical remove from the practices they embraced: he seems not to have tried his hand at any medium of artistic creation, just as he never ventured from the theoretical basis of modern psychology into either individual therapy or clinical training. But even as he ascended into ever more rarefied zones of philosophical speculation, his own private footpath (to borrow Nabokov's excellent metaphor) continued to run parallel to the great road of that troubled decade. The centrifugal tensions that were tearing at the social and political fabric of the Republic registered in his thinking in the very way he struggled to outline the field of a radical philosophical project in those years: philosophy could not claim validity unless it were able to grasp the existential realities of everyday life, and enter into them. In short, philosophy must become *concrete*.

---

3. Marcuse commented on the later period of the Republic in May 1974; cf. 'Heidegger's Politics: An Interview with Herbert Marcuse by Frederick Olafson' in the *Graduate Faculty Philosophy Journal,* vol. 6, no. 1 (winter 1977), p. 34 (hereafter 'Olafson'). The interview took place in San Diego.

The movements of thought that dominated the German universities during the first decades of this century were not equipped to meet the demands of the generation that studied in Germany after the First World War, and with which Marcuse felt a strong identification.[4] Reflecting the disproportionate successes of the natural sciences during the preceding half-century, especially relative to the humanistic disciplines, prevailing intellectual priorities concerned the epistemological foundations of the various sciences. Shallow extrapolations, popularizations, and critiques – the latter often taking the form of calls for a neo-idealist 'renewal of the humanistic disciplines' – became especially conspicuous during the Weimar period.[5]

Among the most extreme of the mainstream philosophical positions concerned to establish philosophy as a rigorously scientific system was the logical empiricism of the Vienna Circle (represented in Germany by Hans Reichenbach), whose militant neo-positivist programme simply dismissed as 'metaphysics' all presumptively philosophical undertakings that departed from strict logical or empirical criteria as the basis of their investigations. More influential in Germany were the competing currents of neo-Kantianism, whose common foundation was the Kantian premiss of the cognitive inaccessibility – and thus the practical autonomy – of the 'things-in-themselves' of the real world of sense and experience. Whether in its logical and natural-scientific orientations or its cultural and historical concerns, the necessary dictate of neo-Kantianism was the radical separation of the *subject* of a priori consciousness from the natural or cultural *object* of knowledge and action.[6]

For Marcuse, the decisive challenge to the prevailing currents of

4. Marcuse on several occasions stressed the 'generational' character of his philosophical restiveness; cf., for example, Olafson, p. 28, and Jürgen Habermas *et al, Gespräche mit Herbert Marcuse,* Frankfurt 1978, p. 10.
5. Cf. Fritz K. Ringer, *The Decline of the German Mandarins,* Cambridge 1969, pp. 305–434 for a lucid survey of themes and thinkers, many of which were raised by Marcuse in his writings of this period in order to be summarily dismissed.
6. These were among those specifically cited by Marcuse as 'the philosophies which at that time had dominated the German universities' (Habermas, pp. 10–12; Olafson, p. 29). For fuller characterizations of the German philosophical milieu and the issues involved, cf. Lucien Goldmann, *Lukács and Heidegger,* London 1977, pp. 1–24; Fritz-Joachim von Rintelen, *Contemporary German Philosophy,* Bonn 1970; for the background of 'the revival of neo-Kantianism in German social and historical thought', cf. Thomas Willey, *Back to Kant,* Detroit 1978.

philosophy unquestionably came from Freiburg. Husserl had been the first to hold out the possibility that rigorous philosophical analysis could regain access 'to the things themselves' closed off by the neo-Kantian dualism of knowing subject and the world to be known and transformed, as well as to suggest the complicity of modern scientific rationality in sustaining and in fact embodying this false dichotomy – a critique that was to survive as a central element throughout Marcuse's later thought.[7] It was in the work of Heidegger, however, that the real breakthrough from 'essences' to a genuinely concrete philosophy of Being appeared to have taken place: this was a philosophy that took as its starting point the *Existenz* of human beings in their world.

The two young Marxists Herbert Marcuse and Alfred Seidemann had not simply *read* Heidegger's *Being and Time*: together they undertook an exhaustive line-by-line critical analysis of the text, and on the basis of this study, Marcuse announced his intentions in his first philosophical essay. Following Marx, whose *Critique of Hegel's 'Philosophy of Right'* had first been published in the same year as *Being and Time*, Marcuse outlined his understanding of the current relation between thought and history: '[Heidegger's] work seems to us to indicate a turning point in the history of philosophy: the point where bourgeois philosophy transcends itself from within, and opens the way to a new, "concrete" science.'[8] Heidegger had returned philosophy to its proper foundations by redirecting it to the concrete conditions of human life in a natural and social world, and in the

7. In *Die Krisis der Europäischen Wissenschaften und die Transzendentale Phänomenologie,* Husserl maintained that post-Galilean science, by virtue of its mathematization (abstraction from empirical reality), in fact abrogates the transcendence of Reason and submits to a hidden '*lebensweltliche a priori*' which is thoroughly empirical, historical, and normative. Although the first part of the *Crisis* was not published until 1936, Aron Gurwitsch states that 'some of his preparatory studies for that book . . . date from the late twenties when Marcuse was still his student; cf. *Boston Studies in the Philosophy of Science,* New York 1965, vol. 2, p. 291.

8. Herbert Marcuse, 'Beiträge zu einer Phänomenologie des historischen Materialismus', *Philosophische Hefte,* 1 Berlin July 1928, reprinted in the first volume of Marcuse's *Schriften,* Frankfurt 1978, p. 358; trans. 'Contributions to a Phenomenology of Historical Materialism' in *Telos,* 4 (1969), p. 12. English sources will be cited where available, although I have not hesitated to make frequent adjustments in existing translations, especially in order to render Marcuse's terminology consistent with that of the Macquarrie and Robinson translation of *Sein und Zeit.* Consequently, in this chapter only, page numbers of the original (or, if possible, of *Schriften,* vol. 1) will be cited following the citation of existing English versions (for example, p. 67/42). All other translations are my own.

concept of 'authenticity' (*Eigentlichkeit*), had confronted the possibility of a meaningful existence. For Marcuse, however, philosophy had at that point defined a problem whose solution was a political one. As Marx had written of Hegel, 'it is now the *philosopher* in whose brain the revolution begins'.[9]

The immediate consequence of this discovery was that Marcuse resolved to return to Freiburg and resume his academic career under the direction of Heidegger himself. The task he had undertaken, however, was not solely to bring the practical imperative of Marxism to bear upon Heidegger's 'revolutionary beginnings'. Marxism itself had come to an impasse, as evidenced by its failure to provide theoretical guidance to German socialism in the period following the defeat of the revolution. Indeed, the mechanical subjugation of conscious political *praxis* to the inflexible dictates of historical laws – the theoretical legacy of the Second International associated in varying degrees with the German socialists Kautsky and Bernstein – corresponded to premises not far removed from the dualisms characteristic of academic neo-Kantian and neo-positivist thought, which Heidegger had overthrown.[10] A vital question, then, is why Marcuse appears not to have been equally attracted to the philosophical work that had accomplished a comparable renewal within Marxist theory itself: Lukács's pathbreaking studies published in 1923 as *History and Class Consciousness*.

The dualisms of both academic philosophy and vulgar Marxism, which had in effect removed man from the world of objects and experience and thus limited his power over it, were explicitly attacked throughout *History and Class Consciousness*, which had reintroduced the Hegelian category of 'concrete totality', of 'the all-pervasive supremacy of the whole over the parts',[11] as the

9. Karl Marx, 'A Contribution to a Critique of Hegel's *Philosophy of Right*: Introduction' in *Early Writings*, New York 1975. In general, the recapitulation in the 1920s of the themes of the nineteenth-century Kant-Hegel-Marx transition is often profoundly suggestive.

10. This familiar assessment is sketched briefly but persuasively by Goldmann who notes: 'Although for political reasons, Marxists could not enter the university before 1918, the entry of Marxists into the German-speaking universities did not involve any upheaval: their contribution was limited to the creation of a small number of courses scarcely different from those already in existence.' (p. 3)

11. Georg Lukács, *Geschichte und Klassenbewusstsein* (1923), trans. Rodney Livingstone, *History and Class Consciousness*, London 1971, p. 27. Cf. also the essay by István Mészáros, 'Lukács's Concept of Dialectic', in G. H. R. Parkinson, ed., *Georg Lukács. The Man, His Work, and His Ideas*, New York 1970, pp. 34–85.

epistemological means of transcending this fragmentation. Unlike Heidegger, however, Lukács had drawn the political consequences of this philosophical position: in concrete terms, this appears as a *social* totality integrated under the universal form of commodity production. Under the domination of the commodity structure, a 'phantom objectivity' is conferred upon human relations, transforming social relations into relations between things; subjectively, the consciousness of individuals comes to reflect and reproduce this system of domination, giving it the character of a 'second nature'. Extending Marx's analysis of the fetishism of commodities, Lukács describes this process of the 'reification of consciousness' as the most immediate obstacle to the liberation of the proletariat from these very conditions.[12]

In view of the impact of the book on the radical intelligentsia of Central Europe, and the close affinity between Lukács's concept of reification and his own (admittedly much later) analysis of the mental reproduction of 'one-dimensional' society, Marcuse's posture remains a matter for speculation – and here we are hardly guided by his sparse remarks at the time or his subsequent recollections. It is clear that he knew the book, for he referred briefly to its 'inestimable significance for the development of Marxism' in an essay of 1930,[13] and the *'Lukács-Debatte'* in any case dominated theoretical discussion on the left for ten years after the publication of *History and Class Consciousness*.[14] Marcuse's strident attacks against the philosophers Heidegger and Carl Schmitt a few years hence permit the conjecture that he may have found Lukács to be guilty of an intolerable intellectual compromise (with official Communism), but that political considerations argued for silence rather than adding one more divisive statement. For whatever reasons, the fact remains that he turned not to Lukács but to Heidegger in his search for a properly

---

12. Lukács's analysis is centred in his essay, 'Reification and the Consciousness of the Proletariat' (1922), esp. pp. 83–110. Two recent studies of Lukács's early work are Andrew Arato and Paul Breines, *The Young Lukács and the Origins of Western Marxism*, New York 1979, esp. part 2, and Michael Löwy, *Georg Lukács – From Romanticism to Bolshevism*, London 1979.

13. Herbert Marcuse, 'Zum Problem der Dialektik I', review of Siegfried Marck, *Die Dialektik in der Philosophie der Gegenwart*, Die Gesellschaft, 7 (1930), pp. 15–30; reprinted in *Schriften*, I, p. 421. He would later acknowledge that Lukács's philosophical reconstruction of his dialectical underpinnings of radical thought encouraged him in his belief 'that Marxism can be seen as more than a political strategy and a political goal'. (Habermas, p. 12).

14. For a thorough account, cf. Arato and Breines, p. 163–189.

ontological underpinning for Marxian revolutionary theory.

The project outlined by Marcuse in his essay 'Contributions to a Phenomenology of Historical Materialism' (1928) thus entailed the *reciprocal* critique of existential phenomenology and Marxism.[15] In the broadest terms, phenomenology had penetrated to the essential, underlying structure of human existence and disclosed its fundamental and universal character; historical materialism, enriched by the *ontological* understanding of this structure of life, could grasp its concrete historical variations. The resulting 'dialectical phenomenology' would permit analysis of the concrete possibilities contained within the bounds of any actual historical situation and indicate the scope of the revolutionary *praxis* that would transform it in the direction of this essential humanity. 'This', wrote Marcuse, 'is the extent of the validity of the dialectical phenomenology . . . it points to historical human existence, both in its essential structure, and in its concrete forms and configurations.'[16]

In identifying two planes or dimensions of human existence – the 'essential structure' uncovered by phenomenology and its 'concrete forms and configurations' as analysed by historical materialism – Marcuse had outlined the intellectual project that would occupy him in varying forms throughout the rest of his career: the effective integration of an essential standard of criticism with its material, historical objects. The first anticipations of this project were already evident in the aesthetic dimension portrayed in his 1922 *Doktorarbeit* as the domain of Wilhelm Meister, Keller's Heinrich, and Gustav

15. This essay and its implications have been examined in exhaustive detail: Alfred Schmidt's essay, 'Existential-Ontologie und historischer Materialismus bei Herbert Marcuse' contains the most balanced critical exposition of Marcuse's early *'marxistische Geschichtsontologie'* (in *Antworten auf Herbert Marcuse,* Frankfurt 1968); cf. also Paul Piccone: 'The forced synthesis of the two mechanically juxtaposed frameworks is bound to fail from the very beginning' ('Phenomenological Marxism' in *Telos,* 9, p. 11); Pier Aldo Rovatti writes: 'This is no doubt a non-systematic phase of inquiry.' ('Critical Theory and Phenomenology' in *Telos,* 15, p. 36).

16. Marcuse, 'Contributions to a Phenomenology of Historical Materialism' p. 22/370 (following our English/German convention). Several of Marcuse's early essays appeared in the *Philosophische Hefte,* a rather spirited but avowedly non-partisan philosophy journal edited by his friend Maximilien Beck. Beck was a student of Alexander Pfänder, a prominent member of the Husserl school who sought to gain access to the essence of the human soul and its values through a phenomenological analysis of the structure of the psyche. Pfänder's influence is evident in Beck's one systematic work, *Wesen und Wert,* Berlin 1925. After fleeing first to Prague, Beck emigrated to the United States under the sponsorship of the exiled *Institut für Sozialforschung,* of which Marcuse was by then a member.

von Aschenbach; now, driven more, perhaps, by the internal demands of that rudimentary aesthetic theory than by any external exigencies of the later years of the Weimar Republic, Marcuse prepared to return with his wife and infant son Peter to the birthplace of that project, where it would be reformulated with the rigour of philosophy.

As a post-doctoral student at Freiburg University, Marcuse was able to follow several major currents of contemporary German thought. It may well have been his Hegelian focus on structured 'totalities' that continued to attract him to Gestalt psychology, particularly the work of Max Wertheimer, its leading exponent.[17] He also followed the later writings of Husserl, as well as the work of Max Scheler, the first of Husserl's two phenomenological 'antipodes'.[18] The other 'antipode' was, of course, Heidegger, still very much in favour when Marcuse became one of about a dozen of his advanced students in the transitional year in which the former assumed Husserl's chair in the philosophy faculty.

Most contemporary accounts portray Heidegger as having been a brilliant and exceptionally dedicated teacher, determined 'to bring philosophy home to the students as their own concern *qua* students'.[19] Marcuse and his student colleagues were not exceptions to this general appraisal, learning from him the boundless depth of reading and thinking that can be brought to the study of a text: 'he really could take one sentence in Aristotle or even in a pre-Socratic', he recalled, 'and analyse it not only for an hour or two hours, but half a semester'.[20]

17. The psychological perspective for which 'a whole is more than or different from the sum of its parts' (Rudolf Arnheim), and which expounded a fully dialectical conception of the interaction of a field of objects with the subject of perception was also taken up at this time by Marcuse's later colleagues T. W. Adorno (noted in Susan Buck-Morss, *The Origin of Negative Dialectics,* p. 9) and Max Horkheimer, who discussed it in his important essay, 'Materialismus und Metaphysik' (*Zeitschrift für Sozialforschung,* II, 1, 1933). On Wertheimer, cf. Ringer, pp. 374–9.

18. Husserl's own term, in a letter to Roman Ingarden of 19 April 1931, quoted by Herbert Spiegelberg, *The Phenomenological Movement,* The Hague 1969, vol. 1, p. 230.

19. 'From Husserl to Heidegger. Excerpts from a Freiburg Diary by W. R. Boyce Gibson', Herbert Spiegelberg, ed., in *Journal of the British Society for Phenomenology,* vol. 2, no. 1 (1971), p. 74.

20. Olafson, p. 37. Marcuse added: 'I must say frankly that during this time, let's say from 1928 to 1932, there were relatively few reservations and relatively few criticisms on my part.' (p. 27) This seems overly self-effacing, for his initial approach to Heidegger was as a Marxist, and his writings of the period document areas of substantial dissension.

Such attempts as were made to advance the phenomenological inquiry in the explicitly political directions envisaged by Marcuse were confined to discussions within his circle of friends, however (his radical student colleagues at this time included the Marxists Seidemann and Siegfried Landshut). The hostility of Husserl – still very much a presence at Freiburg – to dialectical thought was well known,[21] and while he was a man of deep humanity, he regarded political, moral, and aesthetic judgements as matters of private belief and practice: true philosophy must be founded as objective, 'rigorous science' and could not be attained through the unstable truths of a 'historicist' or *'weltanschauungliche'* approach.[22] Of greater ultimate significance was Heidegger's indifference to the philosophical analysis of political and social reality. Marcuse recalled no occasions during his four years in Freiburg on which he entered into discussions of a seriously political nature with his teacher, and Heidegger never responded to his attempts to extend the range of phenomenological analysis.[23]

Marcuse's attempts to penetrate beyond the abstractness of the existential framework constructed by Heidegger were sketched out in a series of about a dozen essays and reviews written during this period.[24] These pieces covered a range of contemporary theoretical issues, and, viewing them together, it is possible to identify two thematic concerns. The first entailed the dialectical 'mapping' of the ontological terrain first surveyed by Heidegger, and upon which Marxism would be reconstructed; the second feature of his early essays was an aggressive, and perhaps self-conscious, meta-theoretical defence of the theoretical component of *praxis*. This

21. Cf., for example, Gibson, pp. 69, 73; also Maurice Natanson, *Husserl: Philosopher of Infinite Tasks,* Evanston 1973, pp. xiv–xv.
22. This philosophical conception, which guided Husserl's personal conduct, is formulated with rigorous clarity in 'Philosophy as Rigorous Science' (1911) – cf. Husserl, *Phenomenology and the Crisis of Philosophy,* trans. Quentin Lauer, New York 1965, esp. pp. 122–47.
23. Olafson, p. 29 (confirmed in conversation with HM).
24. Most were published in Beck's *Philosophische Hefte,* in the mainstream *Archiv für Sozialwissenschaft und Sozialpolitik,* and in *Die Gesellschaft.* The latter is significant as it was the theoretical organ of the German SPD, nominally under the direction of Rudolf Hilferding, but in fact edited by Albert Saloman. Marcuse's sympathies were definitely to the left of the establishment socialism of the SPD, and while he recognized the importance of Hilferding's classic *Finanzkapital* (1910), he felt he had little in common with the politics of the later Hilferding (now Finance Minister in the coalition government). The *Gesellschaft* had commissioned his work, and, as he recalled, 'they paid well'.

phenomenological penetration to the underlying structures of human existence, together with the dialectical grasp of material, historical conditions, would be called 'Concrete Philosophy'. Its elaboration followed a course that began with Heidegger and ended with Hegel.

There is surely no place in this analysis for an independent presentation of Heidegger – an attempt that would in any case be futile. Nevertheless, in order to disclose the *progression* of Marcuse's thought across this phase of his life, and to indicate some of the otherwise unlikely reasons for the attraction of a young, left-wing Berlin intellectual to the philosopher whose work was to become equally attractive to activists of the extreme right, it really is essential to examine certain of Heidegger's categories. Heidegger's thought (and his conception of thinking) weighed heavily upon Marcuse, but only because his 'appropriation' of it was critical and selective.[25]

In *Being and Time* Heidegger had undertaken to analyse the structure of Being – not the nature of some class of entities that might 'be', but of the very *be*-ing of entities as such.[26] The analysis of the *Seinsfrage*, the question of what it means for something 'to be', moves into the range of vital human concerns once Heidegger justifies his methodological decision to use 'human being' – the being of that peculiar entity which alone is able to grasp the meaning of being – as the vehicle of his analysis: 'We are ourselves the entities to be analysed. The Being of any such entity is [the kind of Being that is] in each case mine'.[27] A phenomenology thus appears to be possible only as an ontology of human existence: the

25. In the brief discussion which follows, I have tried to sustain a reasonable vocabulary that will stand on its own, without presupposing a prior familiarity with the relevant works of Martin Heidegger's early period. I hope thus to have freed the main text, as far as possible, from 'the jargon of authenticity' (Adorno), reserving the footnotes for more detailed explication and citation, where necessary.

26. The 'ontic' investigation of entities themselves is the task of the special sciences (anthropology, psychology, biology, etc.): 'Ontological inquiry is indeed more primordial as over against the ontical inquiry of the positive sciences'. Martin Heidegger, *Being and Time,* p. 31/11 (the first figure will refer to the Macquarrie and Robinson translation, New York 1962; the second, to the seventh German edition, Tübingen 1953).

27. Ibid., p. 67/42.

transcendental *essence* of (human) Being can be disclosed through a phenomenological analysis of the structure of *existence.* [28]

The phenomenological method, as adapted by Heidegger, demands that the object of analysis be allowed to reveal itself to investigation 'as it shows itself', that is, in a way that includes both the subject and the object of perception in the analysis.[29] Starting not from any external, logical, material, or metaphysical premiss, but from the object of analysis itself, phenomenology characteristically asks, 'How is it possible, what must be presupposed, in order for a thing to be?' For Heidegger, the results of this preliminary inquiry disclose that to *be* means to be a self in a world, with objects and with others (hence his term for human being is *Dasein*, 'being-there').

In this interrelatedness, it is possible for the self to become entirely submerged in the immediate cares and concerns of the everyday world into which – in Heidegger's characteristic jargon – we are 'thrown'.[30] While part of our existence is clearly claimed by the immediate and the actual, part of our being *is* the possible ways of being that have not yet been closed off by reality. There is, in Heidegger's ontology, a definite priority given to this latter mode of the possible;[31] thus, where our being-towards our own possible, free existence is overshadowed by our being-in our actual, determined existence, we may lose sight of the fullness of our being, of what it means for a human being to *be*. This condition of 'fallenness', of acquiescence in 'the real dictatorship of the "they" ' in which the possibilities open to one's own self are 'covered up' in the submission to the actual facts, Heidegger calls the 'inauthentic' mode of being; its positive existential complement is the mode of 'authenti-

28. Thus 'Existential ontology', by which Heidegger simply means the analysis of the Being of *human* being; '*The "essence" of Dasein lies in its existence*', so the investigation of this essence (ontology) is necessarily existential. (Ibid., emphasis original).

29. Heidegger's formal, somewhat more technical definition is 'to let that which shows itself be seen from itself in the very way in which it shows itself from itself'. (Ibid., p. 58/34).

30. 'The expression "thrownness" is meant to suggest the *facticity* of its being delivered over'. (Ibid., p. 174/135, emphasis original).

31. '. . . possibility as an *existentiale* [an *a priori* mode of being of Dasein] is the most primordial and ultimate possible way in which Dasein is characterized ontologically.' (Ibid., p. 183/143–144, and all of sections 31 and 32, for a development of this central doctrine.)

city', being with the full awareness of the significance of what it means to be. [32]

Heidegger's ontology thus has a 'spatial' axis that extends to such trans-historical constants of human existence as a caring self, being-in-the-world, and being-with-others. Superimposed upon these ontological constants are the dimensions of authentic and inauthentic existence. The concept of authenticity, however, tied as it is to one's potentialities and thus to possible future ways of being, makes manifest the *temporal* axis of the existential ontology. [33] We *are* in the present, indebted to the past, and oriented toward the future, and this temporal structure of human being opens up the component of Heidegger's ontology which was to be central for Marcuse: the concept of *historicality*. [34]

Heidegger's ontological-phenomenological analysis of Being revealed that to be is to be in time. From the disclosure of the temporal structure of every possible way of being, Heidegger prepares to conclude his analysis by linking time to history. But we are not permitted to return from ontology to more familiar ('ontic') ground: 'The proposition, "Dasein is historical", is confirmed as a fundamental existential ontological assertion. This assertion is far removed from the mere ontic establishment of the fact that Dasein occurs in a "world-history".' [35] We are pressed behind the common-sense conception to a deeper level, from history (the domain of things and events) to historicality (the very *being* of things and events in *time*).

The method of existential phenomenology stipulates that the

32. Ibid., p. 164/126. Heidegger's terms are *Eigentlichkeit* and *Uneigentlichkeit*; Magda King, in her study of *Heidegger's Philosophy,* New York 1974, pp. 56–9, proposes the English 'owned' and 'disowned' existence. Less familiar and more awkward, these terms nonetheless grasp the root *eigen* = 'own' and thus transmit the individualized meaning of one's awareness of one's *own* self.

33. Temporality (*Zeitlichkeit* or 'time-liness') is the ground of Being, i.e. it is that which makes Being possible: 'Temporality temporalizes itself as a future which makes present in the process of having been.' (Ibid., p. 401/350); also 'The primary phenomenon of primordial and authentic temporality is the future.' (p. 378/329)

34. Most writers have adopted the convention of rendering *Geschichtlichkeit* as 'historicity' which is bound to cause difficulties for readers familiar with the only existing English translation of *Sein und Zeit,* where quite separate meanings are assigned to 'historicity' (*Historizität*) and 'historicality' (*Geschichtlichkeit*); cf. Heidegger, p. 41/20–21.

35. Ibid., p. 381/332.

analysis of history begin not with abstract laws or impersonal forces, but with the being of that entity for whom history is a problem: *human* being-in-a-world becomes the ground of history, that which makes history possible. The existential grasp of history, then, does not take hold of such conceptual processes as 'the class struggle', 'disenchantment of the world', or 'the decline of the West', nor even of a bare sequence of past events. Rather, the inherited possibilities open to the presently existing individual (one's 'heritage'), and the authentic choices and decisions one makes in the light of them (one's 'fate') become 'the *locus* of the problem of history',[36] and the reference point from which the historical 'worlds' of such subjects become significant.[37] 'Historicality', then, the pivotal concept in Heidegger's ontology, refers to the way in which individuals proceed to a self-awareness of the way they live in history; it comprehends the way in which individuals relate to their own past and appropriate ('to makes one's own') the tradition of which they are a part.

Heidegger's ontology, then, as sketched in these broadest of strokes, postulates the essential aspects of human being: as individuals we are thrown into a world populated with others and with objects; we exist in time, lost in the factual limitations of our present circumstances or conscious of our own future potentialities. This structure of being and of the awareness of it, as disclosed by the phenomenological analysis of *human* being, is the immutable essence of human existence: it remains fixed, unaffected by the manifold variety of its existence.

But of what value could such an interpretation be to a Marxist, especially since the philosopher Heidegger was very explicit as to the function of this analytical framework, which seems no less resistant to serving as an 'arm of criticism' than to being used to mount a 'criticism of arms' (Marx)? Notably, since it is our very essence to have both limitations and possibilities (they are 'equiprimordial'), Heidegger does not wish to advance any sort of value-laden claim as to the superiority of authentic self-awareness over inauthentic fallenness in the world. Thus he warns that his existential ontology is

36. Ibid., p. 427/375.
37. The study or science of history is not concerned with the actual facts, for this is the foreclosed ground of inauthenticity; rather, authentic 'historiology will disclose the quiet force of the possible'. (Ibid., p. 446/394).

not to be mistaken for a description of an ideal realm or mode of existence: 'So neither must we take the fallenness of Dasein as a "fall" from a purer and higher "primal" status.'[38] Rather, phenomenology simply takes as ontologically given the dualism of authenticity/inauthenticity, the immersion in the factical world of the present and the awareness of one's future possibilities, and applies it to the ontological analysis of the being (*Dasein*) which exists in these modes. He adds: 'it may not be superfluous to remark that our own interpretation is purely ontological in its aims, and is far removed from any moralizing critique of everyday Dasein and from the aspirations of a "philosophy of culture".'[39]

Despite his repeated disclaimers, however, the extrapolation of the analysis into the domain of ethical or sociological critique does not necessarily violate the fundamental tenets of Heidegger's work, even if it departs radically from his own intentions. Indeed, it was Marcuse's claim that the elaboration of the results of Heidegger's investigations in the direction of political criticism was a step mandated by the internal logic of the fundamental ontology itself. With certain important adjustments, the theory of being could reveal the link between 'the possibilities of authentic being and its fulfilment in authentic action'.[40]

The first of Marcuse's dialectical correctives to Heidegger's ontology was stated with welcome simplicity: 'The individual is not the historical existential unit'.[41] It is true that in a very few years he would finally acquire – from the writings of the young Marx – the completed conceptual framework that would reveal that the opposite is in fact the case: that the goal of the historical process is

38. Ibid., p. 220/176.
39. Ibid., p. 211/167. Cf. also pp. 264–5/222: 'If we are to use (the expression "falling") *in existential analysis,* we must avoid giving it any ontically negative "evaluation".' (emphasis added)
40. Marcuse, 'Contributions to a Phenomenology of Historical Materialism', p. 17/363. Heidegger would himself make the fatal transition from the ontological (historicality) to the ontic (history) in a brief but momentous phase of his career: 1933–34.
41. Ibid., p. 27/376. Lucien Goldmann rightly makes much of this as one of the central points of contention between *Being and Time* (1927) and *History and Class Consciousness* (1923). On substantive grounds, his attempt to link the most influential representatives of contemporary Marxist and existentialist thought is insightful and often profound. His ancillary argument, however, that Heidegger explicitly designed *Being and Time* as a philosophical rejoinder to Lukács's work is not supported by more than circumstantial evidence, and is in any case unnecessary to his thesis (Goldmann, pp. 27–39).

precisely the universal, social individual (*Gattungswesen,* or 'species-being') of post-capitalist society. At this point, however, he was able to point out only that the full realization of human potentialities is not an existential task of individual self-awareness, but the result of a historical struggle which is collective (political) in nature. The subject of the historical process implicit in *Being and Time,* to the contrary, could be identified in its central concept of authenticity which Heidegger virtually defined as the being-aware of the possibilities open to *one's own self.* Marcuse acknowledged the significance of the restoration of individual existence to the centre of philosophy, but as a Marxist it was impossible for him to have considered the achievement of an authentic existence as a solitary act of 'anticipatory resoluteness', of which few would in any case be capable. Heidegger had recognized the existential constant of *Miteinandersein* (Being-with-others), but had failed to make the necessary extrapolation to the social collectivity that is the condition ('ground') of the possible (authentic) realization of the individual.

In the manner of Marx's critique of Hegel, Marcuse claimed that in its individual bias, Heidegger's philosophy had in effect misunderstood itself: where the individual is constrained by a network of reified social relationships, a true philosophy of individualism will address a socio-economic totality and will bring the individual in only at the end. He alludes to the continuity of Heidegger's work with the false individualism characteristic of the tradition of bourgeois thought, which focuses prematurely on the atomized individual of capitalist society: 'Thus it is precisely when philosophy wishes to take seriously its concern with the individual that it has no right to neglect the world in which the existence of the individual is fulfilled . . . In this case, the individual is no longer the point of departure, but rather the *objective* [*Ziel*] of philosophy.'[42] Having assessed the 'fallen' state of modern capitalist society in terms of class differentiation and the social division of labour, he proposes a mediation which advances the existential analytic from the level of the historical individual to historical society, and back again: the call to abolish inauthenticity, to paraphrase Marx, is the call to abolish the conditions that give rise to inauthenticity! The existen-

42. Marcuse, 'Uber konkrete Philosophie', in *Archiv für Sozialwissenschaft und Sozialpolitik,* vol. 62, pp. 111–28, reprinted in *Schriften* 1, pp. 404–5. In the manner of Heidegger himself, we might illustrate the critique with the word-play 'Dasein' = 'das Ein'.

tial ontology thus provided for him an explosive, revolutionary category which presupposes the radical transformation of society.

This directly implies the second of Marcuse's major objections to Heidegger's system, namely its abstractness from concrete conditions: human Being (*Dasein*) remains remote from human beings (*Daseiende*), historicality nowhere intersects with history. Once again, Heidegger's philosophical breakthrough – in this case the interpretation of being through the existential given of time – is not challenged, but only his failure to press his discovery to its *immanent* and radical conclusions. In identifying the essential historicality of human existence, Heidegger had retreated from *history*, and from the material conditions within which an authentic existence might be achieved: 'phenomenology cannot restrict itself to the demonstration of the historicality of its object, and subsequently fall back into abstractions . . .The analysis of an historical object must be grounded in historicality, must always take into consideration the concrete historical situation and its concrete "material condition".'[43] Making a charge that would recur throughout his later work, Marcuse insisted that the value of abstraction is to provide not a point of departure, but a point of return.

Having thus collectivized Heidegger's individual, authentic subject, and concretized his abstract concept of historicality, Marcuse had outlined a 'dialectical phenomenology'. With Heidegger, he accepted the notion of an ontological *Grundstruktur*, a 'fundamental structure' of human existence 'which, although not ahistorical, endures through all historicality';[44] but with Marx, he insisted that analysis cannot leave these existential categories formal and abstract: 'There is no uniform world of meaning related to a uniform existence. The ontological relationship between Dasein and the world is not a disconnected abstraction, but is constituted in concrete historical events.'[45] In his writings in the last years of the Weimar Republic, Marcuse referred to this bivalent analysis, together with the practical political imperatives arising out of it, as 'Concrete Philosophy'.

So-called Concrete Philosophy utilizes an ontology of social life

43. Marcuse, 'Contributions to a Phenomenology of Historical Materialism', p. 21/368–9.
44. Ibid., p. 22/370.
45. Ibid., p. 26/374.

in order 'to confront the threatened existence with its truth'.[46] Though he clung to a conception of Marxism as a theory of revolution, this phenomenological revisionism suggests that Marcuse had not found in any of its prevailing forms an adequate philosophical interpretation of the repressed human potentialities to be liberated by the overthrow of the prevailing conditions. The attempt to derive a transcendent standard of truth based upon an existential ontology finds little support in the known writings of Marx at that time, and was surely not a project that could be rendered compatible either with the immediate questions of strategy and organization that dominated official Communism in the 1920s, or with the philosophically inadequate investigations of the foundations of a socialist society undertaken by Soviet Marxist theorists after Lenin.

But Marcuse's framework was hardly more congenial to other contemporary revisionist attempts to restructure Marxian theory on a philosophical basis. He appears to have been surveying the intellectual landscape of Marxism at this stage in his life, establishing his own position – as he always would – through a series of philosophical confrontations. Among these was the neo-Kantian attempt to secure the ethical and epistemological foundations of Marxism, which had been prominent earlier in the decade through the work of Karl Vorländer and the Austro-Marxist Max Adler. For Marcuse their work represented an abuse of the possibilities of transcendental criticism, and threatened to weaken Marxism politically under the guise of purifying it philosophically. He attacked its characteristic removal from concrete existence in the (objective) social world, but not the notion of transcendental criticism *per se*, for he held the revolutionary possibilities of such a critique to be enormous: 'The concept of "possibility" as the central concept of the transcendental method can certainly, in the last analysis, put reality into question. Concretely, it can lead to the dissolution of the ossified categories of reality, and violently shake this existing reality itself.'[47] The neo-Kantian Marxists did not and could not follow this direction, however, for their work aimed at a transcendental

---

46. Marcuse, 'Uber konkrete Philosophie', p. 395. Although this critical function of social analysis is evidently a Marxian inheritance, the concept of truth as the 'dis-closure' (*Erschlossenheit*) of inherent existential possibilities which have been covered up ('foreclosed') is thoroughly Heideggerian; cf. the important discussion of the meaning of truth in *Being and Time*, pp. 256–73/212–30.

47. Marcuse, 'Transzendentaler Marxismus?' in *Die Gesellschaft*, Berlin 1930, vol. vii,

epistemological basis for the social sciences that deliberately exclud-ed the social reality manifest in time and space. Marcuse continued: 'The division between phenomenon and thing-in-itself does not create two essentially different objective domains, but rather posits one and the same domain of being [*Seinsgebiet*]: reality as the correlate of experience.'[48] Far from challenging the neo-Kantians' creation of a transcendent philosophical (ontological) basis for social criticism, he charged them with the *failure* to do so.

If the neo-Kantian Marxists had reduced reality to the (a-historical) conditions of possible knowledge of it, Karl Mannheim's *Ideology and Utopia*, which appeared in 1929, committed the inverse error: knowledge was stripped of its possible autonomy and reduced to a mere reflection of reified social processes. Marcuse did not slight the accomplishment of Mannheim's important work, for the historicization of knowledge restored to social theory the practical, material dimension that had been closed off by Adler and Vorländer. Still, by relativizing knowledge, Mannheim had denied himself access to the 'external' plane of criticism revealed by phenomenological ontology. Following Heidegger, Marcuse main-tained the conception of a trans-historical 'fundamental structure' of human being, to which corresponds a transcendent dimension of truth: 'As factical realizations, all historical situations are only historical transformations of such fundamental structures [*Grund-strukturen*], which are realized in different ways in any order of life . . . Truth and falsehood would in that case lie in the relation of the factical realization to such fundamental structures.'[49] Concrete Philosophy was defined in terms of this 'linkage'.

If Concrete Philosophy was not to have a strangely metaphysical cast, then, it would be necessary to address the substance of these

part 2, pp. 304–326, reprinted in *Schriften*, 1, p. 449. This essay was a lengthy critique of Adler's *Kant und der Marxismus* (1904) and other writings. Marcuse had confronted Vorländer's work in the previous year: cf. his 'Besprechung von Karl Vorländer: *Karl Marx, sein Leben und sein Werk*', in *Die Gesellschaft*, vol. vi, part 2 (1929), pp. 186–9.

48. Ibid., p. 452. Although the Kantian doctrine of moral autonomy rendered neo-Kantianism 'useless for the purposes of fascism' (the standard is Benjamin's), the latter-day collaboration of Marx and Kant does not appear to have produced lasting theoretical – not to say practical – results. Cf. Tom Bottomore and Patrick Goode, eds., *Austro-Marxism*, Oxford 1978, esp. p. 15f; Willey; for an appraisal of Adler, cf. William Johnston, *The Austrian Mind*, Berkeley and Los Angeles 1972, pp. 109–11.

49. Marcuse, 'Zur Wahrheitsproblematik der soziologischen Methode', in *Die*

essential ontological 'structures' that are held to underlie a 'transcendent dimension of truth'. In this task Marcuse was to be immeasurably assisted by the researches of his fellow student Siegfried Landshut. In 1932, Landshut and J. P. Mayer published Marx's recently discovered *Economic and Philosophical Manuscripts* of 1844, an event which has proved to be decisive for subsequent Marxist studies.[50] In Marcuse's interpretation, the *Manuscripts* provided conclusive proof that philosophy discloses the true basis for a theory of revolution, and even more startling, they revealed that Marx had constructed the critique of political economy upon foundations that had been laid by ontological investigations. Almost with a tone of disbelief, Marcuse wrote: 'Marx's positive definitions of labour are almost all given as counter-concepts to the definition of *alienated* labour, and yet the ontological nature of this concept is clearly expressed in them.'[51] Labour was not simply one human activity among others for Marx – it was 'grasped as the real expression and realization of the human essence'.[52]

Marcuse's argument followed the lead provided by Marx in his transformation of Hegel's concept of labour (*Arbeit*). In the *Phenomenology of Mind* Hegel had expounded an ontological conception according to which labour, broadly conceived as man's historical self-objectification, defined the essence and the existence of human being-in-the-world. For Marcuse, Marx's decisive achievement in the Paris *Manuscripts* was to have identified the *political* content of Hegel's pivotal philosophical categories (alienation, objectification)

Gesellschaft, vol. vi, part 2 (1929), p. 369. Cf. also Martin Jay: 'there is – and here Marcuse the Heideggerian was speaking – a transcendent dimension to truth. Historical facticity was part of a deeper structured reality which had to serve as the final court of appeal for the validity of a theory in the long run.' ('The Frankfurt School's Critique of Karl Mannheim and the Sociology of Knowledge', *Telos*, 20, summer 1974, p. 80.)

50. Mark Poster transmits the claim that Heidegger had a hand in editing the *Manuscripts* (*Existential Marxism in Post-war France*, Princeton 1975, p. 222, n. 25).

51. Marcuse responded almost instantaneously to the publication of the *Manuscripts*, which he immediately recognized as 'a crucial event in the history of Marxist studies'. His review, 'Neue Quellen zur Grundlegung des historischen Materialismus', appeared in *Die Gesellschaft*, vol. ix, part 2, pp. 136–74, reprinted in *Schriften*, I, trans. 'The Foundations of Historical Materialism', by Joris de Brès in Marcuse, *Studies in Critical Philosophy*, Boston 1972; this passage appears on p. 13/519. It might be noted that Marcuse continued to hold to this 'ontological' interpretation of Marx; cf., for example, his comments to Olafson (p. 31) and Habermas (pp. 10–11).

52. Marcuse, 'The Foundations of Historical Materialism', p. 12/518.

while preserving the philosophical (ontological) conception of labour in his critique. Labour is not simply or even primarily an economic activity, which might be contrasted with other activities (play, for example, or intellectual work) as in the manner of bourgeois political economy; it is rather the fundamental event in human existence, the condition of genuine individuation, 'that in which every single activity is founded and to which [it] again return[s]'.[53] It follows that the emancipation of human beings *as such* demands, as a prelude to total revolution, the overthrow of capitalist economic relations.

The revolutionary critique of political economy is thus founded upon a philosophical interpretation of human existence and its potentialities, and a political analysis of their negation under the historical conditions of alienated labour. With this achievement, the demands made upon a dialectical phenomenology appeared to have been met: the linking of the human *essence* with the material conditions of its *existence*: 'For Marx, essence and facticity, the situation of essential history, are no longer separate regions or levels independent of each other: the historical appearance of man is *taken up into the definition of his essence* . . . which can be defined in *history*, and only in history.'[54] Not surprisingly, it is precisely at this point in Marcuse's work that the influence of Heidegger begins to recede; Heideggerian categories would recur over the years – the existential theory of the meaning of death, and the analysis of the structure of aesthetic perception – but from this point on his philosophical function was supplanted by the insight of the young Marx.

Marcuse found in Karl Marx the radical ontology he had sought in Martin Heidegger. The 1844 *Manuscripts* gave him a way to look (ontologically) at the whole human being, to allow his critical gaze to see through and beyond the fragmentation of life in class society and the false individuation of the labour process; on the other side of capitalism – and of bourgeois political economy – lay a vision of what Marx himself repeatedly called 'the human essence', man's 'essential being'. Only when the still-abstract 'species-being'

53. Marcuse, 'Uber die philosophischen Grundlagen des wirtschaftswissenschaftlichen Arbeitsbegrifs', in *Archiv für Sozialwissenschaft und Sozialpolitik* (Tübingen 1933), vol. 69, no. 3, pp. 257–92; reprinted in *Schriften*, I, trans. 'On the Philosophical Foundation of the Concept of Labour in Economics', *Telos*, 16 (summer 1973), p. 13/562.
54. Marcuse, 'The Foundations of Historical Materialism', p. 28/535 (emphasis original).

(*Gattungswesen*) of the individual is portrayed against the real alienation of the labour process of capitalist society could Marcuse's Concrete Philosophy become truly concrete.[55]

Marcuse attempted to press beyond even the radical standpoint of the *Economic and Philosophical Manuscripts*, however. Departing once and for all from the terrain of any possible Marxist orthodoxy, he extended the conception of the ontological centrality of labour into a standard against which *all* 'factical' historical configurations might be judged and condemned: 'Being human is always "*more*" than its present existence. It goes beyond every possible historical situation and precisely because of this there is always an ineliminable discrepancy between the two: a discrepancy that demands constant labour for its overcoming, even though human existence can never rest in possession of itself and of its world.'[56] The perpetual need for labour, and thus its ontological centrality, is based upon the conception of an 'essential excess of Being over existence',[57] of an essential dimension of human being which can *never* attain fulfilment in the historical world. As such, it provides the ontological foundations for a transcendent political critique, for a 'permanent revolution' in a sense much nearer to Goethe's Faust than to the European proletariat:

> Werd ich zum Augenblick sagen:
> Verweile doch! Du bist so schön!
> Dann magst du mir in Fesseln schlagen,
> Dann will ich gern Zugrunde gehn.[58]

Like Faust, Marcuse's philosophical standpoint builds in a fundamental irreconcilability with the prevailing reality principle, with the established society (as two of his later formulations would have it); he has laid the ontological foundations for a truly great refusal.

---

55. Karl Marx, *Economic and Philosophical Manuscripts*, esp. the section on 'estranged labour' at the end of the first manuscript, passim.
56. Marcuse, 'On the Philosophical Foundations of the Concept of Labour in Economics', p. 22/575.
57. 'Dieser wesentliche Uberschuss des Seins über das Dasein . . .', ibid.
58. Johann Wolfgang von Goethe, *Faust* I, ll. 1699–1702; (my translation: 'Should I to any moment say: Linger on! Thou art so sweet! Then must you fasten me in chains, Then my end I gladly meet.') Goethe remained one of Marcuse's great reference points throughout his life.

The immediate historical situation did in fact call attention to the European proletariat, however, and systematic reflection upon his own political obligations as a Marxist philosopher comprised a second theme which ran through Marcuse's writings of the late twenties and early thirties, alongside the ontological investigation. By that time the powerful German Communist Party had long since submitted to the doctrinal hegemony of the Soviet Union where the drive towards 'permanent revolution' had been supplanted by the consolidation of 'socialism in one country', the unprecedented regimentation of labour contrasted sharply with its professed emancipation, and, in Germany, the denunciation of the 'social fascism' of the SPD had replaced the dream of a United Front. The Social Democrats, on the other hand, continued to cling to the prestige of their parliamentary successes of 1928, restricting their demands to modest questions of political and economic reform.[59]

Against this background, Marcuse understood that Marx's insight into the ontological realm of freedom beyond the mere legal suppression of private property or the extension of electoral representation was no mere 'spinning of intellectual webs': 'Indeed, the generally insufficient gravity and lack of seriousness of vulgar Marxism in its attitude towards philosophy signifies very much more than merely a theoretical error: namely, it tears asunder the unity of theory and practice that is decisive for the (theoretical and practical) class struggle. This rupture is not only arbitrary and erroneous, but rather is grounded in its turn in the changed situation of the socialist parties within the changed social situation generally.'[60] The exclusion of the philosophical underpinning, which the 1844 *Manuscripts* had revealed as Marx's route to the theory of revolutionary socialism, was being expressed in concrete political decisions that would prove disastrous equally in their failure (Germany) and in their success (the Soviet Union).

At this critical juncture in European history, when the Great

---

59. On German Communism and the programme of the Comintern, now firmly under the control of Stalin, cf. the relevant sections of Gustav Hilger and Alfred G. Meyer, *The Incompatible Allies*, New York 1953, Kermit McKenzie, *Comintern and World Revolution. 1928–1943*, New York 1964, and Louis Fischer, *Russia's Road from Peace to War,* New York 1969. On the parliamentary program of the SPD between 1928 and the end, cf. Erich Eyck, vol. 2, and S. William Halpering.

60. Marcuse, 'Das Problem der geschichtlichen Wirklichkeit', in *Die Gesellschaft*, Berlin 1931, part, 1, pp. 350–67, reprinted in *Schriften,* I, p. 469; this in the context of remarks on Karl Korsch's *Marxismus und Philosophie*.

Depression had destroyed the 'unshakable foundations of the Republic' which had so recently been celebrated, it had become clear to Marcuse and many other leftist intellectuals that fascism was now in the ascendant, and that the force in German society most likely to be able to disarm it was a unified socialist movement; the elaboration of a theoretical basis for socialist unity, founded upon philosophy rather than strategy, had, in such circumstances, become a difficult priority to defend. Marcuse began by declaring his debt to the Greeks, who were the first in the Western world to define theory as the highest mode of *praxis*: 'We are inclined', he wrote, '(although no longer with such a good conscience!) to maintain this hierarchical order.'[61]

The parenthetical ambivalence expressed in this remark reflects one of the few points in his life at which the defence faltered. Marcuse had consistently maintained an aggressive stance on the importance of theoretical reflection, for spontaneous or even 'tactical' political activism was bound to be co-opted, whereas 'the truths of philosophy are not grounded in facticity, even if it is factical Dasein that must carry them out'.[62] The conception of a Concrete Philosophy, however, carried with it special obligations: it is not permitted to remain abstract, but has for its task 'the scrutiny of every moment of existence: to favour those which represent a movement toward the truth, and to hinder those which lead toward fallen modes of existence'.[63] Nor does advocacy alone entirely fulfil the mandate of Concrete Philosophy, for the existential conditions that engage philosophy are also political conditions. Recognizing this, the philosopher 'who deserves the name' must be prepared to throw the full weight of his life into the struggle in the public domain for the transformation of existence: in the manner of Socrates, Plato, and Kierkegaard.[64]

Herbert Marcuse, however, was somewhat less immersed in the

---

61. Marcuse, 'On the Philosophical Foundations of the Concept of Labour in Economics', p. 31/587.

62. Marcuse, 'Uber konkrete Philosophie', p. 397. Though the conceptions expressed are continuous, the Heideggerian language of this passage (written in 1929) contrasts sharply with that of his essays written under the influence of Marx's 1844 *Manuscripts*.

63. Ibid.

64. The isolated, iconoclastic mission of Kierkegaard described by Marcuse (ibid., pp̀. 400–3) sounds very much like that of the outcast figure of the artist of the *Künstlerroman*, in perpetual struggle against 'the life-forms of the surrounding world'.

public sphere. Although the German universities had been strong-
holds of conservative-nationalist sentiment throughout the nineteenth century and well into the 'liberal' Weimar period, and the
National-sozialistischer Deutscher Studentenbund (founded in 1926 behind
the slogan, 'With the State Against the Professors') had gained
control of the national student movement and of many universities
as early as the semester of 1930–31,[65] Freiburg was subject to the
moderating influence of the Catholic student *Kartellverband* (allied to
the Centre Party) and remained relatively quiet. Where the issue of
academic freedom appeared to be involved, Marcuse would attend
such political demonstrations as did take place at the university, but
most of his final years in Germany were taken up with the
preparation of his major interpretation of Hegel, which he had once
hoped would qualify him for an academic career.

Hegel's Ontology and the Foundations of a Theory of Historicality is
clearly not in the spirit of Marx's critique of Hegel – it is, of course,
indebted to the teaching of Heidegger, and conveys this indebted-
ness explicitly, as also in its language and philosophical categories.[66]
Further, the texts which it analyses – Hegel's early theological
writings, the *Phenomenology of Mind*, and the *Science of Logic* – are those
which at first approach seem most distantly removed from political
concerns. Even so, it may well be excessive to state that in *Hegel's
Ontology* Marcuse 'interrogates Hegel from a perspective scarcely
reconcilable' with that of his later work,[67] for although it is cast in

---

65. Cf. Wolfgang Zorn, 'Student Politics in the Weimar Republic', in the *Journal of
Contemporary History,* vol. v, no. 1 (1970), pp. 128–43; also Hans Peter Bleuel and
Ernst Klinnert, *Deutsche Studenten auf dem Weg ins Dritte Reich,* Gütersloh 1967.

66. Herbert Marcuse, *Hegels Ontologie und die Grundlegung einer Theorie der Geschichtlichkeit,* Frankfurt 1932; my translations are from the third edition of 1976. The book
was to have been Marcuse's *Habilitationsschrift,* the scholarly publication prerequisite to an academic position. Interest in *Hegels Ontologie* has, unfortunately, been
confined to specialists, but there is a summary discussion of it by Jean-Michel
Palmier in his enormous tome, *Herbert Marcuse et la nouvelle gauche,* Paris 1973, pp.
42–54 and 90–5. Palmier considers it less in its own intellectual-historical context
than in contrast with Marcuse's later *Reason and Revolution* (1941): 'En l'interro-
geant ici, nous n'avons aucunement l'intention de discuter en détail l'interpréta-
tion que donne Marcuse du système hégélien, mais plutôt de souligner ce qui
oppose ces deux interprétations de Hegel', the one 'Heideggerian' and the latter
'Marxist' (p. 42). Paul Robinson mentions it very briefly in *The Freudian Left,* New
York 1969, pp. 154–5.

67. Palmier, p. 91. Palmier maintains that a 'decisive rupture' separates *Hegels
Ontologie* from the rest of Marcuse's work.

the expository form mandated by the academic conventions of the *Habilitationsschrift*, it in fact contains virtually all the concepts that powered the revolutionary Concrete Philosophy.

To recognize its political implications, one need only recall the prominence of academic and Marxist neo-Kantianism in the preceding decades: the duality of subject and object, which lay at the heart of the Kantian system, had appeared to Marcuse to promote a philosophical impasse with direct political overtones, and Hegel's resolution of this state of alienation in the concept of the *verlebendigte Welt*, an objective world penetrated by subjectivity, pressed him toward a critique of the divided world within which Kantianism survived. The critical transformation of Kantian metaphysics indeed proves to be one of the principal themes of Marcuse's analysis, which demonstrates the way in which Hegel raised the hitherto *epistemological* schism of subject and object, self and other, finitude and infinitude to fully *ontological* status: the unification of these 'moments of Being' is shown to lie in the concept of *life* – practical human activity – and 'not in some sort of pure apperception'; its ground is always *history.*[68]

Throughout his analysis of the evolution of Hegel's early thought, Marcuse stressed this grounding in and commitment to the concrete historical world and its modes of material life. '*Das Wesen*', he writes, '*muss erscheinen*'[69] – the concern of the Hegelian ontology ultimately rests neither with abstract human 'essence' nor with the transitory forms in which it 'appears', but precisely in the historical modes of their interdependence. Despite his Heideggerian propensity to permit the analysis to drift to an abstract dimension of pure Being, the fact that Marcuse always renders this interrelation as a dynamic process – *Bewegtheit*, the 'being-in-motion' of life which partakes of both ontological essence and historical existence – already presses at the limits of static existential ontology.

More broadly significant, however, is Marcuse's abiding interest in the overall conception of Hegelian philosophy: 'the task of philosophy, as Hegel conceives it, arises from a necessity, a need of human life in a determinate historical situation: the situation of division'.[70] The 'situation of division' – so clearly reminiscent of the 'problematic civilization' he had seized upon ten years earlier in his

---

68. Marcuse, *Hegels Ontologie*, p. 303.
69. Ibid., p. 91 (quoting Hegel).
70. Ibid., p. 18.

reading of the early Lukács – is for Hegel an ontological principle of human existence. The unifying power of philosophy, in conjunction with creative human *praxis*, confronts the objective (objectified) world, and the Being-in-motion (*Bewegtheit*) towards the resolution of this alienation constitutes the dialectic of history. The 'end' of this process – expressed in the central ontological concept of *Sichselbstgleichheit-im-Andersein* (selfsameness-in-otherness)[71] – is the overcoming of the division between subjectivity and objectivity, actuality and potentiality, abstract (ontological) essence and concrete (historical) existence. The pursuit of this '*Reich der Freiheit*', in its various guises from Hegel's earliest theological writings throughout the *Phenomenology of Mind* and the *Logic*, is really the structural theme of *Hegel's Ontology*, and this overarching concern with human freedom links it with the larger contours of Marcuse's thought.

Marcuse's interpretation does in fact permit the anti-metaphysical possibilities of Hegel's thought to survive, even if the radicalization of the idealist synthesis would not be completed for another decade (by which time the existential ontology of Heidegger would have long been supplanted by that of the young Marx). In focusing upon the 'two-dimensionality' (*Zweidimensionalität*) of Hegel's ontology, he stresses that ontological essence and historical fact 'are not two independent "worlds", for-themselves and posited in isolation, which will ultimately be brought into a relation with one another, but rather, dimensions of Being' which only have existence in their unity.[72] His demonstration of the actual and potential 'dimensions of Being' has a fundamental philosophical meaning that is also a political meaning: 'the opposition thus presupposes for its part a prior signification which is its ground, an originary synthesis (!) which is the "measure" of all comparison and of all opposition.'[73] This notion of a permanent, transcendent standard of criticism, a trans-historical 'measure of all comparison and of all opposition', has already been identified as a distinctive feature of Marcuse's thought.

---

71. This is the language of Hegel's *Science of Logic* (1812–16); this pivotal concept is illuminated with great lucidity by Albert Hofstadter, 'Ownness and Identity: Rethinking Hegel', in *The Review of Metaphysics*, vol. xxviii, no. 4 (June 1975), pp. 681–97.

72. Marcuse, *Hegels Ontologie*, pp. 84–5. There is evidently much more than a terminological continuity with his famous analysis of the fractured totality of 'one-dimensional' society (1963).

73. Ibid., p. 236 (punctuation original).

But there is discontinuity as well. In his later years of internationalal recognition, Marcuse always tried to deflect attention away from his own intellectual accomplishment (usually by disparaging the opposition, for, as Marx had once quipped, on the level plain even anthills look like mountains). As an ambitious young scholar, however, he submitted to no such restraint: when his family visited Freiburg to celebrate the publication of *Hegel's Ontology*, he climbed onto the base of a statue and announced to his incredulous visitors, 'ICH BIN BEDEUTEND!' – 'Now I'm somebody!'

It is the scepticism engendered by the book itself, of course, that is more significant. The manifestly expository format and Heideggerian categories of *Hegel's Ontology* caused leftist reviewers to wonder about the politics of the young scholar whose writings had thus far appeared in the official Social Democratic press and other even more mainstream philosophical journals.[74] From Frankfurt, Theodor Adorno chided Marcuse, 'who usually holds onto Heidegger's public dogma with the rigour of a disciple', but acknowledged that a decisive and promising revision had begun to take place.[75] Marcuse now 'inclined from the "meaning of Being" to the disclosure of beings; from fundamental ontology to philosophy of history; from historicality to history'.[76] Although Adorno did not suppress the wish that the link with the philosophical dimension of ontology might have been severed altogether (rather than simply grounded in concrete history and historical *praxis*), he and his colleagues of the Frankfurt Institute for Social Research were interested.

This was fortunate, because Marcuse's academic career was about to end before it had begun. *Hegel's Ontology* had been accepted by Heidegger's publisher, Klostermann, but he never formally submitted it to Heidegger himself, and the latter probably never read it. By 1932 the academic *Habilitationsschrift* seemed a useless formality to Marcuse: he was Jewish and a Marxist, and the Nazis, with 230 deputies in the Reichstag, thousands of SA-men in the streets, and millions of unemployed supporters throughout the

74. Such reservations were recalled by Leo Löwenthal in conversation. The *Archiv für Sozialwissenschaft und Sozialpolitik*, for example, was founded by Max Weber and Werner Sombart.

75. Theodor Wiesengrund-Adorno, 'Besprechung von Herbert Marcuse's *Hegels Ontologie*', in *Zeitschrift für Sozialforschung* (Frankfurt-am-Main 1932), Band 1, p. 409.

76. Ibid., pp. 409–10.

country, were preparing to take over the fate of Germany.

Heidegger, at this time, appears to have revealed nothing of his political sensibilities: no anti-semitism or pro-Nazi sympathies have been reported in his personal life or in the execution of his academic duties, and his conduct remained entirely unpolitical. Relations between the professor and his radical *Privatdozent* never broke down, and toward the very end of the Republican era, Marcuse was even entrusted with a delicate mission: Heidegger was to be offered the historic Fichte-Hegel-Schelling Chair at the University of Berlin, and Marcuse was asked by a friend in the Prussian Ministry of Education to act as intermediary! Heidegger, of course, declined this and subsequent calls, but whether this was because his celebrated *Naturgefühl* rooted him in his Black Forest environment, or because he too anticipated that the government that had made him the offer would fall, cannot now be known. Heidegger's notorious entry into the Nazi Party as Rector of Freiburg University took place during the *Revolution-Semester* (spring 1933), by which time Marcuse and his family had already been safely out of the country for several months. The news came as a complete shock.[77]

Marcuse's cordial relations with Husserl, however, were never rendered uncertain. Their acquaintance extended as far back as Marcuse's outstanding defence of his *Künstlerroman* dissertation before Husserl and other members of the Freiburg faculty in 1922, and he would periodically visit the Husserls in their apartment on the Lorettestrasse while he was working on the Hegel book. They evidently regarded one another with mutual esteem, and it is very likely that it was Husserl who interceded on his behalf, recommending Marcuse to his friend Kurt Riezler, a prominent Weimar

---

77. Most of the preceding details emerged in conversation with HM. I have omitted details of 'der Fall Heidegger' and discussion of the difficult problem of the relation between his philosophical ideas and his political disgrace, for I am satisfied that all of the events in question took place following Marcuse's emigration and did not directly affect him. Further, it was only later that he began to reflect on the vulnerability of Heidegger's thought: 'Now, from personal experience I can tell you that neither in his lectures, nor in his seminars, nor personally was there any hint of his sympathies toward Nazism . . . So his openly declared Nazism came as a complete surprise to us.' (Olafson, p. 32). Though I cannot entirely follow the somewhat apologetic tone of his conclusions, the most comprehensive single source on the Heidegger case is undoubtedly Karl August Moehling, 'Heidegger and the Nazis', unpublished dissertation (De Kalb 1972). The fullest primary documentation is to be found in Guido Schneeberger, *Nachlese zu Heidegger: Dokumente zu seinem Leben und Denken*, Berne 1962.

political figure and educator, then *Kurator* of the University of Frankfurt.[78] Marcuse was already known to Riezler, and to Max Horkheimer, director of the neo-Marxist Institute for Social Research affiliated with the university, and so, out of this network of interconnections, Leo Löwenthal was sent to Freiburg to interview Marcuse. Their discussions initiated a life-long friendship, and a confirmation from Horkheimer and Friedrich Pollock resulted in an invitation for the Freiburg philosopher to enter the Frankfurt Institute.

At the time of the onset of the Great Depression in Germany, the Institute had undertaken an empirical survey of skilled and unskilled workers in the Rhineland and Westphalia, and its researchers had been shocked to find, underneath the 'overt' attitudes of good democrats, the 'covert' psychological profile of the passive authoritarian character. They conjectured that this would mean that little resistance could be expected, fears that were heightened by the Nazi victories in the elections of the first depression year, in September 1930. Since 1931, then, 'when the clouds had already begun to gather',[79] they had begun preparing their evacuation, gradually shifting the Institute's activities to its Swiss branch.

The imminent danger had already touched Marcuse personally as well: in Berlin, the family chauffeur had just left the service of his father, joined the SS, and become Goebbels's private driver. Although Marcuse had never been a particularly astute forecaster of political developments, the signs of the coming catastrophe were clear enough, and he immediately accepted his new assignment to the Geneva office. He left Germany with his family several weeks before Hitler was named Chancellor.

78. Some interesting remarks about Riezler's relations with Horkheimer, Heidegger, and others are to be found in Riezler's published diaries; cf. Kurt Riezler, *Tagebücher-Aufsätze-Dokumente,* Eingeleitet u. hrsg. von. Karl Dietrich Erdmann, Göttingen 1972, esp. pp. 143–53.

79. International Institute for Social Research: *Ten Years on Morningside Heights. A Report on the Institute's History 1934 to 1944* (n.p., n.d.), p. 2. The summary of the Institute's 1929–30 survey was provided by Leo Löwenthal.

3
HORKHEIMER AND
CRITICAL THEORY
(1933–1941)

From Freiburg, Marcuse and his family went first to Zurich; by the time they resettled in Geneva, six months later, the consolidation of the one-party state and the 'coordination' (*Gleichschaltung*) of social and political life in Germany was practically complete. While still in Switzerland, Marcuse wrote the last of his pieces to be published in Germany for decades, a brief study of the fate of Karl Jaspers's 'philosophy of foundering': 'All talk of historicality remains abstract and detached as long as the wholly concrete, "material" situation is not stressed . . . From the very outset, this *Existenzphilosophie* has the potential to sanction as "historical" *any* situation of Being [*Dasein*].'[1] Against the unnamed backdrop of German fascism, which survived behind 'the transcendence that transcends all determinate beings',[2] Marcuse initiated a sober reappraisal of his search for an Archimedean standpoint.

Of necessity, his philosophical criticism was to become increasingly allied to a pragmatic political criticism directed towards the existing situation in Europe. Like many of his new colleagues in the exiled Institute of Social Research, Marcuse had no illusions that National Socialism would prove to be a transitory 'stage' or that after an initial outburst of violence and bellicosity it would spend its fury. A few days before the 'Night of the Long Knives' consolidated Hitler's total dictatorship, Marcuse finally left Europe. He arrived in New York on Independence Day 1934, and – speaking '*ein bisschen Englisch*' – immediately took out American naturalization papers.

1. H[erbert] M[arcuse], 'Philosophie des Scheiterns. Karl Jaspers Werk', *Unterhaltungsblatt der Vossischen Zeitung*, Number 339, 14 Dezember, 1933, p. 6. Three months later this historic liberal newspaper – founded in 1704 and owned by the Jewish House of Ullstein – was forced out of business, one of the first victims of the Reich Press Law of October 1933.
2. Ibid.

It has been said that 'the history of National Socialism is the history of its underestimation',[3] a charge that applied to political parties and trade unions in Germany, as much as to foreign diplomats and journalists. The newly renamed International Institute of Social Research, to the contrary, regarded the processes of authoritarian rule and obedience as the central phenomena of modern times. From 1931, once the directorship of the Institute had passed to the Frankfurt social philosopher Max Horkheimer, virtually all its intellectual resources were channelled into the study of the sources of authoritarianism. Following the terminology proposed by Horkheimer in a seminal essay of 1937, the set of theoretical assumptions that guided their collective researches became known as Critical Theory, and its elaboration as an alternative to the currents of thought underlying the authoritarian state was Marcuse's main contribution to their work.

In Germany, the Institute had been affiliated with the University of Frankfurt-am-Main, and in the purge of spring 1933, which saw the dismissal of nearly one-third of the latter's faculty, it was finally closed by the Nazis 'for tendencies hostile to the state'. It had come to function by this time on a distinctively collaborative basis, and this legacy was preserved when its membership largely reassembled in New York – via Geneva, Paris, and London – as guests of Columbia University.[4] One of their public relations statements reported: 'It has been a standard practice of the Institute, since the Frankfurt days, to meet regularly for discussion of the various problems arising out of separate branches of investigation. Every contribution by any member of the staff has, prior to publication, had the advantage of frequent discussion and criticism by members representing different disciplines. Thus the Institute has constantly been a collective entity and not merely a more-or-less artificial and

3. Karl Dietrich Bracher, *The German Dictatorship*, New York 1970, p. 199.
4. For the origins of the *Institut für Sozialforschung*, and details of its subsequent history in New York (as the International Institute of Social Research) I have drawn upon three of its own reports: 'IISR. A Short Description of its History and Aims', New York 1935; 'IISR. A Report on its History, Aims, and Activities, 1933–1938', New York 1938; 'IISR. Ten Years on Morningside Heights. A Report on the Institute's History, 1934–1944', (unpub., 1944, in U. C. Berkeley collection). Indispensable is Martin Jay's *The Dialectical Imagination. A History of the Frankfurt School and the Institute of Social Research, 1923–1950*, New York 1973; cf. also Phil Slater's *Origin and Significance of the Frankfurt School. A Marxist Perspective*, London 1977; for an 'institutional' perspective, cf. Helmut Dubiel, *Wissenschafts-organisation und politische Erfahrung*, Frankfurt 1978.

haphazard gathering of scientists working in related fields.'[5] Indeed, when the Institute's finances fell on hard times after the start of the war, and it was forced to request outside grants to maintain the $4,200 salaries of Marcuse and Franz Neumann, applications were based on the claim that should either of the two permanent associates have to seek outside employment, his departure 'would greatly disrupt the cooperative work of the Institute which requires the full activity of each of its staff members'.[6]

Consequently, Marcuse's work during this period cannot be considered in isolation. To be sure, the progressive development of his thought continued in its course, but just as it had adopted Heideggerian categories in Freiburg, it was now shaped by the priorities of the exiled Frankfurt Institute under the leadership of Horkheimer. It is possible to follow the 'inner' movement of Marcuse's thought only by first accounting for his contribution to their collective projects.

I

The primary activity of the Institute was the publication of its German-language journal, the *Zeitschrift für Sozialforschung*, in which a comprehensive analysis of the dominant trends in social thought and practice was undertaken.[7] As the 'resident philosopher' in this period, Marcuse was assigned the task of reviewing current literature in the various fields of European philosophy. This otherwise unexceptional duty is worth mentioning both because it frequently constituted his major activity – he often treated dozens of books in a volume – and because the course of his reviews vividly documents the disintegration of intellectual life in Nazi Germany.

Professors in the German universities had historically been regarded as public officials, and the basic 'Act for the Reform of the Civil Service', promulgated on 7 April 1933, led to the dismissal of over 1,600 Jewish, leftist, and republican scholars in the first year of

5. 'ISSR. Ten Years on Morningside Heights', p. 10.
6. Letter from Asst. Director Friedrich Pollock to Stephen Duggan, Chairman of the Emergency Committee in Aid of Displaced Foreign Scholars, 7 June 1941; files in Archives of N. Y. Public Library.
7. Paris, vols. I–VIII, 2 (1932–39) hereafter *ZfS*; continued in English as *Studies in Philosophy and Social Science*, vols. VIII, 3–IX, 3 (1939–41), hereafter *SPSS*.

its operation. In the resulting 'intellectual migration' from Central Europe, unprecedented in modern times, the German universities were decimated – a price acknowledged by Hitler, who nonetheless declared his willingness to pay it – and the philosophical work that survived was frequently a disgrace to an almost legendary heritage of scholarly intelligence and imagination.[8] The range of options left to those who remained was reflected in the very tones in which Marcuse reviewed a decade of philosophical writing under National Socialism.

Those scholars who undertook an 'internal migration' were often accorded a generous measure of sympathetic respect, as in his collective consideration of a dozen seemingly unrelated studies in the history of philosophy which, he wrote, 'is perhaps justified today by the fact that in these works the interpretation is not determined by an accommodation to the ideology of the authoritarian state, but rather by the attempt at an objective treatment of their topics'.[9] Passive resistance easily merged into acquiescence, however, as Marcuse intimated in his review of a new edition of Aquinas and related modern texts: 'The three Catholic publications appear as a grossly apologetic literature: the present attack against Christianity is answered with the secure and self-confident demonstration of what the Christian culture of the West has been.'[10] And outright intellectual capitulation could be met with bitter sarcasm: 'The following works serve as representative publications of German psychology in the present time. This fact, and not the scientific

8. To the protests of Max Planck, President of the Kaiser Wilhelm Society for the Advancement of Science, Hitler is reported to have replied, 'If the dismissal of Jewish scientists [read 'scholars'] means the annihilation of contemporary German science, we shall do without science for a few years.' Cited in E. Y. Hartshorne, *The German Universities and National Socialism*, Cambridge 1937, pp. 111–2. Cf. also Bracher, pp. 266–72. Some relevant studies of the emigration: Norman Bentwich, *The Rescue and Achievement of the Refugee Scholars*, The Hague 1953; Robert Boyers, ed., *The Legacy of the German Refugee Intellectuals*, New York 1972; Stephen Duggan and Betty Drury, *The Rescue of Science and Learning*, New York 1952; Laura Fermi, *Illustrious Immigrants*, Chicago 1968; D. Fleming and B. Bailyn, *The Intellectual Migration*, Cambridge 1969; Kurt Grossman, *Emigration: Die Geschichte der Hitler-Flüchtlinge*, Frankfurt a.M. 1969; H. Stuart Hughes, *The Sea Change*, New York 1975; Franz Neumann *et al.*, *The Cultural Migration*, Philadelphia 1953; Helge Pross, *Deutsche akademische Emigration*, Berlin 1955; Joachim Radkau, *Die deutsche Emigration in den USA*, Düsseldorf 1971.

9. Herbert Marcuse, 'Besprechungen', *Zeitschrift für Sozialforschung*, Jahrgang V, Heft 3 (1936), p. 411.

10. *Zfs* V, 1 (1936), pp. 109–10.

value of the two publications, justifies a detailed examination.'[11]

Marcuse always recognized 'the superhuman courage and loyalty' demanded of those intellectuals 'who carry on their fight for freedom in the authoritarian states',[12] and as the violence in Germany escalated, resignation before the apparatus of censorship, intimidation, and dismissal was accordingly treated with generosity. He reserved his most uncompromising condemnations for those German thinkers whom he believed to have betrayed the intellectual calling itself by their attempt 'to make use of philosophy for the current ideology of German fascism':[13] Carl Schmitt, whom he attacked with particular severity, the right-wing nationalist Hans Freyer, and such outright Nazi propagandists as Erich Rothacker, Ernst Krieck, and Franz Böhm.

In these polemical reviews for the *Zeitschrift*, Marcuse participated in the Institute's ongoing confrontation with National Socialism as it was expressed (or resisted) in works of logic, metaphysics, and the history of philosophy. His more systematic argumentation took place in his own essays for the journal; while juristic and socio-economic aspects of the authoritarian state were analysed by Franz Neumann, Otto Kirchheimer, and Friedrich Pollock, and its cultural and psychological aspects by Adorno, Fromm, and Löwenthal, Marcuse dealt primarily with its ideological underpinnings.

The collective nature of this undertaking is evident in Marcuse's work, which reflects the Institute's characteristic analysis of fascism as fundamentally continuous with its liberal past.[14] The attack of the new 'heroic-folkish' world-view on liberalism, he argued, is understandably conducted on the ideological plane: analysis of the deeper social and political realities reveals 'the reason why the total-authoritarian state diverts its struggle against liberalism into a struggle of "Weltanschauungen", why it bypasses the social structure basic to liberalism: it is itself largely in accord with this basic structure. The latter was characterized as the organization of society through private enterprise on the basis of the recognition of private property and the private initiative of the entrepreneur. And this

11. *ZfS* V, 1 (1936), p. 121.
12. *SPSS* IX, 1 (1941), p. 147.
13. *ZfS* VII, 3 (1938), p. 406.
14. The evolution of the views of the different members of the Institute on this problem is traced in Jay, ch. 5.

very organization remains fundamental to the total-authoritarian state.'[15] The difference is that at the authoritarian (monopolistic) stage of capitalism, the total mobilization of individual and economy is required. In such conditions, the formal and indeterminate character of even the most progressive ideas of the bourgeois era renders them serviceable to the fascist state, or they are proven to have been ideological masks for their opposites.

This analysis of the fate of the bourgeois heritage of 'progressive' liberalism reflects the profound influence exerted upon Marcuse's thought by Max Horkheimer, his closest collaborator and the member of the group to whom he acknowledged his greatest intellectual debt. Above all, it was Horkheimer's attempt to construct a modern theory of rationality situated in 'the unbridgeable gulf between reality and reason'[16] that constituted their common ground. Horkheimer's guiding conception – which would recur throughout Marcuse's own career – was that the battle against forms of irrationalism conducted by the philosophical representatives of the militant bourgeoisie was transformed in the course of the consolidation of that class into a new irrationality, that is to say, into a new rationalization of the existing order of social domination.

The ideological (and political) consequences of this process, which would later be summarized as 'the dialectic of enlightenment', were elaborated in the 1930s in Horkheimer's philosophical and historical studies in the *Zeitschrift*. Taken together with those of Marcuse, they exemplify the distinctive brand of dialectical criticism developed by the members of the 'Frankfurt School' in those years: the dominant concepts of modern thought and ideology were dismantled, traced back to the material circumstances in which they originated (characteristically as the progressive requirements of an ascending middle class), and then systematically reconstructed so as to reveal their changed political functions in new circumstances. The truth as well as the falsehood of the concepts that guide philosophy, science, and social *praxis* is thus exposed, and their ideological hold is loosened.

This philosophical analysis, which sought to substantiate the

15. Marcuse, 'Der Kampf gegen den Liberalismus in der totalitärer Staatsauffassung', *ZfS* III, 1 (1934), trans. Jeremy Shapiro, 'The Struggle Against Liberalism in the Totalitarian View of the State', in Marcuse, *Negations*, Boston 1968, p. 10.
16. Max Horkheimer, 'Materialismus und Metaphysik', *ZfS* II, 1 (1933), trans. Matthew O' Connell *et al.*, in Horkheimer, *Critical Theory*, New York 1972, p. 12.

characteristic position of the Frankfurt School that 'the turn from the liberalist to the total-authoritarian state occurs within the framework of a single social order',[17] had its direct correlate in the work of the second of the major influences on Marcuse in this period, namely that of the Institute's economist Friedrich Pollock, who had proposed the concept of 'state capitalism' in his contribution to the Frankfurt School's analysis of fascism.[18] In brief outline, Marcuse credited Pollock with the demonstration that what the 1930s witnessed was not the breakdown of the capitalist system, but its consolidation at a higher level of organized planning, state intervention, and authoritarian control of private economic initiative: fascism did not signify the collapse of capitalism, but only of its 'liberalist' phase.[19] It is clear that in their analyses of the transfer of individual autonomy to 'large-scale units' and ultimately to the state, Pollock and Marcuse were offering economic and philosophical descriptions of the same historical process.

In addition to his writings for the *Zeitschrift für Sozialforschung*, Marcuse's participation in two other collaborative undertakings may be mentioned. In 1936, the Institute had been invited to offer an annual course for the Extension Division of Columbia University on 'Authoritarian Doctrines and Institutions in Europe'. Here he had the opportunity to present his findings in a more concrete manner (his lectures included 'The Individual and Modern Society' and 'State and Individual under National Socialism') as part of a collaborative presentation dealing with 'the genesis of the authoritarian state in the history of modern society, analysed from economic, psychological, sociological, juristic, and philosophical viewpoints'.[20] The most substantial of the Institute's projects in this period, however, in which the findings of philosophy were regarded as integral, was the *Studien über Autorität und Familie*, published in 1936. This was a massive multi-disciplinary project that sought to

17. Marcuse, 'The Struggle Against Liberalism . . .', p. 19.
18. For a valuable survey of the largely neglected positions of the Institute's economists Henryk Grossman and Friedrich Pollock in the Frankfurt School's 'discussion of the collapse of the capitalist system', cf. Giacomo Marramao, 'Political Economy and Critical Theory' *Telos*, 24 (summer 1975), pp. 56–80; also Jay, esp. pp. 152–5.
19. Cf. especially Pollock's essays, 'Die gegenwärtige Lage des Kapitalismus und die Aussichten einer planwirtschaftlichen Neuordnung', *ZfS* I, 1/2 (1933), and 'State Capitalism: Its Possibilities and Limitations', *SPSS* IX, 2 (1941).
20. 'IISR. A Report on its History, Aims, and Activities, 1933–1938', p. 16; also

demonstrate the centrality of the institution of the family in rendering the individual receptive to the influence of authority, and assuring its renewal. To the sociological and psychoanalytical frameworks, supplied by Horkheimer and Erich Fromm respectively, Marcuse contributed a 'History of Ideas' section situating the whole problematic within the evolution of the religious and philosophical systems in which modern structures of authority have their sources.[21]

A high degree of methodological self-consciousness informed every stage of this undertaking, as was the case with most of the Institute's work. Indeed, Marcuse's contribution to the elaboration of a theoretical framework of dialectical social analysis – the 'critical theory' of society – is perhaps the most enduring legacy of his collective work with the Institute of Social Research. As a philosopher grounded in the tradition of Hegel and Marx, Marcuse had been recruited to the avowedly scientific research institute out of the conviction that the empirical researches of the social sciences must be guided by correct theoretical and methodological principles: 'The Institute considers, therefore, the European philosophies of the eighteenth and nineteenth centuries as important for the theory of society as are political economy and statistics.'[22] In the cautious language of emigrés, 'the philosophies of the eighteenth and nineteenth centuries' referred specifically to the incorporation of the rationalist epistemology of the Enlightenment into Hegel's system, and the subsequent transformation of philosophical idealism into the critical social theory of Marx. Indeed, in their commitment to recovering the allegedly 'external' conditions of scientific knowledge,

mentioned is a seminar – undoubtedly led by Marcuse – on 'selected chapters of Hegel's *Logic* in connection with the discussion of the basic concepts necessary in the social and cultural sciences'. The two lectures are listed in 'IISR. Ten Years on Morningside Heights', pp. 23–36; also noted are several unpublished manuscripts: 'The Impact of Rationality on Modern Culture', 'Private Morale in Germany' (with Adorno), and 'German Re-education' (with Adorno). The latter appear to have been contributions to a projected study of post-war German reconstruction, one of several projects which the Institute planned but never completed.

21. Marcuse, 'Ideengeschichtlicher Teil', in *Studien über Autorität und Familie,* Paris 1936, trans. Joris de Bres in Marcuse, *Studies in Critical Philosophy* (London 1972), pp. 49–155; also his survey of 'Autorität und Familie in der deutschen Soziologie bis 1933' in the last section of the *Studien* (pp. 737–52). On the background, structure, and reception of the *Studien,* cf. Jay, pp. 117–33.

22. 'IISR. A Short Description of its History and Aims', p. 3.

and to incorporating these into the theoretical concepts themselves, the 'scientists' of the Institute echoed Hegel: 'Let the other sciences try to get somewhere by doing without philosophy as much as they please; without it they cannot contain life, spirit, or truth.'[23]

With Critical Theory, Marcuse, Horkheimer, and their colleagues had sought to build a bridge between the concern of empirical social science with the material conditions of life, and the transcendent truths embedded in the abstractions of idealist philosophy. This implied a thoroughgoing critique of both traditional Cartesian theory and idealist metaphysics, each of which failed to grasp the material conditions of its existence, and thus ultimately betrayed its avowed pursuit of objectivity and rationality.

The refusal or inability of the positivist social sciences to transcend the empirical givens of the social reality of which they are a part not only contradicts their own condition of objectivity, but renders their concepts and findings plainly ideological, 'a factor in the continuous renewal of the existing state of affairs'.[24] In fact, Marcuse and Horkheimer held that the empiricist programme remained at that primitive stage of cognition described by Hegel where 'the worship of "observable facts"' precludes a critical understanding of the essentially contradictory character of existence: 'The real field of knowledge', however, 'is not the given fact about things as they are, but the critical evaluation of them as a prelude to passing beyond their given form.'[25]

Philosophical idealism, by contrast, had indeed grasped *potentiality* as an integral moment of actuality, preserving in its structure the tension between reason and reality. By constructing an autonomous dimension of abstract rationality, where the images of freedom and happiness might find a refuge from the 'false materialism' of the present, the progressive currents of the idealist philosophy of the bourgeois era had contained a protest against this order. But this protest could have no material consequence: truth – in the sense of the full realization of human potentialities – is secured, but transferred to the realm of pure subjectivity, and freedom 'rather

23. G. W. F. Hegel, 'Preface' to the *Phenomenology of Mind,* trans. Walter Kaufmann, New York 1966, p. 102.

24. Max Horkheimer [and Herbert Marcuse], 'Traditionelle und kritische Theorie' in *ZfS* VI, 2 (1937), in Horkheimer, *Critical Theory,* p. 196.

25. Marcuse, *Reason and Revolution. Hegel and the Rise of Social Theory* (1941), revised edition, Boston 1960, p. 145.

modestly sets up house within necessity'.[26]

The result in both cases – idealist metaphysics and positivist social science – is the surrender to the power of the given. Against this capitulation, Marcuse and Horkheimer attempted to construct a theoretical framework that would confront the antagonistic character of the existing society and point beyond it. In the 1930s this effort took the form of studies of society as an integrated (but still contradictory) historical totality whose ruling ideas had their origins in a defunct liberal past, but which preserved in them a demand whose realization points into the future. The 'regulative ideas', which engaged the inherent partisanship of the theory, were those whose authentic realization would explode the framework of the established reality, and which could exist within it only in a truncated and ideological form: mind, happiness, individualism, beauty, morality, and above all, Reason.

It has appeared to some later critics that the positing of abstract concepts as political goals, rather than rallying the social forces that could realize them, is evidence of a journey from Hegel to Marx that was arrested at the stage of Young Hegelianism.[27] This ahistorical assessment must be weighed against the realities of the mid thirties, however, when the structure of the theory was being elaborated: Germany was manifestly preparing for war, the European proletariat – the potential agent of social change – had been crushed in Central Europe and was on the defensive in Spain, and in Moscow Stalin's trials had significantly discredited the socialist ideal. The Marxian injunction of the ultimate unity of theory and practice retained its force, but the miserable fates of more practically minded groups testified to the fact that this unity was not to be immediate, but must be transferred to the future. In fact, Horkheimer

26. Marcuse [and Max Horkheimer], 'Philosophie und kritische Theorie', *ZfS* VI, 3 (1937), trans. 'Philosophy and Critical Theory', in *Negations,* p. 138. This theme is fully developed in two complementary essays: Horkheimer, 'Egoismus und Freiheitsbewegung', *ZfS* V, 2 (1936), where it is described as the 'affirmative Charakter der Kultur' (p. 219), and Marcuse's essay by that title, *ZfS* VI, 1 (1937).

27. Alastair MacIntyre, *Marcuse,* London 1970, and – more substantially – Leszek Kolakowski, *Main Currents of Marxism,* vol. 3 (Oxford 1978) both direct this charge against Marcuse in particular. From the very different perspective of 'scientific' Marxism, Göran Therborn accuses Marcuse of a 'self-destructive intellectual hyper-radicalism', a charge which he extends to the Frankfurt School enterprise of *Ideologiekritik* generally. Cf. his detailed critical analysis of 'The Frankfurt School' in *New Left Review* 63 (Sept – Oct 1970), pp. 65–96.

anticipated this challenge when he inveighed against those leftist intellectuals who 'cannot bear the thought that the kind of thinking which is most topical, which has the deepest grasp of the historical situation, and is most pregnant with the future, must at times isolate its subject and throw him back on himself.'[28] Just as the Institute insisted upon maintaining the *Zeitschrift* as a refuge for the German language in exile, they acknowledged the depth of the crisis and sought to safeguard as well as transcend the progressive heritage of liberalism in '*eine dürftige Zeit*'. It has also been argued that the Institute's theoretical programme remained imprecise, purely negative, or that 'Critical Theory had a basically insubstantial concept of reason and truth'.[29] This can, perhaps, be acknowledged, but with the caveat that Marcuse ventured further than any of his colleagues in attempting to 'arm' the critical concept of reason. In this he pursued a course that was distinctively his own.

II

The concept of reason, and of a rational society, undoubtedly constitutes the major leitmotif of Marcuse's work within the Institute of Social Research; at the same time, however, his writings for the *Zeitschrift* carry the weight of previous stages of his thought. From the university years at Freiburg, Marcuse's treatment of the aesthetic dimension of the *Künstlerroman* and his ontological investigations under Heidegger demonstrate that he had already been groping for a transcendent standard of criticism, immune to the restrictions imposed by the factual world while nonetheless preserving its basis in – and power over – it. Now, confronted in his daily review work with the fascist transformation of categories that he had himself applied without dialectical sophistication in his earlier writings – nature, community, spirit, being – and under the influence of Horkheimer's militant mistrust of metaphysics, he

28. Max Horkheimer, 'Traditional and Critical Theory', p. 214; cf. also Lewis D. Edinger's depressing account of *German Exile Politics* (Berkeley and Los Angeles 1956). It should be noted that although its effective organizations had been destroyed and its leadership murdered, exiled, or imprisoned, there is little evidence that the German working class was ever significantly anti-semitic or sympathetic to fascism.

29. Jay, p. 63.

became acutely sensitive to the power of irrationalism and the vulnerability of reason itself.[30]

The autonomy and authority of reason appeared to Marcuse to be threatened from two apparently opposing forces. On the one side, the positivist conception of rationality came to look increasingly like the narrowly instrumental 'rationalization' to which Max Weber had attributed the progressive 'disenchantment of the world'. For Marcuse, the functional rationality maintained in the positivist tradition of thought was the philosophical correlate of larger social and economic processes, and as Weber himself had demonstrated, the expansion of the formal-legal rationality of means tended to deliver society over to irrational ends.[31] If the *autonomy* of reason was undermined by rationalist thought itself, its *authority* was under attack from less subtle constellations of irrationalism: claiming an ancestry in German *Lebensphilosophie*, the theoreticians of National Socialism proffered a range of concepts designed to justify the authoritarian state on a plane to which critical reason is denied access: 'Decisive here is that irrational givens ("nature", "blood and soil", "folkhood", "existential facts", "totality", and so forth) are placed prior to the autonomy of reason as its limit *in principle* (not merely in fact), and reason is and remains causally, functionally, or organically dependent on them.'[32] Confronted with a world situation in which 'existential' political realities had become the standard of what is rational, Marcuse undertook to restore to reason its authority as the independent standard of what is real – it was to

30. The attack on metaphysics, as a *complement* to the attack on positivism ('These divergences do not signify a structural difference in ways of thinking.'), was a persistent theme for Horkheimer throughout the 1930s; cf. esp. his essays 'Materialismus und Metaphysik', *ZfS* II, 1 (1933); 'Zum Rationalismusstreit in der gegenwartigen Philosophie', *ZfS* III, 1 (1934); 'Der neueste Angriff auf die Metaphysik', *ZfS* IV, 1 (1937). 'Post-war metaphysics', he wrote, 'paved the way intellectually for the authoritarian state', (*Critical Theory,* p. 139).

31. Marcuse never made the simplistic claim that positivism was or could be an authoritarian ideology, both because of the scientific criterion of freedom of inquiry, and because 'Positivism is of its very nature *ex post*'. ('Review of John Dewey', *SPSS* IX, 1, 1941, p. 145). Rather, the relation between positivism and authoritarianism is one of detached compliance with the 'objective' world order. Cf. also his 'Besprechung von der *International Encyclopedia of Unified Science*', *ZfS* VIII, 1/2 (1939), pp. 228–32, and his analysis of the historical shift from 'critical' to 'technological rationality' in 'Some Social Implications of Modern Technology', *SPSS* IX, 3 (1941), pp. 414–39.

32. Marcuse, 'The Struggle against Liberalism in the Totalitarian View of the State', p. 15.

become the ultimate 'critical tribunal'.

Marcuse's long-standing effort to find a vantage point from which to evaluate society and history was not displaced by his entry into the Institute of Social Research; rather, as the rationalized irrationalism that was 'the fate of the West' (Weber) closed over Europe, Reason itself acquired the status of a transcendent value. Transcendent ideas had traditionally served the progressive function of 'setting reality against its potentiality and what exists against what could be',[33] but they had also coexisted alongside that reality and acquiesced in it from an ontological realm of security. Marcuse now sought to recover the dialectical connection between reason and revolution: the tension between actuality and potentiality was not to be frozen into an immutable ontological difference but grasped as 'a historical relationship which can be transformed in this life by real men'.[34] The claims of later critics notwithstanding, Marcuse did indeed follow the course of Reason from Hegel all the way to Marx, but with some characteristic detours.

From the structure of the materialist dialectic, Marcuse knew that transcendence of the given social reality must be 'in the direction of another historical structure which is present as a tendency in the given reality'.[35] The more the realization of human potentialities is stifled, however – by the extension of the (alienated) labour process and the integration of ever larger spheres of social and personal life – the further these potentialities retreat from the primary concerns of life, and the more utopian becomes the search for 'the counter-image of what occurs in social reality'.[36] The truths embodied in the intellectual and aesthetic culture of the bourgeois era have not been realized in the ascent of their middle-class carriers, and thus their demands upon the present survive. In a programmatic passage, Marcuse wrote: 'More and more the culture that was to have been abolished [*aufzuhebende Kultur*] recedes into the past. Overlaid by an actuality in which the complete sacrifice of the individual has become a pervasive and almost unquestioned fact, that culture has vanished to the point where studying and

---

33. Marcuse, 'Zum Begriff des Wesens', *ZfS* V, 1 (1936), trans. 'The Concept of Essence' in *Negations*, p. 60.
34. Ibid., p. 69.
35. Ibid., p. 86.
36. Marcuse, 'Uber den affirmativen Charakter der Kultur', *ZfS* VI, 1 (1937), trans. 'The Affirmative Character of Culture' in *Negations*, p. 102.

comprehending it is no longer a matter of spiteful pride, but of sorrow. Critical theory must concern itself to a hitherto unknown extent with the past – precisely insofar as it is concerned with the future.'[37] Critical thought turns not to the misery of the industrial worker for its image of liberation, but to the past ideals that remain true because the moment of their realization has been suspended, and to those few spheres of the present in which bourgeois society has been willing to tolerate these ideals: the individuating principle of sexual love,[38] the bourgeois conception of the personality which 'exempts a concrete region of private life from domination',[39] phantasy, whose capacity 'to create something new out of the given material of cognition' is bounded only by technical limits,[40] and above all, the ideal forms of classical bourgeois art, whose materialization would demand 'a leap into a totally other world'.[41]

Herein lies the philosophical basis of much of the 'elitism' which is so frequently attributed to the person and the politics of Marcuse – a charge which he all too defiantly accepted. His adolescent disdain for the *zeitgemässe* popular novels of the *Wandervogel* and his perfunctory treatment (in 1922) of the militant *Zeitromane* of Young Germany now find a theoretical justification, for it is in the enduring triumphs of the European cultural inheritance that the deepest human drives have been expressed, not in the propaganda or partisan *Tendenzliteratur* of day-to-day struggles.

Emphatically, Marcuse's gesture towards art as the concrete embodiment of an ideal dimension of truth and beauty is not for its momentary fulfilment of suppressed pleasures and forgotten truths. Like sports and popular culture, art possesses an 'affirmative' character that has in fact been a powerful ideological force sustaining the deprivations of material life, for 'unlike the truth of theory, the beauty of art is compatible with the bad present, despite and within which it can afford true happiness'.[42] Rather, the beauty

37. Marcuse, 'Philosophy and Critical Theory', p. 158. Also Hegel: 'It is, then, the memory alone that still preserves the dead form of the spirit's previous state as a vanished history, vanished men know not how.' (*Phenomenology of Mind*, trans. Baillie, pp. 564–5).

38. Marcuse, 'The Affirmative Character of Culture', p. 111.

39. Ibid., p. 124.

40. Marcuse, 'Philosophy and Critical Theory', p. 154.

41. Marcuse, 'The Affirmative Character of Culture', p. 99.

42. Ibid., p. 118.

of art is to be grasped as 'the presage of possible truth',[43] the material embodiment (*Verkörperung*) of life beyond the rule of commodity production, of arduous labour, of material and sensual renunciation.

'A foretaste of such potentialities', he wrote, 'can be had in experiencing the unassuming display of Greek statues or the music of Mozart or late Beethoven';[44] but it can also be detected in the need for the social and economic management of sexuality, whose 'unpurified, unrationalized release' would subvert the consciousness of individuals and shatter the social system of the bourgeois world.[45] As little as Marcuse turned to art merely to enrich the soul within the poverty of class society, was he supplanting politics with a snobbish aestheticism. The dialectical pursuit of 'what is present as a tendency in the given reality' points to oppositional social forces other than great art; in one of his most significant passages, Marcuse again struck a programmatic note: 'Those social strata . . . which are kept back in semi-medieval forms, pushed to the lowest margin of society, and thoroughly demoralized, provide, even in these circumstances, an anticipatory memory [*vordeutende Errinerung*]. When the body has completely become an object, a beautiful thing, it can foreshadow a new happiness. In suffering the most extreme reification, man triumphs over reification. The artistry of the beautiful body, its effortless agility and relaxation, which can be displayed today only in the circus, vaudeville, and burlesque, herald the joy to which people will attain in being liberated from the ideal, once humanity, having become a true subject, succeeds in the mastery of nature.'[46] Like the medieval mimes, minstrels, and itinerant scholars who had prefigured the estranged artist of the *Künstlerroman*, the outcast types of modern society – the prostitute, the clown, the

43. Ibid., p. 117.
44. Ibid., p. 131.
45. Marcuse, 'Zur Kritik des Hedonismus', *ZfS* VII, 1/2 (1938), trans. 'On Hedonism', in *Negations,* p. 187. Nietzsche, as much as Freud, had recognized the 'hunger for wholeness' expressed in sexual relations: 'At the very climax of joy there sounds a cry of horror or a yearning lamentation for an irrevocable loss'. (*The Birth of Tragedy,* trans. Kaufmann, New York 1967, p. 40).
46. Marcuse, 'The Affirmative Character of Culture', p. 116 (trans. slightly altered). Freud, whose works Marcuse had begun to read ten years earlier, had a profound sensitivity to the wisdom exiled from the mundane world: 'In all ages those who have had something to say and have been unable to say it without danger to themselves have gladly donned the cap and bells.' – *Interpretation of Dreams,* trans. Brill, New York 1938, p. 422.

acrobat, play a very different role here from that of Marx's lumpenproletariat. They offer 'a presage of possible truth', a 'foretaste of potentialities', *'une promesse de bonheur'*, in short, the 'anticipatory memory' that projects into future society the generalized satisfaction of the progressive demands and ideals of the past.[47]

Despite the centrality of art and beauty in the evolution of his own critical theory, an independent aesthetic does not appear to be struggling to emerge from beneath the surface of Marcuse's writings of this period. Nor has he left evidence of having entered directly into the aesthetic controversies that animated relations between his colleagues Adorno and Walter Benjamin, and to which so many Marxists had retreated in the thirties. A further indication that he was not yet ready to follow the implications of his ideas on art and beauty to their conclusions at this point is his striking failure to confront the substance of Absolute Spirit in his final work within the Institute, *Reason and Revolution: Hegel and the Rise of Social Theory*. One of the great enigmas of the book is Marcuse's unanswered question, 'Does the rule of the state extend over art, religion, and philosophy, or is it rather limited by them?'[48]

The second Hegel book – which stands to *Hegels Ontologie* as a *Kampfschrift* to a *Habilitationsschrift* – was a defence of Hegel against statist distortions current both in Nazi Germany and among hostile Anglo-American philosophers, and it also served as a defence of Hegel against himself. More specifically, Marcuse sought to show that although Hegel's avowedly universal concepts of reason and freedom ultimately express the social content of a particular order of society, 'the method . . . that operated in this system reached further than the concepts that brought it to a conclusion'.[49] The *truth* of Hegel's 'political philosophy' is actually contained less in his doctrine of the state than in the *Science of Logic*, an ontology whose purpose is to demonstrate the negative and dynamic structure of all existence. Dialectic, in contrast to formal logic and common-sense

47. Only in the 1960s did Marcuse begin to search for the outcasts specific to industrialism as an active social force (as distinct from an 'image'), so producing some of his most characteristic and controversial contributions to radical social theory.
48. Marcuse, *Reason and Revolution. Hegel and The Rise of Social Theory*, Oxford 1941; revised edn Boston 1960, p. 87.
49. Ibid., p. 257.

thinking, 'shows latent in common sense the dangerous implication that the form in which the world is given and organized may contradict its true content, that is to say, that the potentialities inherent in men and things may require the dissolution of the given forms.'[50] The true heir to the negative dialectic, then, is Marx, in whose hands it transcends its philosophical basis in ontology, and becomes a social theory inextricably linked to history: the task of rendering the world the proper dwelling-place of reason is not an ideal (cognitive) but a material (political) one.[51]

By demonstrating the transformation of philosophy into social theory, Marcuse also reformulated the history and structure of critical theory. The Marxian dialectic shares with the Hegelian – *mutatis mutandis* – a conception of the negative character of reality, of the gap between appearance and essence, of actuality and potentiality. By projecting the resolution of this contradiction into 'the future', he in effect assigned to dialectical reason the status of an autonomous and transcendent critical ideal. With (another?) silent bow towards Mephistopheles, *der Geist, der stets verneint*, Marcuse describes the dialectical method itself as the 'uncompromising "spirit of contradiction".'[52]

It is possible, on the basis of the foregoing analysis, to assemble a summary characterization of the central concept of 'autonomous reason' that guided Marcuse's thought through a decade of irrationalism. In essence, reason pertains to the processes of thought and action oriented toward the conditions within which the human potentialities of a free mind and a free body can be realized.

The earliest and most 'formal' conception he expressed implied – not at all tautologically – that the goal of reason is a society that is

50. Ibid., p. 131.
51. A second great enigma of *Reason and Revolution:* by 1940, Marcuse had secured American citizenship and cautious, Aesopian references to 'the materialist dialectic as social theory' finally yielded to a direct and thoroughgoing analysis of Marxism (pp. 273–322). Although the early writings of 1843–46 are analysed in depth, he ignored Marx's important essay, 'Zur Judenfrage' even though this work would have contributed decisively to a refutation of the Nazi appropriation of Hegel's *Staatslehre.* Hegel's *Rechtstaat* was to have been the universalization of the particular interests of civil society; the National Socialist *Machtstaat* was the premature, forced reconciliation of contradictory forces in which they were preserved, not *aufgehoben.*
52. Marcuse, *Reason and Revolution,* p. 400, where he surreptitiously quotes Goethe's *Faust* I, 1. 1338.

safe for reason, understood as 'the human faculty of comprehending, through conceptual thought, the true, the good, and the right. Within society, every action and every determination of goals as well as the social organization as a whole has to legitimate itself before the decisive judgement of reason and everything, in order to subsist as a fact or a goal, stands in need of rational justification.'[53] Where the free exercise of autonomous, critical rationality is constrained by the totalitarian administration of politics and knowledge, its truths must take refuge in heretical doctrines and oppositional forces. They are disclosed by critical (dialectical) social theory which sustains them as goals of and against the present.

The conditions presupposed by Marcuse are the possibilities of adapting human existence to human needs at a given level of development of society's productive forces. Neither the needs nor the technical possibilities for their satisfaction are fixed, however. Following Marx's 1844 *Manuscripts*, he denied that authentic happiness could simply be designated as the subjective gratification of present drives and needs, 'for as such they are beyond neither good and evil nor true and false . . . They are the drives and needs of individuals who were raised in an antagonistic society.'[54] And just as Marx had premissed the emergence of 'true' needs on the full liberation of human sensuality, Marcuse conjectured that 'under the system of scarcity, men developed their senses and organs chiefly as implements of labour and competitive orientation'.[55]

If the senses, organs, and appetites of individuals have actually become factors of the apparatus of commodity production, consciousness itself has been subjected to the same violation. A pervasive 'technological rationality', corresponding to the requirements of industrialism, has transformed freedom into submissiveness and rendered protest harmless or irrational; even at the level of thought, feeling, and conscience, 'there is no escape from the apparatus which has mechanized and standardized the world'.[56]

---

53. Marcuse, 'The Affirmative Character of Culture', p. 14. Jürgen Habermas's theory of a rational society as one characterized by 'communication free of distortion' carries this thought into the 'second generation' of the Frankfurt School; see his *Knowledge and Human Interests,* trans. Jeremy Shapiro, London 1971.
54. Marcuse, 'On Hedonism', pp. 189–90.
55. Marcuse, 'Some Social Implications of Modern Technology', *SPSS* IX, 3 (1941), p. 437.
56. Ibid., p. 419.

Under conditions of nearly total mobilization – and here Marcuse is speaking not only of the fascist countries, but of the advanced, industrialized world generally – only the liberation of technology, its redirection toward the *objective* human interest in general freedom, could produce qualitatively new needs and new wants. 'Modern technology', he wrote, referring always to the whole technical, institutional, and social apparatus of production, 'contains all the means necessary to extract from things and bodies their mobility, beauty, and softness in order to bring them closer and make them available . . . The development of sensuality is only one part of the development of the productive forces; the need to fetter them is rooted in the antagonistic social system within which this development has taken place.'[57] The liberation of individuals, then, of the fullest potentialities of their minds and their bodies, is a social process, conditional upon the total liberation of society as an integrated totality, an 'inherently multi-dimensional (*vieldimensional*), organized structure.[58] In the present era, the technological means are available which could abolish the material basis of competitiveness, compliance, and complicity; the phantastic, utopian potentialities they could release became the standard of Marcuse's condemnation of the given realities.

III

These given realities had by this time lost their merely threatening aspect and degenerated into total war. In 1939, Marcuse's parents and brother finally made their belated flight to London, where they joined Else and her husband. Throughout the 1930s, while Herbert worked in America (reassuring them – as late as 1939! – that at least there would be no war), his family in Germany had been suffering increasing privations and intimidation. His grandparents, utterly disillusioned, had abandoned their religious practices after 1933, and Carl Marcuse was now retired, ill, a 'good German' bewildered by the violent turn of events.

Herbert's brother Erich, the student radical who had been the

57. Marcuse, 'On Hedonism', p. 184.
58. Marcuse, 'The Concept of Essence', p. 70. Again, the recurrent image of the 'multi-dimensional' character of liberation anticipates the later thesis of 'one-dimensional society', most of whose elements were by this time present.

last Jew to receive the PhD from Berlin University (in 1933), was running the family business as best he could, picking up odd consulting jobs wherever such opportunities remained, and gradually assuming full responsibility for the maintenance of the family. Frightening anti-semitic demonstrations were taking place with increasing frequency in front of their house – a number of high-ranking Nazi officials had their residences in Dahlem – and as the grip tightened around the European Jews, he managed to manoeuvre his wife and parents (and some of their money) out of Germany; this was in March 1939, at the last possible moment. Although he had been trained in Germany as an economist, in London Erich Marcuse was obliged to open a small business (it was later to become a fashionable ladies' boutique) in order to support the family. The rest of their relatives died in Theresienstadt.

The situation in New York was also a precarious one, for the Institute's financial autonomy had been imperilled by the war, and the small salaries of Marcuse and Neumann could only be maintained in 1941–42 by virtue of an outside grant from the Emergency Committee in Aid of Displaced Foreign Scholars.[59] Horkheimer had, on medical advice, already left the New York office for the Santa Monica area, which had become an important centre of refugee culture during the war – the community of emigré Weimar luminaries included Thomas and Heinrich Mann, Lion Feuchtwanger, and Bertolt Brecht (with whom the 'Tui-Intellektuellen' got on quite well on a personal level).[60] He was soon joined by Adorno, who had formally become a member of the Institute in 1938, and, upon the completion and publication of *Reason and Revolution*, by Marcuse; Friedrich Pollock followed shortly thereafter.

Financial pressures had disrupted plans for several projected studies that the Institute had begun or outlined in New York, and

59. This information is from the files of the Emergency Committee (in the archives of the New York Public Library). The published account of the Committee by its Director (Stephen Duggan) and Executive Secretary (Betty Drury) conveys a sense of the privileged situation of the independently endowed Institute compared with other refugee scholars in the 1930s: *The Rescue of Science and Learning,* New York 1952.

60. Cf., for example, Klaus Völker, *Brecht-Chronik,* München 1971. In a famous project, inspired by the philosophers of the Frankfurt School, Brecht mercilessly lampooned those intellectuals 'who always get everything backwards' (hence *T*ellekt-*u*ellen-*i*n).

throughout much of 1941 and 1942 the group in California held discussions about a new collaborative undertaking:[61] Marcuse's contribution to a large-scale study of materialist dialectics was to have been a historical survey of doctrines and movements of opposition, conceived in terms of the interrelation of heresy, revolt, and materialism in history, an analysis that would have permitted him to systematize the themes of his separate studies of the fate of rationality in the totalitarian era. In fact, the projected work appeared in a much abbreviated form a few years later as the now-classic *Dialectic of Enlightenment*, co-authored by Horkheimer and Adorno, with help from Löwenthal.

There were, of course, differences of intellectual temperament and theoretical perspective among the *Mitarbeiter* of the Institute. Marcuse's closest personal friendship was with Neumann, whereas his analysis of the transformation of critical into technological rationality allied him more closely with the philosophical perspectives of Horkheimer, Adorno, and Pollock.[62] But there is no evidence that intellectual or personal incompatibility was a serious issue in the last years of the Institute. It was rather the case that in the emergency situation of the early 1940s, even Horkheimer's considerable administrative skills could not be counted upon to ensure the continued funding and institutional cohesiveness of the group. In addition, it was gradually being recognized in other quarters that the European emigré scholars possessed skills that were urgently required elsewhere. These were the circumstances in which Marcuse accepted a more pressing engagement and joined Neumann in Washington – where his friend had just left the Board of Economic Warfare to join the newly formed Office of Strategic Services.

61. A number of these projects are described in the pamphlet 'IISR. A Report on its History, Aims, and Activities, 1933–1938', pp. 19–25. For the changed intellectual and financial circumstances of the Institute by the late 1930s and early 1940s, cf. Jay, esp. pp. 167–72.
62. A few further details may be culled from the pages of H. Stuart Hughes, *The Sea Change*, pp. 171, 174–5, and Buck-Morss, p. 289, n. 6.

INTERREGNUM

ART AND POLITICS IN THE TOTALITARIAN ERA (1942-1951)

For about a decade, 'between the reigns' of pre-war and post-war liberalism, Herbert Marcuse lived in Washington, DC, where he served as an intelligence analyst in three agencies of the US government. Although commentators and critics have variously characterized these years as a period of intellectual 'latency'[1] or as the first stage of 'G-Man Marcuse's' allegedly unbroken government involvement,[2] the period was one of active political engagement and the development of advanced theoretical formulations.

I

In July 1941, some six months before the United States entered the war, Roosevelt had issued an Executive Order creating the office of 'Coordinator of Information' (CoI); it was to be headed by William J. Donovan, a conservative Wall Street lawyer with close ties to the President, whose task it would be 'to collect and analyse all information and data which may bear upon national security', and make it available to the White House, the armed forces, and other government agencies, and 'to carry out . . . such supplementary activities as may facilitate the securing of information important for national security'.[3] With the entry of the United States into the war, the need for a centralized and comprehensive intelligence network

1. H. Stuart Hughes, *The Sea Change,* New York, 1975, p. 174.
2. 'Marcuse: Cop-out or Cop?', *Progressive Labor,* 6:6 (February 1969), p. 61. This article has accurately been designated as marking the lowest point in the fortunes of the New Left; cf. Paul Breines, ed., *Critical Interruptions,* New York 1970, 'Introduction'. It will be dealt with later, not as an argument but as a phenomenon.

became apparent, a need that was acknowledged in a major reorganization on 13 June 1942: the overt or 'white' propaganda functions of Donovan's office were severed and autonomously constituted as the Office of War Information (Owi) under the playwright Robert Sherwood, while a special 'operational branch' was added to intelligence gathering and analysis in a new Office of Strategic Services (Oss). It was to be headed by Donovan, who was authorized to hire 'such personnel as may be required', and was responsible only to the President and the Joint Chiefs of Staff.

Field agents could be given fairly rapid training for specific missions of espionage, subversion, liaison, or sabotage, but it is in the nature of the analysis of intelligence data that extensive technical or regional knowledge, linguistic competence, research skills, and other specialized abilities are required. Such trained experts had long been part of most of the European intelligence agencies, but the only immediate reservoir of this level of professional expertise in the United States was the scholarly community, and it was Donovan's great innovation to draw upon this ready-made field of intellectual talent and experience. Accordingly, James Phinney Baxter, President of Williams College, and the eminent Harvard historian William L. Langer were summoned to Washington in August 1941, to build a Research and Analysis Branch (R&A). Working with Archibald MacLeish (then Librarian of Congress), representatives of the National Archives, the American Council of Learned Societies, and the Social Science Research Council, and tapping the time-honoured academic grapevine, they assembled a staff of distinguished scholars unprecedented in American political or intellectual history.[4]

Herbert Marcuse had been in contact with Oss officials from the latter half of 1942, and had expressed an interest in coordinating his work with theirs. In July, while still in Santa Monica, he had sent to the Chief of the Psychology Division manuscripts he had written on 'Private Morale in Germany' and 'The New German Mentality', followed several months later by the preliminary findings of an

3. The Presidential Order of 11 July 1941, creating America's first centralized intelligence service is reproduced in the internal history of the OSS written in 1947, declassified 17 July 1975, as the *War Report of the OSS,* New York 1976, p. 8. Although it suffers from the predictable limitations of an internal history, this is the most valuable source of documentary material on the OSS.

4. Among the members of Langer's R&A staff who were or would become major

Institute study on 'The Elimination of German Chauvinism'.[5] From the outset, the attempt to develop a comprehensive conception of the psychology culminating in the Nazi regime, and to make a psychoanalytical evaluation of conditions in Germany, had been part of the US intelligence strategy, and appeared to be a common concern.[6]

In the general conception and in the methodologies they had devised, the Oss psychologists' plans had affinities with the work that had already been undertaken by the Institute at Columbia, and Marcuse's inquiries were intended to explore the grounds of possible cooperation. The initial response from Psychology Division Chief Robert C. Tryon was favourable but non-committal, however, and no concrete arrangements resulted. Nonetheless, with the effective suspension of the Institute's activities, Marcuse left California and on the advice of Neumann and Kirchheimer, made himself available to the burgeoning intelligence community then taking shape in the capital. Before long, Neumann was able to recommend him to the political scientist Gabriel Almond, then a recent PhD from the University of Chicago who had been brought to Washington to set up an 'Enemy Section' within the newly-formed Office of War Information.[7] In the latter part of 1942 Marcuse went to work in the Bureau of Intelligence of the Owi, the internal and external propaganda arm of the wartime government.

Ideological differences tended to be suppressed within the agency

academic figures were Paul Baran, Norman O. Brown, John K. Fairbank, Franklin Ford, Felix Gilbert, Hajo Holborn, H. Stuart Hughes, Leonard Krieger, Barrington Moore, Jr, Arthur Schlesinger, and Carl E. Schorske. Donovan had 'assembled the best academic and analytical brains he could beg, borrow, or steal from the universities, libraries, and museums' of America: Allen Dulles to the Erie County Bar Association, 4 May 1959, quoted in R. Harris Smith, *OSS,* New York 1972, p. 13. Former OSS operatives Stewart Alsop and Thomas Braden wrote that 'in the peculiarly amateur atmosphere of OSS, friends chose friends, had them security-checked, and installed them in a Washington office or sent them overseas.' (*Sub-Rosa,* New York 1946, p. 23.)

5. Correspondence of 7 July 1942; 11 July 1942; and 7 December 1942 in the files of the Research & Analysis Branch, OSS (in the National Archives).

6. As early as 1941 a Field Psychoanalytical Unit had been established in the office of the Coordinator of Information (*War Report of the OSS,* p. 31). Working with published sources, refugees, and psychoanalysts in neutral countries, the FPU was to undertake psychoanalytical studies of: 1. conditions in pre-Nazi Germany, 2. Nazi writings and early speeches, and 3. patients in this country with strong Nazi or Fascist tendencies. Among other uses, it was hoped that the results would contribute to the Allied propaganda campaign.

7. I am grateful to Professor Almond for sharing his recollections with me.

during this period, and although Marcuse seems never to have missed an opportunity to *épater les bourgeois*, his colleagues appreciated his ironical, and even cynical, attitude. This was expressed also in his official duties, which, in the estimation of his Bureau Chief, he often did not take seriously. He received German newspapers, transcripts of radio broadcasts monitored by a branch of the Fcc, and the text of every speech made by Hitler and Goebbels, with the assignment of keeping Owi policy-makers informed about the relation between private morale and public policy in Nazi Germany, but he did not see in this activity a major threat to the stability of the fascist regimes. In the aftermath of the campaigns of the winter of 1942–43 (the Battle of Stalingrad, the Allied invasions of El Alamein and French North Africa), Goebbels delivered a major address on the 'Conduct and Morale' to be expected of the German people, and Marcuse was asked to prepare an interpretation of the German term '*Stimmung*' (morale, mood). His satirical 'class analysis' of the *Stimmung* to be found from the petty-bourgeois beer halls to the fashionable Berlin hotels contributed to the morale of his colleagues, but it may well have been with mutual relief that his career in the Office of War Information ended shortly thereafter, as he accepted an invitation to join the Europeanists in the Research & Analysis Branch of the Office of Strategic Services.

In contrast to the experience of many European refugees, Marcuse's leftward movement continued unabated into the 1940s, and indeed outstripped that of Horkheimer and Adorno, whose writings of those years were beginning to reveal traces of what has been called '*metaphysischer Pessimismus*'. Still, it is not at all surprising that he should have entered into the service of the US government, for in the crisis years of the Second World War, it was widely recognized that the collapse of European fascism would come about through external military defeat, at best aided by internal oppositional forces. Just as Donovan – a registered Republican – had vigorously defended the recruitment of Communist agents and Marxist analysts by referring conservative Congressional critics to their common enemy, Marcuse and dozens of other leftist intellectuals understood that the tolerant, and even *ad hoc* nature of the Oss might provide them with an opportunity to contribute effectively to an anti-fascist alliance.

It is also the case that certain 'structural' affinities between the Research & Analysis Branch of Oss and the Institute of Social

Research may have eased the transition – quite apart from the overlap of personnel.[8] R&A was a high-level interdisciplinary community of scholars who, like the members of the Institute, had assembled around an explicitly partisan common purpose. And like the Institute, the R&A Branch protected the independence of its partisan scholarship by avoiding any binding affiliations that might prejudice this factional neutrality: 'R&A was primarily a service so conceived that it could be of value to many agencies but subject to none . . . It was in an organization free of policy-making responsibilities and therefore separate from any particular point of view advocated in any other quarter or agency.'[9]

The scale of operations, however, was vastly greater than that of the Institute, and the coordination of the work of some 800 Washington-based analysts was achieved through a flexible division of intellectual labour: four regional Divisions constituted the Branch, each containing functional sub-divisions (Economic, Political, and Geographical) which were themselves composed of sections designed to handle special subjects.[10] These four Divisions formed the core of the R&A Branch, which in turn 'was the very core of the agency'.[11]

Until the end of 1944, when the advance of the Allied armies finally made the defeat of Germany a realistic prospect, the highest priority of American military – and, consequently, intelligence – activity had been on the European continent and on the intentions and capabilities of Germany in particular. The analysts in the

---

8. Besides Marcuse, both Neumann and Kirchheimer had come to work in the Europe-Africa Division of R&A, and Neumann's wife Inge was on the staff of the Biographical Records Section which produced informational profiles of thousands of key political figures in German and occupied territories; Leo Löwenthal had been serving as a part-time consultant to the German Section of the neighbouring OWI (he later became Section Chief), and Friedrich Pollock had served – with Neumann – as a confidential consultant to the Board of Economic Warfare; Sophie Marcuse had a position as a statistician for Naval Intelligence (G–2).

9. *War Report of the OSS,* pp. xii–xiii.

10. This structure, which lasted until the end of the war, was created by the major reorganization of OSS in January, 1943, after it had been given a formal charter by the Joint Chiefs of Staff on the basis of its success in 'softening up' North Africa in preparation for the Allied invasion (see the appendix to this chapter).

11. Corey Ford, *Donovan of OSS,* Boston 1970, p. 148. After the war Donovan quipped, 'We did not rely on the "seductive blonde" or the "phony moustache". The major part of our intelligence was the result of good old-fashioned intellectual sweat.'

German unit of R&A's Central European Section, then, engaged in the continuing study of changing political conditions within the Reich, were in a potentially important position within American intelligence operations.[12]

During this two-year period Marcuse's group worked on the analysis of political tendencies in Germany, and he was specifically assigned to the identification of Nazi and anti-Nazi groups and individuals; the former were to be held accountable in the war crimes adjudication then being negotiated between the four Great Powers, and the latter were to be called upon for cooperation in post-war reconstruction. For his source materials he drew upon official and military intelligence reports, extensive Oss interviews with refugees, and special Oss agents and contacts in occupied Europe; it was his duty to evaluate the reliability of each of the items of intelligence that reached him, and assemble them all into a coherent analysis of points of strength and weakness in the Reich.

While the war was in progress, Marcuse's political reports (which were almost all written as team projects) were sent up to Section Chief Neumann, and then on to the Current Intelligence Staff where they were further analysed, edited, and disseminated to the appropriate military or civilian authorities (or Oss field operatives). Their work thus figured significantly in the attempt to mount a programme of psychological warfare against Germany, as well as in evaluating possible sources of resistance within Germany that might be susceptible to propaganda or even contacts.

After the reversal of the German counter-offensive in the Ardennes by the end of January 1945, and the advancing encirclement of the Reich by the Allied military forces, the Oss shifted its principal 'operational' activities to problems in the Far East. The German Section of the Europe/Africa Division, however, remained one of the most active units, both in assisting the penetration of German territory by some 200 agents prior to the final military invasion,[13] and – of greater importance – in preparing for the post-war military regulation and military governance of Germany.

This latter project was the second of Marcuse's major assign-

---

12. 'Prior to VE-Day, and to some extent thereafter by reason of the many post-war problems which came within the purview of R&A, highest priority was on Europe.' *War Report of the OSS*, p. 172.

13. Joseph E. Persico's *Piercing the Reich*, New York 1978, recounts some of the OSS operations within Germany in the last year of the war.

ments as a senior intelligence analyst. America's post-war position in Europe with respect to Germany had been an issue in government and intelligence circles almost from the beginning of the war, and the Central European Section of R&A bore the responsibility for much of the preparation. Late in 1944, a series of political and administrative 'Civil Affairs Handbooks' were prepared under the nominal direction of the young historian Carl E. Schorske (responsible to Hajo Holborn) to provide social, political, economic, and geographical background information for the use of military government authorities in occupied Germany.[14] Marcuse's group – which at this time effectively meant Neumann, Kirchheimer, and himself – prepared an extensive *Denazification Guide* within the framework of this overall effort, probably the most important project in which he was involved as part of Oss: specific names were given, instances of wartime criminality and complicity cited, and concrete recommendations made, such as the prohibition of German rearmament.[15] The *Guide* was primarily concerned to discourage cooperation with former Nazi officials in the post-war reconstruction of Germany, and the return of many of these people to commanding positions in German industry and politics may serve as an accurate measure of the real influence exerted by this tiny group of leftist scholars over US policy.

With the conclusion of hostilities in Europe, and the Allied occupation of Germany, Oss responsibilities increased further, and on 3 May 1945, within days of Hitler's suicide in Berlin, Central European Section Chief Franz Neumann circulated a plan for the reorganization of the German and Austrian Unit to meet the new intelligence requirements of the post-war situation.[16] The focus was to be on the reaction of local populations to the establishment of military government over Germany and Austria, which the staff would study from a regional and functional point of view. Marcuse was to be assigned the US Zone (with Kirchheimer and Barrington Moore Jr responsible for the French and Soviet zones respectively), as well as the analysis of the impact of denazification policies generally. He was additionally instructed to coordinate the investigation of the surviving Nazi and nationalist underground, and the

14. R. Harris Smith, *OSS,* New York 1972, p. 222; *War Report,* p. 178.
15. Conversations with HM; correspondence with Professor Carl Schorske.
16. Neumann memorandum of 3 May 1945 to members of the Central European Section, R&A (file of the OSS, National Archives).

European ramifications of Nazism, as well as the prospects of political parties of non-Nazi strata of the population.

This overall research and analysis programme passed largely into the hands of Marcuse when Neumann left for occupied Europe in the summer of 1945 to begin the investigation of Nazi war criminals (he was to be the first chief of research of the International War Crimes Tribunal at Nuremberg). Intelligence reports reached Marcuse in Washington from the Oss staff who had moved into Germany from neutral Switzerland, where Allen Dulles had been coordinating secret intelligence activities during the last two years of the war. The Chief of German R&A in particular was Lt-Col H. Stuart Hughes, and Marcuse's memos to the young Harvard-trained historian served as a reminder of the distance that remained between the Frankfurt School and the empirical research techniques of American social science: 'We have recently received three reports which were an oasis in the desert . . . May we reiterate our humble request that instead of indulging in personal interviews of isolated personalities you concentrate your efforts on such reports . . . covering one decisive, larger area, integrating political and economic developments?'[17] At the foot of this mildly sarcastic (and thoroughly Marcusean) request for current intelligence, written at the end of August, Marcuse added some intelligence of his own: 'As far as the future of this agency is concerned, nothing has so far been decided. There are only rumours, some of which to the effect that R&A may be continued in one form or another in a new central intelligence agency.' One month later the Oss, 'half cops-and-robbers and half faculty meeting',[18] was formally dissolved and dismembered, but Marcuse's information was ultimately to prove correct.

By the autumn of 1944, Roosevelt had begun to anticipate the post-war configuration of international politics, and instructed Donovan 'to submit his views on the organization of an intelligence service for the post-war period'.[19] Donovan responded on 18

17. Marcuse memorandum to Lt. Col. Stuart Hughes, Germany, 17 August 1945 (OSS files, National Archives).
18. McGeorge Bundy, 'The Battlefields of Power and the Searchlights of the Academy', in E. A. J. Johnson, ed., *The Dimensions of Diplomacy,* Baltimore 1964, p. 3.
19. *War Report of the OSS,* p. 115.

November with a draft memorandum in which he proposed the liquidation of the existing organization but insisted upon the need to preserve its intelligence functions during peacetime in a permanent, centralized authority. He added his opinion, referring specifically to the scholarly staff of R&A, that immediate preparations be made: 'We have now in the Government the trained and specialized personnel needed for the task. This talent should not be dispersed.'[20]

The unexpected prolongation of the hostilities deferred such plans, but in August of the following year, Donovan once again took up his case for a centralized intelligence agency that would be adequate to the new responsibilities the United States had assumed in the post-war world. As Donovan himself had recognized, however, 'it is not easy to set up a modern intelligence system. It is more difficult to do so in time of peace than in time of war.'[21] He was indeed proven correct, for by this time the favourably-disposed Roosevelt had been dead for several months, and proposals for some sort of 'Super-Spy System for Post-war New Deal', an 'all-powerful intelligence service to spy on the post-war world and pry into the lives of citizens at home', were beginning to be fiercely attacked by the right-wing, isolationist press.[22]

In addition, the Oss had had no shortage of enemies to contend with in the government. The petulant J. Edgar Hoover, outspoken in his jealousy of the FBI's jurisdiction over the Western hemisphere, had ostentatiously boycotted all planning sessions of COI/OSS,[23] and similar jurisdictional claims over intelligence functions were made in other politically conservative quarters: the Coordinator of Inter-American Affairs (CIAA), Nelson Rockefeller, created frequent obstacles to Oss intelligence needs in Mexico and Latin America, and both Army and Navy intelligence (G–2) repeatedly opposed any diminution of their own authority.[24]

The most sustained and damaging attacks against Oss, however – from Hoover, from HUAC, and from the public and the press – were grounded not in threats to institutional hegemony but in

20. Exhibit W–43 in ibid., p. 116.
21. Donovan to the Director of the Bureau of the Budget, 25 August 1945, Exhibit W–44, *War Report of the OSS*, p. 117.
22. Chicago *Tribune,* New York *Daily News,* and Washington *Times-Herald,* 9 February 1945; discussed in Ford, p. 302f.
23. Stewart Alsop and Thomas Braden, p. 15.
24. Cf. *War Report of the OSS,* p. 22; Ford, pp. 109, 130.

alleged questions of security. The agency's staff did indeed include avowed Communists and Marxist scholars, which contributed to the ascending temper of paranoia: in the Labour Branch of Oss, in Morale Operations, and in the R&A Branch in particular, 'the political tenor . . . began at predominant New Deal liberalism and then travelled left on the political spectrum'.[25] This conspicuous feature of America's first intelligence agency – plus the simple fact that Oss had, in the words of one astute journalist, 'too many professors' – was not calculated to enhance its status in the crucial months when United States foreign policy was shifting its attention from German fascism to Soviet communism, and on 20 September 1945, President Truman's Executive Order 9620 recorded the nation's appreciation of its wartime accomplishments and terminated the Office of Strategic Services as of 1 October; Marcuse's R&A Branch was transferred more or less intact to the Department of State, and Secret Intelligence (SI) and Counter-espionage (X–2) became the Strategic Services Unit of the War Department.[26]

II

In September 1945, with the chill of autumn and the Cold War already perceptible in the Washington air, Herbert Marcuse took stock of the period just closed. The false objectivity of conventional historiography had already revealed to him its inherent bias in favour of the status quo, and an alternative philosophy of history, one that measured the factical world by aesthetic norms and technological potentialities, was coming tentatively into focus. In a somewhat chaotic burst of intellectual creativity, repressed during three years of urgent political work in the Oss, Marcuse compressed his thoughts into an extraordinary treatise on the avant-garde writers of the French Resistance, subtitled 'Art and Politics in the Totalitarian Era'.[27]

25. Smith, p. 14. In a privately printed autobiographical memoir, R&A Chief Langer recalled the German Section and Herbert Marcuse in particular, 'whose later revolutionary role was then indiscernible'. *Up From the Ranks,* New York 1975, p. 183 (obtained through Mr. Ray Cline, National Intelligence Study Centre).

26. For more 'inside' information, cf. Dean Acheson, *Present at the Creation,* New York 1969, pp. 161–2.

27. [Herbert Marcuse], 'Some Remarks on Aragon: Art and Politics in the

Above all, the fascist period represented to Marcuse the massive intensification of the processes of domination and coordination that were already characteristic of industrial capitalism, even in its pre-monopolistic, 'liberal' phase. Thus the central problem of modernity had become the winning of a critical standpoint not subject to the total administration of physical and psychical life. Marcuse's aesthetic theorizing was still very much contained within this critical framework, but the background against which it was elaborated in 1945 was the disclosure of the extent of the totalitarian violence.

To Marcuse, the violent suppression of oppositional doctrines and actions was ultimately less terrifying than their 'being assimilated to the all-embracing system of monopolistic controls'.[28] Against this seamless totality, the indictments of revolutionary theory remain helplessly academic, and revolutionary art, once antagonistic and transcendent to the prevailing order, becomes fashionable' and classical: 'The intellectual opposition is thus faced with the apparent impossibility of formulating its task and goal in such a manner that the formulation breaks the spell of total assimilation and standardization and reaches the brute foundations of present-day existence.' As the revolutionary *content* of theory or art came increasingly to be adjusted to the prevailing order, the alienation from this order, which transmits the critical force of the *oeuvre*, was transferred to the aesthetic form itself.[29] The second stage of the 'solution' to the problem of the work of art, and its unique capacity to liberate suppressed needs, faculties, and desires, thus lay in the creation of aesthetic forms discontinuous with the realities of repressive existence. Where no 'subject' is left that is really revolutionary, no 'theme' so hostile that it cannot be accommodat-

---

Totalitarian Era' ([Washington, DC] September 1945); unpublished manuscript in personal possession of HM (cited with permission of the author). A few minor editorial changes have been made.

28. Ibid. Unless otherwise indicated, all passages quoted in this section are from the original typescript, pagination irregular.

29. Marcuse pencilled in a passage from Whitehead: 'The truth that some proposition respecting an actual occasion is untrue may express the vital truth as to its aesthetic achievement. It expresses the "great refusal" which is its primary characteristic.' *Science and the Modern World* (New York, 1967), p. 158. The original source of this oft-repeated phrase, which may be considered to represent the Frankfurt School's most concise reading of the dialectic, is Canto III of Dante's *Inferno*.

ed, a new aesthetic imperative arises: 'Free the form from the hostile content, or rather, make the form the only content by making it the instrument of destruction. Use the word, the colour, the tone, the line in the brute nakedness, as the very contradiction and negation of all content.'

But when this reality became more of a shock than Dadaism, abstract expressionism, epic theatre, or atonality, when, in the fascist period, 'the surrealistic terror was surpassed by the real terror', the avant-garde negation proved to be not negative enough: 'The formless form was kept intact, aloof from universal contamination. The form itself was stabilized as a new content.' The betrayal of reason by the once-progressive bourgeoisie called forth the latest stage to the solution of the problem of art and politics, represented by the return to the severely classical metrics of the ascendant bourgeoisie itself: where language could not talk without talking the language of the enemy, the surrealist writers of the Resistance made it sing.

In their attempt to reveal the system of totalitarian domination in its totality and negativity, the Resistance poets returned, with French philosophy, to the free individual, the one ultimate denominator, the sole absolute negation: 'The work of art must, at its breaking point, expose the ultimate nakedness of man's (and nature's) existence, stripped of all the paraphernalia of monopolistic mass culture, completely and utterly alone . . . The most esoteric, the most anti-collectivistic one, for the goal of the revolution is the free individual.' But again, this is no serviceable, bourgeois aestheticism: the liberated individual is, after all, 'the ultimate principle of socialist theory', and the abolition of the capitalist mode of production is only the means to this goal. In the field of reality, access to liberation lies through political action; in art it is approached through aesthetic form, 'the artistic a priori which shapes the content'.

The form or style that is 'the artistic a priori' of which Marcuse writes is conceived not as a technical category but as that dimension of the work of art that actually sets the content and governs the interrelations (interactions) between its components (members). Style transmits the sensuality of the *oeuvre*, and sensuality expressed 'the individual protest against the law and order of repression'. Only because of its manifestly unpolitical character does it preserve the political goal of liberation. Marcuse quotes Baudelaire's *Invitation au voyage* to illuminate the esoteric and anti-political forms to which art is driven in order to free itself from all contents controlled by the monopolistic reality: 'C'est une grande destinée que celle de la poésie! Joyeuse ou lamentable, elle porte toujours en soi le divin charactère utopique. Elle contradit sans cesse le fait, à peine de ne plus être.' The paradox that the political content demands a manifestly unpolitical form was revived in the bitter discussions among the founders of French surrealism at the beginning of the fascist period.[30] Accordingly, the language of the Resistance poets became increasingly remote from the language of the oppositional avant-garde during the occupation. It was their use of the classical vocabulary, paraphernalia, and rituals of love that Marcuse saw as the artistic-political a priori of their work: 'as an element of the aprioric artistic form of this poetry, the language of love emerges as the instrument of estrangement; its artificial, unnatural, "inadequate" character is to produce the shock which may lay bare the true relationship between the two worlds and languages – the one being the positive negation of the other.' *La patrie, la résistance, la libération* are only the carriers of the revolutionary goal which is the true content, and in this artistic negation of the manifestly political, art and politics find their common denominator. Nowhere was this more plainly evident than in *Aurélien*, the fourth novel in Louis Aragon's series, 'Le monde réel'.[31]

The theme that Marcuse drew from the novel is that of a sensual love that embodies the revolutionary promise of transcendence, and the *Aufhebung* of that love – its fulfilment and destruction – when confronted with the revolutionary demands of politics. After many

30. A few years later, Marcuse took issue with the essays in Lukács's *Goethe und seine Zeit* (1947): 'his method fails in so far as it connects literary works more or less externally with the social reality instead of tracing these societal indices in the very style and content of these works.' *Journal of Philosophy and Phenomenological Research*, XI (1949), p. 14.

31. In his draft, Marcuse mistakenly identifies it as the third. Aragon's career to that point – turning largely on an attempt to honour his loyalties to Surrealistic poetics and Communist politics – made him a well-suited subject for Marcuse's analysis; for a characteristically thorough treatment of the polemics of the 1920s and 1930s, cf. Maurice Nadeau, *History of Surrealism*, London 1965. A further attraction was that Aragon never doubted the place – indeed, the priority – of poetry as a combative weapon: he once delivered a severe tongue-lashing to a promising young writer who had briefly abandoned his literary work to take up arms with a Maquis unit. For details of his literary-political work as a Resistance leader, cf. the essays by Malcolm Cowley and Peter Rhodes in H. Josephson and M. Cowley, eds., *Aragon. Poet of the French Resistance*, New York 1945.

years of estrangement, Aragon's lovers find themselves reunited by events amid the fall of France in 1940 and the emergence of a national resistance. But once they are finally alone, 'politics stands between them. They no longer speak the same language, or, the language of politics silences the language of their dead love which they still try to speak . . . Nothing apparently can be more hostile to the *promesse du bonheur* than this language and the activity which it denotes.' Political action demands for its efficacy an immediate confrontation with the unfree world, but the adjustment of the transcendent boundaries of love to that tainted reality is its destruction.

Marcuse's literary criticism, however, remained dialectical criticism. It does not rest with the mere demonstration of the tension between the two realities, but presses toward their final identity: 'The beloved is "enfant craintif", "soeur", and *Geliebte*; her free weakness, laxity, and compliance evoke the image of the victim as well as the conqueror of the fascist order, of the sacrificed utopia which is to emerge as the historical reality.'[32] Political action is shown to have as its goal the winning of the ground upon which the revolutionary *promesse* can be fulfilled. A historical coincidence had transformed the struggle for absolute liberation into a struggle for national liberation, the fight against the mundane life-forms of the surrounding world in general into the fight against Vichy and the Gestapo. The poetical form has negated the political content in Aragon's novel, but in doing so it reveals their identity, the common requirements of Resistance action and Resistance art.

The philosophical analysis of *Aurélien* corroborates the thesis that Marcuse's intellectual career – perhaps as early as his adolescent fascination with the poetry and prose of the French avant-garde – has been regulated by the search for an external, critical standpoint that could cancel the totality of existence without being cancelled by it. The radicalism of the artistic effect of estrangement, however, 'cannot cancel the reconciliatory element involved in this nega-tion'.[33] The very freedom of the artistic *oeuvre* from the prevailing

32. The sources of Marcuse's later feminism should be noted in this passage.
33. The affinity of this conception to Brecht's central principle of the V[erfremd-ungs]-Effekt should neither be overlooked nor overstated. For Brecht, the estrangement effect was a dramatic device created consciously and purposively; inherent in the aesthetic form itself. Cf. Brecht's contemporaneous notes on 'a new technique of acting' in *Brecht on Theater,* trans. John Willett, New York 1969, pp. 143–45.

reality also ensures its accommodation to that reality: 'In the medium of the artistic form, things are liberated to their own life – without being liberated in reality. Art creates a reification of its own. The artistic form, however destructive it may be, stays and brings to rest. In the artistic form, all content becomes the object of aesthetic contemplation, the source of aesthetic gratification.' The artistic presentation of the total fascist terror – Aragon's 'Monde réel', Paul Eluard's 'Sept poèmes d'amour en guerre', Picasso's 'Guernica' – remains a work of art.

Marcuse's search for transcendence in a separate, immediately sensual *'ordre de la beauté'* thus retains its dialectical character, against any romanticist overestimation or cheap escapism. Art is inseparably linked to the historical totality of which it is a part (and from which it is apart), and only thus is it allied to political processes by which that totality may be transformed. The conception of the 'vordeutende Errinerung', the 'anticipatory memory' of forgotten truths that may yet be realized in the future, reappears here ten years after it was initially outlined: the political function of art is the 'awakening of memory, remembrance of things past'.[34] The incompatibility of the artistic form with the real form of life 'may promote the alienation, the total estrangement of man from his world. And this alienation may provide the art-ificial (*sic*) basis for the remembrance of freedom in the totality of oppression'.

These frequently reiterated characterizations of fascism as 'the totality of oppression' are much more than a rhetorical flourish, for they illuminate Marcuse's appreciation of the radical individualism of the Resistance writers. The individual, 'completely and utterly alone, in the abyss of destruction, despair, and freedom', had appeared to be the last impenetrable refuge against the system of monopolistic controls that integrated and coordinated every sphere of social life; he often referred to the 'monopolistic culture' of fascism, and to the intrinsically free individual as 'the sole absolute negation' of that culture.

In the poetical evocation of the individual as the political *a priori*, the literary underground had been accompanied during the war by French existentialism – the most distinct philosophical resonance of

34. Marcuse had begun work on a Proust manuscript several years earlier, but it remained unfinished and unpublished.

the literary image of the individual as the substratum of liberation was the '*pour-soi*' of Sartre's *L'Etre et le Néant*, which came out in 1943, during the German occupation. With the defeat of fascist totalitarianism, however, philosophical individualism seemed to Marcuse to lose much of its urgency, and when he came to grips with the existential 'reconstruction of thought on the ground of absurdity' in the immediate post-war era, he retreated rather considerably from his earlier sympathies.[35]

The '*realité humaine*' upon which the new existential ontology was built served as a powerful bulwark against the *un*reality and *in*humanity of the fascist terror. Confronted with the omnipresent threat of enslavement or annihilation, the art and philosophy of the Resistance had sought a 'transcendental stabilization' of the free subject, a sphere in which freedom could be preserved as an intrinsic attribute of humanity. With the partial redress of the overwhelming odds, however, and the passing of the crisis in which Sartre's ontology had its origins, existentialism came to look increasingly like a helpless idealism, another '*Philosophie des Scheiterns*'. Marcuse's argumentation against Sartre revived the recurrent theme of so much of his pre-war philosophical criticism: 'In so far as Existentialism is a philosophical doctrine, it remains an idealistic doctrine: it hypostatizes specific historical conditions of human existence into ontological and metahistorical characteristics.'[36] Viewed against the conditions of its own existence, the radicalism of existential thought proves as illusory as its dialectical pretensions. Worse than its metaphysical and meta-historical errors, however, Marcuse found that Sartre had not merely posited an ontological essence, but had identified it with historical existence. The demonstration that absolute freedom is operative in actuality, that there are always grounds for the exercise of individual choice, may be ontologically correct and may carry some moral force when the totalitarian organization of life offers the 'choice' of complicity, enslavement, or death. But clearly, it reflects at this stage a historical world in which 'freedom has shrunk to a point where it is wholly irrelevant and thus

---

35. Herbert Marcuse, 'Existentialism: Remarks on Jean-Paul Sartre's *L'Etre et le Néant*', *Philosophy and Phenomenological Research*, vol. VIII, no. 3 (March 1948), p. 309. A slightly abridged version appears in Marcuse, *Studies in Critical Philosophy*, London 1972, with his brief 1965 postscript. The essay was originally written in 1947 or the latter half of 1946.

36. Ibid., p. 311.

cancels itself'.[37] In this light, existentialism ceases to be merely another quiescent idealism, and becomes plainly ideological: reality has the last word.

Marcuse's characteristic dialectics of liberation always direct him to the most unlikely reserves of resistance to the prevailing order, and he finds, in Sartre's favour, a point at which this order negates itself: his existential ontology has disclosed the *'attitude désirante'* which permeates human relations as a transcendent *'désir d'un corps'*, and had thus indubitably penetrated to a dimension of sensual and sexual concreteness to which traditional ontologies (Heidegger) could only aspire. Once again, it is at the unlikely point of *greatest* reification, when the body is lived as mere flesh, that a new image of freedom and happiness is suggested.[38] Referring back to the language of his work on Hegel, Marcuse calls this 'the negation of the negation'; referring programmatically forward, he speaks of the supersession of 'an incessant moral and practical *performance*' by a principle that 'makes the reality of freedom a *pleasure*'.[39]

In his polemic against the 'hidden positivism' in Sartre's work,[40] Marcuse went beyond a critique of the *content* of *L'Etre et le Néant*: with the aesthetic problematic of Resistance poetry fresh in his mind, he also took up certain far-reaching questions of philosophical *form*. The limits of both the theoretical and the artistic critique of the established reality had been a central issue for him at least since his contribution to the aesthetic theory of the Frankfurt School, and the stylistic experiments of the French writers whom he had been studying during the war – Sartre, Camus, Simone de Beauvoir – provided him with the opportunity to refine his own thinking on these issues.

37. Ibid., p. 322.
38. Thirty years later, during which time his estimation of Sartre had been revised dramatically upwards, Marcuse praised the concreteness of Sartre's existential ontology over that of Heidegger: 'In *L'Etre et le Néant* gibt es z. B. eine wirkliche charmante Phänomenologie des Popos. Das hat mir gefallen.' Cf. Habermas et al., *Gespräche mit Herbert Marcuse,* Frankfurt 1978, p. 21.
39. Marcuse, 'Existentialism . . .', pp. 332–3 (emphasis added).
40. To avoid misplaced objections, it might be noted that 'positivism' for Marcuse always denotes an ultimate accommodation to the posited facts of objective reality. It is thus to be contrasted with the 'negativism' (dialectical critical theory) attributed to Hegel in *Reason and Revolution*, rather than identified with a particular philosophical movement. This 'highly personal' interpretation, as Kolakowski has called it, was in fact shared by his Institute colleagues.

In developing the theory of 'affirmative culture' in the 1930s, Marcuse had insisted that while the work of art contains a sensuous dimension which alone can penetrate to the deepest structures of human existence, it is also inescapably bound to the material structures of that existence: 'The beauty of art', he had written, 'unlike the truth of theory, is compatible with the bad present'.[41] The power of criticism, as the editors of *Das Dreieck* had intimated twenty-five years earlier, was liberated neither by collapsing artistic protest into philosophical explanation, nor by suspending thought 'between the "sentiment of absurdity" and its comprehension, between art and philosophy'.[42] Sartre had attempted to banish the '*esprit de sérieux*' from philosophy in order to reflect the assertion of the 'free play' of the existentialist '*pour-soi*', the '*jouer à l'être*' of the creative subject: 'Existentialism plays with every affirmation until it shows forth as negation, qualifies every statement until it turns into its opposite, extends every position to absurdity, makes liberty into compulsion and compulsion into liberty, choice into necessity and necessity into choice, passes from philosophy into *Belles Lettres* and vice versa, mixes ontology and sexology, etc. The heavy seriousness of Hegel and Heidegger is translated into artistic play. The ontological analysis includes a series of "scènes amoureuses", and the novel sets forth philosophical theses in italics.'[43] For Marcuse, this is not an avant-gardist contribution but a retrograde confusion, the disintegration of philosophical style and the corruption of artistic expression. More decisively, it reflects not the 'free play of the creative subject', but the inability of existentialism to grasp the concrete conditions of human existence.

This clarification of the limits of philosophical criticism has its roots in Marcuse's earlier intellectual history of 'the rise of social theory' out of Hegelian philosophy. The transition from abstract universals to the critique of the concrete structures of existence (Sartre's '*réalité humaine*') took place not within philosophy, but in theology and religion (Kierkegaard), the critique of political economy and the theory of socialist revolution (Marx), and artistic creation which refuses to '*raisonner le concret*' (Camus). For a true 'existentialist philosophy' in this sense it would be necessary to turn not to Sartre, but to Hegel and Heidegger in whose thought

41. Marcuse, 'Uber den affirmativen Charakter der Kultur', *ZfS* VI, 1 (1937), p. 79.
42. Marcuse, 'Existentialism . . .', p. 310.
43. Ibid., p. 333.

ontological essence and historical existence are never confused. Just as Hegel had remained self-consciously within the terms of philosophical abstraction, Heidegger's existential ontology eschewed all ethics and politics. More perceptively than Sartre, he had recognized that since Hegel, 'the gap between the terms of philosophy and those of existence has widened' – a perception confirmed by 'the experience of the totalitarian organization of human existence'.[44]

III

But Heidegger, of course, had had other problems, and these lent a bitter irony to Marcuse's exploitation of him as a corrective to the militantly anti-fascist Sartre. In 1946 and 1947, while the writers of *Les Temps Modernes* were debating '*Le cas Heidegger*',[45] Marcuse made an official trip to Germany of several months' duration. Travelling with another former Oss officer, the mission was to collect evidence pertaining to the strength of Nazi sentiments under the controlled conditions of the occupation, to determine the state of the socialist organizations, and generally to assess the stability of the highly artificial equilibrium in post-war western Germany against actual social and political forces. A confrontation with his former mentor had been on the agenda since the shock of 1933, and Marcuse's post-war duties as Research Analyst within the State Department gave him the opportunity to make the arduous side-trip to Todtnauberg, the tiny village in the Black Forest where Heidegger had his mountain cottage.[46]

The reunion must have been something of an anti-climax. The two men discussed the activities and understandings of the Rectorate, and according to Marcuse, Heidegger admitted his misjudgement while maintaining a dignified refusal to join the post-war chorus of supposed 'anti-Nazis' among his academic colleagues. If Marcuse's subsequent recollections of a 'friendly encounter', some-

44. Ibid., p. 335.
45. Cf. Karl Löwith, 'Les implications politiques de la philosophie de l'existence chez Heidegger' (November 1946), pp. 343–60; Alphonse de Waehlens, 'La philosophie de Heidegger et le Nazisme' (July 1947), pp. 115–27; Eric Weil, 'Le cas Heidegger' (July 1947), pp. 128–38.
46. Interested readers should compare the following episode with the one described by Günter Grass in his novel *Hundejahre*, translated by Ralph Manheim as *Dog Years*, New York 1965, pp. 401–3.

what stiff and generally unproductive, do indeed sum up the meeting, it is possible that Heidegger at this time seemed a sorry figure, a victim of his own misjudgement, and genuinely mystified by his harsh treatment at the hands of the French military government in Baden.[47]

Upon his return to Washington Marcuse sent his former mentor a 'care package' (supplies were short everywhere, and the military authorities had commandeered Heidegger's house in Freiburg), and then a letter bluntly putting the question as to why Heidegger had joined the NSDAP. In his response, Heidegger once again acknowledged his 'political error' in supposing Hitler and the Nazis to have heralded the '*Aufbruch*' (awakening) and the '*Erneuerung*' (renewal) he had proclaimed in his Rectoral Address of 1933, but added an astonishing comparison of the fate of the East Germans after the war to that of the Jews under Nazism. This response was politically and philosophically unacceptable to Marcuse, and there was no subsequent communication of any sort.[48]

For about two years after the conclusion of the war, Marcuse continued his work for the American denazification programme, collecting documentary materials and assessing evidence. He occupied a somewhat anomalous position within the State Department's Office of Intelligence Research during this period, along with

47. In November 1945, Heidegger submitted lengthy statements to the Rector of Freiburg University and to the *Bereinigungsausschuss,* the University's denazification committee. Although the latter cleared him of any involvement with the Nazis after his 'political error' (a very common phrase in Germany even today) of 1933–34, his teaching rights were suspended; he was not, however, dismissed from the university (the prohibition was lifted in September 1949). The relevant documents are included as appendices to Karl August Moehling's unpublished PhD dissertation, 'Martin Heidegger and the Nazi Party' (Northern Illinois University 1972).

48. Conversations with HM. Heidegger died in May 1976; his final testament – which contains nothing not previously made public – was printed posthumously in Der Spiegel (31 May 1976) under the title, '*Nur noch ein Gott kann uns retten*'. Recalling Heidegger's 'politische Fehler' in conversation, Marcuse snapped, 'You can make a *mistake* adding figures!' Cf. also his interview with Frederick Olafson in May 1974, reprinted in the *Graduate Faculty Philosophy Journal,* vol. 6, no. 1 (Winter 1977): '[A philosopher] certainly can and does commit many, many mistakes, but this is not an error and this is not a mistake; this is actually the betrayal of philosophy as such, and of everything philosophy stands for.' (pp. 33–4) That Marcuse never ceased to hold Heidegger accountable is evident in his memorial statement: 'Enttäuschung', in Günther Neske, ed., *Erinnerung an Martin Heidegger,* Pfüllingen 1977, pp. 161–2.

Neumann, Kirchheimer, and about 900 other men and women who had been transferred from the R&A Branch of Oss at the end of 1945. An Interim Research and Intelligence Branch had been created under the direction of Army Intelligence expert Alfred McCormack, but it enjoyed neither the budget, the influence, nor the political immunity it had under the wartime Oss organization. When McCormack resigned in April 1946, Colonel William Eddy succeeded him with the explicit task of dismantling the former R&A group as a unit. Each of the four geographical divisions was assigned to regular State Department desks where, in the words of the director of Marcuse's Division of Research for Europe, they 'floated in limbo, distrusted by the State Department professionals and seldom listened to'.[49]

Within this new structure, Marcuse's work naturally began to take on a new significance. Studies of the Socialist and Communist parties in Germany had been a central focus of Oss research into points of possible resistance, and were also relevant to the post-war concern that was occasionally voiced that a destabilizing alliance might be struck between Soviet-oriented Communists and conservative industrialists around the issue of German reunification.[50] By the latter half of 1947, however, the rhetorical warnings that 'an iron curtain has descended across the Continent', and that 'we are in the midst of a cold war', signalled the policies and attitudes that were ascendant in the State Department under the Truman administration.

The shift of American foreign policy from anti-fascist to anti-

49. H. Stuart Hughes, 'The Second Year of the Cold War', *Commentary,* vol. 48, no. 2 (August 1969), p. 27. Hughes left the State Department early in 1948, 'after two years of bureaucratic frustration'. His impression is that anti-Cold War sentiments could no longer gain a serious hearing after the middle of 1947. Despite the obvious seniority of many of the emigré intellectuals, Hughes – Marcuse's 'supervisor' – recalled that 'only the native-born . . . could head the new research divisions that had been inherited from the OSS' (San Diego *Daily Guardian,* 5 November 1974).

50. In a symposium held at the University of Chicago in May 1950, Marcuse stressed the 'negative prospects' for such a development, but observed that German history provides noteworthy instances of 'this famous alliance between right and left, between Communists and conservative militaristic forces'. Published as 'Anti-Democratic Popular Movements' in H. J. Morganthau, ed., *Germany and the Future of Europe,* Chicago 1951, p. 111. For a particularly relevant study of post-war conditions in Germany, see the two essays in Hoyt Price and Carl Schorske, *The Problem of Germany,* New York 1947; Schorske had been Chief of the Central European Section of the OSS.

communist priorities was not particularly abrupt, of course – one of the regional sections of R&A had been solely concerned to monitor the Soviet Union, especially to assist in the regulation of Lend Lease arms transfers by strict wartime requirements. With the end of the war, however, and the incipient stabilization of the new international system, the intentions and capabilities of the USSR and dependent Communist parties moved squarely into the foreground of the State Department's concerns (as well as those of the fledgling Central Intelligence Agency, which had been created in 1947).

To be sure, Marcuse's own analysis of the Soviet Union at this time was not a particularly friendly one, although there is no trace of any sort of anti-communism in his official or private work during this period. No more convincing evidence could be produced than a major research project for the OIR Interdivisional Committee on World Communism in which he subjected the assets, liabilities, and prospects of representative European Communist parties to a detailed analysis.

On 1 August 1949, as senior member of a research team that also included Bernard Morris of the neighbouring Division of International and Functional Intelligence and an assortment of regional specialists, Marcuse submitted a 532-page confidential intelligence report on 'The Potentials of World Communism'.[51] His opening 'Summary Report' first reviewed the theoretical and historical background to the postwar situation: 'The major appeal of Communism stems from the paradoxical situation of the coexistence of immense social wealth, technological mastery of the productive forces, and widespread want, toil, and injustice . . . According to the original Marxian concepts, the locus of the Socialist revolution was to be in the highly industrialized countries of the Western world . . . This concept postulated the full development of all material and intellectual forces basic to a higher culture as the pre-requisite for Socialism.'[52] The isolated victory and consolidation of the first stage of the socialist revolution in the relatively backward Soviet Union

51. [Herbert Marcuse, Bernard Morris, et al.], 'The Potentials of World Communism', OIR Report, §4909 (4909.1 – 4909.6), 1 August 1949 (declassified 5.23.78). Although R&A reports were generally team efforts and not individually authored or signed, and despite obvious efforts to suppress theoretical elaboration, the sections for which Marcuse himself was responsible are simply unmistakable. I am grateful to Professor Morris for his assistance in identifying this report, and for further confirming Marcuse's seniority in its preparation.

52. Ibid., 'Summary Report', §4909, pp. 3–4, 12.

thus mandated an accelerated drive toward competitive industrialization, which entailed the coercion of the 'immediate producers' and the subordination of traditional working-class demands to the foreign and domestic requirements of the Soviet state.

Although the Western Communist parties were not discredited by the sacrifice of the immediate interests of the proletariat, and in general retained an important measure of autonomy from Soviet leadership, their base was eroded by other circumstances: the Marshall Plan for European recovery, the American policy of containment, coexistence and the early development of East-West trade all contributed to the economic and political stabilization of the post-war situation. Throughout Western Europe, including France and Italy where the size, strength, and prestige of the Communist parties had risen so dramatically immediately after the war, 'the success of the efforts of the West to promote substantial and lasting recovery has gone far to dissipate the effects of Communist propaganda and weaken the support that Communists have found outside the ranks of their own militants.'[53]

In case after case, the report (accurately) predicted the limits of the growth of the Communist parties, and their integration into the mainstream of established Western European politics:[54] 'Short of an economic collapse which would make it impossible to satisfy minimum social demands, or belief on the part of labour that their socialist leaders have failed them, Communism has no future in Britain.' (4909.2, Part I, p. 4) 'The Communists' chances of increasing their strength and prestige by non-violent methods are being checked by the basic economic improvements now taking place in France.' (4909.2, Part II, p. 25) 'The Austrian Communists have no prospect of achieving power either by legal or illegal means.' (4909.2, Part III, p. 14) 'As an indigenous political force, Communism in the Western Zone of occupied Germany has declined to such a degree that its real popular strength and support are at present not significant . . . it seems likely that in a new economic crisis, the pauperized and declassed strata of the population would again join a neo-fascist rather than the Communist

53. Ibid., §4909, p. 22.
54. 'The Potentials of World Communism' also contains fascinating (and substantially accurate) analyses of the prospects of Communist movements in the Middle East, Latin America, and such Asian countries as Vietnam. These did not, however, fall under Marcuse's purview.

movement.' (4909.2, Part IV, pp. 3, 19)

Although this report may well be the most 'objective' piece that Marcuse ever wrote (in the academic sense he was later to denounce), it should be recognized that these conclusions imply a very definite and dissident policy recommendation: they undermined and directly contradicted the assumptions upon which the policies of the administration were predicated, namely that world communism represented an imminent and overwhelming danger that could be counteracted only with expanded military, political, and ideological mobilization.[55] Marcuse and his few remaining friends in the Office of Intelligence Research were attempting to offset the steady drift into the policies and politics of the Cold War. There is little reason to believe that their work was seriously discussed at higher levels in the government.

As former R&A scholar-analysts with leftist sympathies (Senator McCarthy's ubiquitous 'Communist infiltrators in the State Department') sought to return to private, academic or professional life, Marcuse was pushed upward into vacancies of increasing seniority – by April 1948, he had been made acting Chief of the Central European Branch of the department's Division of Research for Europe. He had, however, become intellectually and politically isolated: with the departures of Neumann, Schorske, Hughes, and many others, he found himself increasingly surrounded by individuals whose political perceptions were narrowly fixed on 'the Communist threat to Europe' and whose concept of intellectual work entailed the projection of possibilities with cybernetics rather than dialectics. His own reasons for remaining several years into the Truman administration had nothing to do with any residual loyalties, or with the ever more dubious hope that US foreign policy could be moderated: Sophie Marcuse had cancer, and they could not think of moving. With her death in 1951, he left.[56]

---

55. Much later, in a work that could not be further from the needs of the State Department, Marcuse maintained this position unchanged: 'In important aspects, this coexistence has contributed to the stabilization of capitalism; "world communism" [sic] has been the Enemy who would have to be invented if he did not exist – the Enemy whose strength justified the "defence economy" and the mobilization of the people in the national interest.' *Essay on Liberation,* Boston 1969, pp. 84–5.

56. Conversations with HM; he has briefly commented on this unhappy period in *Revolution oder Reform,* Munich 1971, p. 6, and Jürgen Habermas, et al., *Gespräche mit Herbert Marcuse,* pp. 20–1.

One of the unexpected by-products of the original R&A Branch of the Oss came to fruition not in the government, but in the academic world to which many of the intelligence analysts were now returning. This was the concept of interdisciplinary 'area studies' programmes, such as the Russian Institute at Columbia University, headed by former Oss Sovietologist Geroid T. Robinson, and the Russian Research Centre, under Langer at Harvard.[57] To be sure, if university scholars had brought academic skills into the government, it was equally the case that many analysts returned to the universities with newly acquired strategic interests. Even so, the eastern academic establishment was clearly preferable to the defence establishment, and in lieu of a decent job offer – a situation also experienced by Kirchheimer and numerous other German emigré scholars – Marcuse divided the next four years between New York and Cambridge, refining his ideas on art, sexuality, and dialectics.

57. McGeorge Bundy: 'it is a curious fact of academic history that the first great centre of area studies in the United States was not located in any university, but in Washington, during the Second World War, in the Office of Strategic Services. In very large measure, the area studies programmes developed in American universities in the years after the war were manned, directed, or stimulated by graduates of OSS.' (in E. A. J. Johnson, pp. 149-52). Both the Columbia and Harvard institutes were initially endowed by the Carnegie Foundation in 1945.

Appendix A: The Structure of the American Intelligence Agencies, Office of Strategic Services (December 26, 1944)

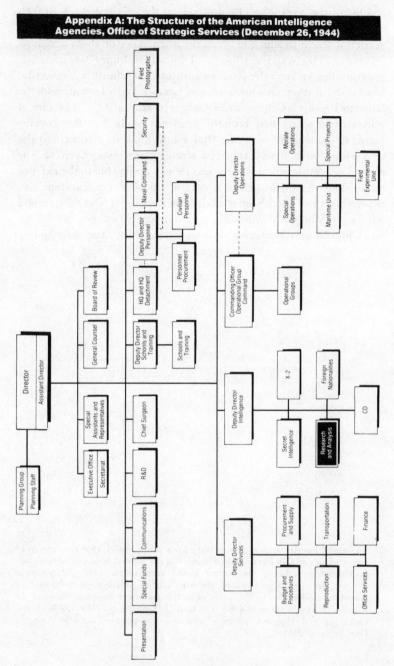

Source: *War Report of the O.S.S.*, p.126.

Appendix B: The Structure of the American Intelligence Agencies, Research and Analysis Branch, O.S.S.

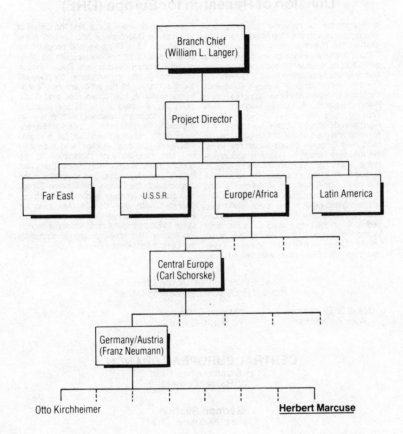

Source: *War Report of the O.S.S.*, p.126.

ORGANIZATION OF THE DEPARTMENT

Division of Research for Europe (DRE)

Is responsible for assuring that the policy-making officials of the Department (and officials of the National Intelligence Authority/Central Intelligence Group) are provided with sufficient positive intelligence reports, studies, and estimates pertaining to all of Continental Europe (except European Turkey and Greece); the Union of Soviet Socialist Republics; Great Britain, Ireland, Australia, Canada, New Zealand, and the Union of South Africa; Algeria; and European dependencies in South America and the Caribbean to enable them to carry out their policy objectives; and performs the following functions: (a) plans and implements a program of research and analysis, pursuant to standards established by the Advisory Committee on Intelligence and maintained by the Office of Intelligence Coordination and Liaison; (b) provides evaluated positive intelligence on the European countries to meet the Department's requirements for the formulation of the foreign policy of the United States Government towards those countries; (c) collaborates with the Advisory Committee on Intelligence and the Office of Intelligence Coordination and Liaison in the formulation of a Departmental program for basic research; (d) collaborates with the Office of Intelligence Collection and Dissemination in planning and implementing the Department's program for the procurement of intelligence materials from all sources, and evaluating, as an integral part of the research process, incoming materials with a view to improving the relevance, accuracy and timeliness of the reporting services; (e) prepares intelligence reports, studies, and estimates for, and supplies spot information to the geographic divisions of the Office of European Affairs, and other authorized recipients in the Department, the Central Intelligence Group, and other Government agencies; and (f) cooperates with the Special Assistant for Research and Intelligence in providing assistance to Departmental and interdepartmental intelligence and research groups, including the Central Intelligence Group.

H. Stuart Hughes, *Acting Chief*
Richard P. Stebbins, *Reviewing Officer*

Isabel G. Blackstock	Marian C. Conroy	Mary F. Hembry
Alice A. Coffman	May I. Ferrari	

CENTRAL EUROPEAN BRANCH
H. Stuart Hughes, *Chief*
W. Russell Bowie, Jr.

German Section
Franz L. Neumann, *Chief*

Beatrice Braude	Coburn B. Kidd	**Herbert H. Marcuse**
Robert Eisenberg	Otto Kirchheimer	Arnold H. Price
John H. Herz		

Austria/Czechoslovakia Section

Hans Meyerhoff   Paul Zinner

Economic Section
Fred Sanderson, *Chief*

Albert G. Capet	Arthur L. Horniker	Murray Ryss
Claire P. Doblin	Miriam E. Oatman	Erwin Strauss

Source: *Register of the Department of State* (Washington. 1946). p.13.

**Appendix D: Office of Intelligence Research
(Department of State), April 1, 1948**

REGISTER OF THE DEPARTMENT OF STATE 1948

Division of Research for Europe (DRE)

Is responsible for planning and implementing a program of positive-intelligence research pertaining to all of continental Europe (except European Turkey and Greece), Union of Soviet Socialist Republics, Great Britain, Ireland, Australia, Canada, New Zealand, Union of South Africa, Iceland, Greenland, Algeria, European dependencies in South America and the Caribbean, and secondary interests, in collaboration with the appropriate research divisions, in countries which are closely related to the area of primary responsibility, to meet the intelligence requirements of the Department in the formulation and execution of foreign policy and the intelligence requirements of the Central Intelligence Agency and other authorized agencies. It maintains continuous, close, and informal relationships with officials of the Office of European Affairs and of other offices in the Department, to encourage the exchange of information and provide them with immediate and timely intelligence for their operations.

Philip J. Conley, *Acting Chief*
Marian C. Conroy, *Administrative Officer*

Isabel G. Blackstock   May I. Ferrari   Mary F. Hembry

CENTRAL EUROPEAN BRANCH
Herbert Marcuse, *Acting Chief*

German Section
Otto Kirchheimer, *Acting Chief*

Robert Eisenberg   John H. Herz
Manfred Halpern   Arnold H. Price

Austria/Czechoslovakia Section
Hans Meyerhoff   Paul E. Zinner

Economic Section
Fred H. Sanderson, *Chief*

M. June Boeckman   Arthur L. Horniker   Murray Ryss
Albert G. Capet   William N. Parker   Erwin Strauss

EASTERN EUROPEAN BRANCH
William B. Ballis, *Chief*
Vladimir Kalmykow

Political Section
———— ———— *Chief*

Rudolf O. Altroggen   Pearl Joseph   Vladimir Prokofieff
John C. Guthrie   Boris H. Klosson   Stanley Wilcox

Economic Section
Herbert Block, *Acting Chief*

William Gffoane   Elizabeth N. Landeau   George J. Rothwell
Stanley Graze   Paul A. Lifantieff-Lee   M. Gordon Tiger
Vladimir B. Grinioff   Helen J. A. Lincoln   Leon S. Wellstone
Samuel Hassman   Eugene Rapaport   Howard M. Wiedemann
Jacob Horak   Ruth T. Reitman

Source: *Register of the Department of State* (Washington, 1948), p. 76.

PART THREE

DEPARTURES
(1950~1958)

4
MATTERS OF
LIFE AND DEATH
(1950–1958)

By the time Herbert Marcuse finally left the government, the military struggle against German fascism had been entirely supplanted by the political struggle against Soviet Communism. The stability of the capitalist countries in the period of reconstruction suggested that with the redirection of the technological apparatus to the post-war economy, a level of material affluence could be promised that was the reward of compliance; in the socialist world, progress remained bound to terror to such a degree as to provoke deep examination of the dimension that had been lost to revolutionary theory and practice.

Still, Marcuse refused to consider that Stalinism (or fascism) had 'eradicated the roots of a different kind of communism in industrial society'.[1] Honouring his intellectual debts to Horkheimer and the Frankfurt School, he regarded the Soviet Union less as an alternative to the Western democracies than as a competitor within a common framework whose features included 'the triumph of technological rationality, of large industry over the individual; universal coordination; the spread of administration into all spheres of life; and the assimilation of private into public existence.'[2] In his view, the Marxian theory of the revolutionary subject had fared badly in the confrontation with Nazism and Stalinism and their post-war survivors. 'Perhaps no other theory,' he reflected later in the decade, 'has so accurately anticipated the basic tendencies of late industrial society – and apparently drawn such incorrect conclusions from its analysis.'[3]

1. Herbert Marcuse, 'Recent Literature on Communism', in *World Politics* (July 1954), p. 521.
2. Ibid., p. 517.
3. Herbert Marcuse, Preface to Raya Dunayevskaya, *Marxism and Freedom*, New York 1958, p. 7.

The fugitive ideas he had been harbouring while working in the US Department of State, and which were finally expounded in his writings of the 1950s, have often been characterized as 'utopian'. Although this appraisal – whether friendly or hostile in intent – is seriously misleading, the misunderstanding upon which it rests points toward the most fundamental structures of his thought. Marcuse's intentions were in fact the very opposite, for he sought to *rescue* a sub-tradition of intellectual culture from defamation as 'mere utopia' and return it to the centre of a critical social theory. Concluding a major cycle of lectures delivered in Germany on the centenary of Freud's birth, he defended his highly speculative manner of reasoning: 'It may be less irresponsible today to depict a utopia that has a real basis than to defame as utopia conditions and potentials that have long become realizable possibilities.'[4] Radical ideas cease to be 'utopian' once the means to realize them exist, and at that point they become subversive of the social order that denies their political content.

Accordingly, Marcuse's philosophical investigations in the post-war decade took the form of a historical assessment: he proposed that we are living at the historical moment in which it is for the first time possible to envisage the global conquest of scarcity, and thus of the political and psychological repression it has demanded. The theoretical anticipations of this qualitatively different mental and material existence that lies within reach, and the political analysis of why the transition to it is not taking place, are tasks that are eminently concrete.

The technological forces mobilized during the world war suggested the triumph over the restraints of nature and of culture – if in its negative, inconceivably destructive form – and it was to the newly stabilized industrial superpowers that had emerged from the war that Marcuse turned to disclose the emancipatory possibilities of that conquest.

---

4. Herbert Marcuse, 'Die Idee des Fortschritts im Licht der Psychoanalyse', lecture delivered 10 July 1956 in Frankfurt a. M., published in 'Freud und der Gegenwart', *Frankfurter Beiträge zur Soziologie,* vol. 6 (Frankfurt 1957), trans. Jeremy Shapiro and Shierry Weber, in Marcuse, *Five Lectures,* Boston 1970, p. 43. Cf. also his remarks in the 1960 Preface to his *Soviet Marxism*: 'Critical analysis has the task of keeping [historical] alternatives in mind, no matter how utopian they may appear in the status quo' (p. xvi).

I

The coexistence of the developed capitalist and socialist superpowers that shaped the international situation in the 1950s also created the problems that determined the shape of Marcuse's research during that decade. His final severance from the State Department, and the pragmatic, policy-oriented research his position had entailed, did not, however, entirely mitigate his restlessness. This was partly due to his new academic surroundings which, despite the company of close former colleagues such as Neumann and Barrington Moore, offered neither a common set of theoretical assumptions such as had characterized the Institute of Social Research, nor the shared sense of purpose that had permeated the community of scholarly analysts in the Oss. In addition, the somewhat mundane empirical research into the ideological foundations and consequences of the Cold War was not the only claim on his attention.

In 1950, while still in the capital, Marcuse had been invited by Dr Edith Weigert to deliver a series of lectures at the Washington School of Psychiatry, elaborating for the first time the contours of his long-standing consideration of Freud.[5] The small group that made up his audience included the psychologist Karen Horney and Marcuse's friend, the international lawyer, Joseph Borkin, who encouraged him to develop his strikingly original reading of Freud into a book. The next four years, when he was not honouring the terms of his Rockefeller Foundation grant by conducting research into Soviet Marxism at Columbia (1952–53) and Harvard (1954–55) were spent writing *Eros and Civilization*, the work that was to assure him of a place in the intellectual history of the radical left. It was published in 1955, by which time the 57-year-old Marcuse – now remarried and already a grandfather – had taken up his first academic appointment as professor of politics and philosophy at Brandeis University. He must have looked forward to a productive but tranquil conclusion to his scholarly career when he and Inge Marcuse, the widow of his recently deceased colleague, moved to suburban Newton, Massachusetts.[6]

Marcuse's 'Philosophical Inquiry into Freud' is indebted, as its original preface acknowledges, to the theoretical position of Hork-

---

5. The School sponsors an annual distinguished visiting lecturer in the humanities, a programme which is ongoing.
6. Franz Neumann died in a car crash in Switzerland in 1954. For three relevant

heimer and the Institute.[7] Once again, however, he is too diffident, for the theories he expounds and the images upon which he draws here had served as prominent leitmotifs in the development of his thought long before he had encountered Horkheimer (or, for that matter, either Marx or Freud).

The Frankfurt School had been drawn to the body of psychoanalytic writings for reasons that were substantially pragmatic, namely to supplement neo-Marxian theory by providing it with an access to the depth dimension of the individual psyche. The pressing task had been to interpret the events of the 1930s: why had the 'revolutionary class' been largely reduced to acquiescence or even complicity? How could the potency of mass propaganda and crude ideologies be explained? What further trends may be anticipated?[8] Apart from several important studies contributed by Fromm to the Institute's *Zeitschrift*, psychoanalytic theory did not itself become the object of critical investigation.[9] Marcuse's interpretation of Freud now supplied this neo-Marxian framework (though Marx remained a silent partner throughout), but it also served to assemble the major themes that had surfaced and resurfaced in his work over the previous thirty years into the theoretical position that was to become associated with his name.

Marcuse's overall purpose was not so much to criticize the errors or shortcomings of Freud's thought as to establish its place within the development of Western rationality and to indicate those of its possibilities which Freud had either neglected or denied. The

appreciations of Neumann's intellectual accomplishment, cf. Herbert Marcuse, 'Preface' to Neumann, *The Democratic and the Authoritarian State*, New York 1957, pp. vii–ix; Otto Kirchheimer, 'Franz Neumann: An Appreciation', in *Dissent*, IV, Autumn 1957, pp. 382–6; H. Stuart Hughes, 'Franz Neumann between Marxism and Liberal Democracy', D. Fleming and B. Bailyn, eds., *The Intellectual Migration*, Cambridge 1969, pp. 446–62.

7. For the Institute's relationship to psychoanalysis, see Jay, ch. 3.

8. Cf. Jay, ch. 3 for a survey of the general concerns and particular positions taken up by the Institute in the 1930s.

9. Fromm's early essays, which Marcuse continued to endorse as 'admirable' even at the height of their polemic (cf. pp. 9–11 below) included 'Uber Methode und Aufgabe einer analytischen Sozialpsychologie', *ZfS* I, 1/2 (1932), 'Die sozialpsychologische Bedeutung der Mutterrechtstheorie', *ZfS* III, 2 (1934), and 'Die gesellschaftliche Bedingtheit der psychoanalytischen Therapie', *ZfS* IV, 3 (1935), as well as Fromm's contribution to the Institute's *Studien über Autorität und Familie*. A selection of Fromm's early papers may be found in *The Crisis of Psychoanalysis*, Greenwich, Conn., 1970.

premiss of this historical contextualization of psychoanalysis was essentially that Freud's thought is subject to 'the dialectic of enlightenment', the historico-philosophical process described by Horkheimer and Adorno by which the liberation from irrationality becomes a new form of domination – domination that reproduces itself, but, in the late phase of industrial civilization, also undermines itself.[10] In its mission of enlightenment, the rationality disclosed by Freud seemingly accommodated itself to the actuality of repressive civilization. At the same time, however, it released forces that cannot be contained within the framework of existing ideas and institutions.

The pattern of this interpretation runs parallel to that laid out in the study of Hegel published fifteen years earlier. This formal congruence, however, is not, as has been frequently remarked, due primarily to a common attempt to 'vindicate' Hegel and Freud, but because substantively their work participates in the same history and shares the same fate. For Marcuse, both Hegel and Freud were epochal figures in the history of thought because they had amplified the concept of Reason beyond traditional religion and metaphysics on the one hand, or a narrowly technical-empirical rationality on the other. In *Reason and Revolution* Marcuse had demonstrated the manner in which Hegel elaborated the concept of reason to embrace subjectivity as well as objectivity, sensuousness as well as intellect, nature as well as history. Marcuse suggested that the resolution of this alienation 'animates the history of Western metaphysics', and in *Eros and Civilization* he brought the same logical and ontological priorities to the interrogation of Freud: 'In its most advanced positions, Freud's theory partakes of this philosophical dynamic. His metapsychology, attempting to define the essence of being, defines it as Eros – in contrast to its traditional definition as Logos.'[11] Freud's thought, like Hegel's, penetrated to the deepest levels of human existence and returned with an image of irreducible gratification and fulfilment, frustrated though they might be within the prevailing order of political, psychological, and epistemological repression. But unlike psychoanalysis and idealist philosophy, Marcuse's thought maintained a vital link with concrete historical conditions

10. Max Horkheimer and Theodor Adorno, *Dialektik der Aufklärung* (1944), trans. John Cumming, London 1972, esp. 'The Concept of Enlightenment', pp. 3–42.
11. Herbert Marcuse, *Eros and Civilization: A Philosophical Inquiry into Freud,* Boston 1955, pp. 124–5.

and with the radical *praxis* prescribed by Marx, and thus remained alert to the collapse of rationality into actuality (the 'reality principle', the 'world of positivity') that had ultimately undermined both systems.

Along with this interpretation of the philosophical context of psychoanalysis went an attempt to uncover its historical and political content. In this undertaking Marcuse was drawn not to Freud's personal statements on current social issues, nor even to his theoretical investigations into the origins of society and civilization. Rather, it was that branch of Freud's thought seemingly furthest removed from social and political life, the so-called 'metapsychology', that suggested to him the most far-reaching social and political critique.[12] The instincts, whatever their historical 'vicissitudes', are the incorruptible governors of a realm in which the laws of gratification are rigidly enforced.

The vicissitudes or modifications of the instincts – ultimately those of Life and Death – to which Freud had directed his attention were, by definition, rooted in individual mental processes: reversal, reversion, sublimation, and out-and-out repression are purely and narrowly psychological categories, alterations visited upon an immutable instinctual structure in the course of its own internal development.[13] It was precisely on this 'basal' substratum that Marcuse took his stand. Against revisionist currents which he loosely characterized as left (Wilhelm Reich), right (Jung), and 'centre' (Erich Fromm), Marcuse insisted that the theory of the instinctual infrastructure remain intact, but be expanded to embrace the *historical* as well as biological character of the influences to which its content is subject: 'The reality which shapes the instincts as well as their need and satisfaction is a socio-historical world.'[14]

The 'cultural' revisionism of Erich Fromm, Marcuse's former colleague, was singled out for an especially harsh attack along these lines, and a somewhat acrimonious public debate ensued, whose first

12. For a survey of the evolution of Freud's theories of the instincts and of the dynamic, 'topographical' description of mental processes, cf. Ernest Jones, *The Life and Work of Sigmund Freud,* New York 1957, vol. III, pp. 165–286, and Richard Wollheim, *Freud,* London 1971, pp. 157–218. Most of the relevant essays of Freud himself are collected in a volume entitled *General Psychological Theory,* New York 1963.

13. Cf. 'Instincts and Their Vicissitudes' (1915) in Freud, esp. pp. 91–103.

14. *Eros and Civilization,* p. 12.

stage dragged on for several months. In their otherwise laudable determination to provide psychoanalysis with a sociological foundation, Marcuse charged that Fromm and the neo-Freudians had postulated secondary, environmental factors as primary, and thus displaced the explosive role given to the instincts. They had taken the 'total personality' as given, and concerned themselves with its happiness and fulfilment without regard to the instinctual constitution of the personality: 'Whereas Freud, focusing on the vicissitudes of the primary instincts, discovered society in the most concealed layer of the genus and individual man, the revisionists, aiming at the reified, ready-made form rather than at the origin of the societal institutions and relations, fail to comprehend what these institutions and relations have done to the personality that they are supposed to fulfil.'[15] A radical, critical theory is thus not only weakened, but rendered ideological – serviceable to the status quo. Fromm shot back with numerous instances of Freud's personal accommodation to contemporary society – an argument constructed on the *ad hominem* grounds that Marcuse explicitly rejected in *Eros and Civilization* (unbeknownst to Fromm, who had not yet seen it) – and mounted his own counter-offensive against Marcuse's 'human nihilism disguised as radicalism'.[16] Rebuttal was followed by counter-rebuttal – none of them very satisfying – and relations between the two 'Freudian leftists', which were never very close, even in the period of their collaboration, steadily deteriorated; to the end, they referred to one another with unconcealed disdain.

The central point in Marcuse's general position was that Freud had revealed the inherent conflicts of the instincts – with one another and with the constraints of the external world – but by failing adequately to distinguish between the biological and the historical, he had defused an explosive theory. This was the defect that Marcuse had identified in the ontologies of Hegel, Heidegger, and Sartre, and his conclusion followed the same lines, namely that the radical politicization of the theory did not require the disman-

15. Marcuse, 'The Social Implications of Freudian "Revisionism" ', *Dissent* (summer 1955), reprinted in slightly revised form as an 'Epilogue' to *Eros and Civilization*, pp. 240–1.

16. Erich Fromm, 'The Human Implications of Instinctivistic "Radicalism" ', *Dissent* (fall 1955), p. 320. It might be noted that Marcuse regards the early work of the 'left-revisionist' Wilhelm Reich, especially the explorations of sexual politics in 'What is Class Consciousness?' (1934), with great admiration.

tling of its basic concepts, but rather presupposed them, in fact pressing them to their limits.

Chief among the environmental variables that condition the prevailing repressive organization of the instincts is the brute fact of material need, *Ananke*: the condition of scarcity that has dominated the whole history of civilized society has dictated that a considerable part of the instinctual (libidinal) endowment of the population be diverted from enjoyment into productive labour. In the present era, however, both theory and practice provide evidence suggesting that the historical limits of a reality principle dominated by scarcity have been reached. In practical terms, the unprecedented productivity of the industrial civilizations of both the West and the East, and the lessening of the time and toil that must be expended on it, permits a corresponding lessening of social demands upon instinctual energy (which has not been forthcoming); in theory, Hegel's thought – which Marcuse always took as 'the representative philosophy of Western civilization' – has mirrored the progress of history as necessary domination but points toward its negation.

Where the rationality of 'repression' ceases to be bound up with the collective survival of the species, its psychological significance becomes political: restrictions imposed upon instinctual gratification in excess of what is objectively required ensure only the survival of an obsolete system of social domination. Drawing his terminology from Marx's critique of political economy (which he felt to be the proper basis of any 'Marxist humanism') Marcuse proposed that the increment of renunciation demanded by the interest in social domination be conceived of as 'surplus-repression'. Referring to Marx's theory of exploitation, he added that from a political point of view, 'the only pertinent question is whether a state of civilization can reasonably be envisaged in which human needs are fulfilled in such a manner and to such an extent that surplus-repression can be eliminated.'[17]

The Promethean world of Marx was soon left behind, however, for psychoanalysis had opened to Marcuse a theoretical perspective which pointed beyond the critique of capitalist political economy. The (political) transformation of the 'environmental' demands made upon instinctual energy suggested the possible transformation

17. Marcuse, *Eros and Civilization*, p. 151; also p. 35f. This explanation was offered in conversation. A central concept in Marx's *Capital* is, of course, 'surplus-value', the portion of a worker's productive labour appropriated by the capitalist.

of the instincts themselves, or rather, of the instinctual value historically assigned to the alleged 'facts' of life (and death): alienated work could be reduced to a point where it becomes continuous with the free play of essential human faculties; sexuality could be restored to its primary, pregenital fullness; the instinctual balance of life and death could itself be radically shifted 'the closer life approximates the state of gratification' (Nirvana) stipulated by Freud as the goal of the death instinct.[18] Not only is the capitalist ruling class to be deposed, but even the powers allegorized in the mythologies of ancient Greece could lose their hostile and alien character: Eros, Thanatos, Kronos could themselves be 'liberated' by the redirected accomplishments of mature civilization.

Although he has stretched them to their outermost limits, Marcuse has thus far remained within the framework of the basic psychoanalytic concepts; above all, his concern has been to demonstrate that the theory is capable of intersecting actively with history and politics, and is not immune to radicalization. Ultimately, *Eros and Civilization* (which Marcuse himself felt to be his most important book) must stand or fall on the basis of its own intentions and the strength of its argument in realizing them.[19] In the wider view, however, it clearly marks a stage in the evolution of the critical social theory that he had been constructing in Europe and America, and through which he was trying to salvage the critical, revolutionary possibilities of Marxism.

Throughout the fascist period, Marcuse had been haunted by the paradox that the greater the potentialities for a hitherto unimagined degree of emancipation, the more total the mobilization of the forces of political and psychological repression arrayed against them. Consequently, he had allowed his thinking to be pressed to the margins of the established society in his search for a refuge of future

18. Ibid., p. 235. Cf. also his distinction between the 'ontological' and 'biological' significations of death, which is the subject of his essay on 'The Ideology of Death' in Herman Feifel, ed., *The Meaning of Death,* New York 1959, pp. 64–76.

19. As noted earlier, the present study does not aim at detailed analyses of individual texts. For other approaches to *Eros and Civilization,* cf. Jean-Michel Palmier, *Herbert Marcuse et la nouvelle gauche,* Paris 1973, pp. 335–412; Paul Robinson, *The Freudian Left,* New York 1969, pp. 147–244; Morton Schoolman, 'Marcuse's Second Dimension', *Telos* (spring 1975), pp. 89–115; Gad Horowitz, *Repression: Basic and Surplus Repression in Psychoanalytic Theory,* Toronto 1977, passim; Sidney Lipshires, *Herbert Marcuse: From Marx to Freud and Beyond,* New York 1974, passim.

liberation, for a political base from which to resist the totalitarian controls. The distinctive insight of the post-war decade, however, was that with the conclusion of peace, these controls had not substantively been lifted and the problem of the 1930s and 1940s – the discovery of an autonomous principle of political functioning – remained acute. In Freud's metapsychology he now found a correlative principle of *mental* functioning that appeared to retain an important measure of freedom from the prevailing reality.

The specific historical content of the prevailing reality-principle is linked with the total administration of inner and outer life, and the analysis of this process which Marcuse had begun with the Frankfurt Institute of Social Research now began to acquire a depth dimension. Under such conditions, critical thought must draw its concepts from outside the system of totalitarian controls, and it now seemed that Freud had indicated the starting-point for all such investigations: in the course of the supersession of the pleasure-principle by the reality-principle, he had written, 'one mode of thought-activity was split off; it was kept free from reality-testing and remained subordinated to the pleasure-principle alone. This is the act of *phantasy-making*, which begins already in the games of children and later, continued as *day-dreaming*, abandons its dependence on real objects.'[20] The illicit rationality of fantasy, dreams, the imagination, and even the sexual perversions – those *fleurs du mal* which 'seem to reject the entire enslavement of the pleasure ego by the reality ego'[21] – argues for the existence of 'a fundamental, independent mental process' with 'a truth value of its own which corresponds to an experience of its own'.[22]

The idea that the 'strange truths' kept alive in the imagination are not merely escapist 'affirmations' but also correspond to a conceivable reality had preoccupied Marcuse since his earliest probings into the suppressed human potentialities of the present. Psychoanalytic theory now gave him the scientific basis for conjecturing that they correspond to an *experienced* reality as well. Fantasy and the imagination provide immediate access to the reservoir of the unconscious, and to the archaic, onto- and phylogenetic memory of

20. 'Formulations Regarding Two Principles of Mental Functioning' (1911) in Freud, *General Psychological Theory,* p. 24 (emphasis in original). This key passage was also cited in *Eros and Civilization,* p. 140.
21. *Eros and Civilization,* p. 50.
22. Ibid., p. 143.

the whole individual, prior to the 'civilized' alienation of psychic and social functions. As such, the instinctual striving 'for a gratification which culture cannot grant' takes over the function he once attributed to existential ontology. And again, as in the early critique of Heidegger, there is no question of a mystical juxtaposition of two hostile 'worlds', but of the raising of a transcendental standard of criticism whose terms are immune to cooptation into existing structures of intellectual and institutional life.

Repression thus revealed its deep structure, but so, then, did rebellion. Marcuse had long been working under the basic dialectical principle that the foreshadowing of liberation is to be sought not through utopian exercises in futurological forecasting, but in tendencies existent – if suppressed or distorted – in the given world. In the present theoretical context, this required the interpretation of manifestations of deep instinctual demands on the surface of modern life, and psychoanalysis confirmed his earlier inclinations to allow the faculty of memory – 'as a decisive mode of cognition' – to guide the analysis.

It is the unconscious, he wrote, that 'preserves the memory of past stages of individual development at which integral gratification is obtained. And the past continues to claim the future: it generates the wish that the paradise be recreated on the basis of the achievements of civilization.'[23] This is clearly a psychological reformulation of the concept of the 'anticipatory memory' which, as he had proposed it in 1937, projects into the future images of liberation drawn from the past. But now a content and a context is provided: what is to be re-membered, re-collected, is the archaic infancy of the individual and the genus under the unchallenged dominion of Eros. And there is no mystical sentimentality in this

23. Ibid., p. 18. The priority of memory in Marcuse's work may also be seen as one of many posthumous tributes to Walter Benjamin, for whom it was the decisive vehicle of emancipation; cf. especially *Einbahnstrasse* and *Berliner Chronik*: 'and now remembrance advances from small to smallest details, from the smallest to the infinitesimal, while that which it encounters in these microcosms grows ever mightier. Such is the deadly game that Proust began so dilettantishly.' *One-Way Street*, London 1979, p. 296. Also Freud, in *The Ego and the Id* (1923), where the decisive movement of ideas from the unconscious to the light of consciousness is entirely a function of memory: 'it dawns upon us like a new discovery that only something that has once been a Cs. perception can become conscious . . . : this becomes possible by means of memory-traces.' (New York 1960, p. 10.) For an original study of the primacy of memory for Marxism, cf. Christian Lenhardt, 'Anamnestic Solidarity', *Telos*, 25 (fall 1975), pp. 133–54.

evocation of the primal unity of pregenital prehistory, for 'the rediscovered past yields critical standards which are tabooed by the present . . . The *recherche du temps perdu* becomes the vehicle of future liberation.'[24]

The recognition of the primal stage of polymorphous gratification offends against the prevailing rationality of toil, renunciation, and forbearance which sustains the reality principle of the present epoch – the 'performance principle' in Marcuse's adaptation. Accordingly, it has suffered the fate of the truly revolutionary opposition: imprisonment (in this case 'repression') or exile to the sheltered redoubts of art, mythology, and fairy tale, where an unreal 'aesthetic' rationality is admitted to pertain.

This conception of a 'total' rationality is perhaps the principal leitmotif of Marcuse's ongoing philosophical work to have survived into the 1950s. Indeed, the centrality of Eros, which he derived from psychoanalytic theory, and the consequent grounding of being in the logic of gratification, allowed him to situate Freud as an heir to the underground current of metaphysical protest which had challenged the ideologies and institutions of repression from at least the time of Plato's philosophy. Their shadowy status in the (orthodox) history of philosophy – to which Marcuse had referred throughout his work – only reflects the advancing hegemony of the narrow system of Western rationalism which finally surfaced after Hegel as positivism and empiricism, and which has exercised a repressive tyranny over the logic and order of sensuousness and gratification.

For the rest, 'the insights contained in the metaphysical notion of Eros were driven underground. They survived, in eschatological distortion, in many heretic movements, in the hedonistic philosophy',[25] were relegated to the margins of respectable thought, as in the 'irrational' philosophies of Schopenhauer and Nietzsche, or managed to secure refuge in the theory of art. For Marcuse, it was precisely this philosophical counter-trend that had sustained the vision of a liberating rationality and the order of freedom corresponding to it. 'Their history', he added, 'has still to be written', and at that time Marcuse still planned to write it: with the philologist Jacob Taubes (who was his editor at the Beacon Press) he had again begun to formulate plans for an epic *Corpus Hereticorum* which, if

24. *Eros and Civilization,* p. 19.
25. Ibid., p. 126. Cf. also his *Soviet Marxism,* pp. 183–4, where he suggests that 'Marxism is an integral part of the same tradition'.

their discussions had come to anything, would have surely offered a unique challenge to the conventional account of the history of philosophy.

In the only other contemporary work to explore the uncharted landscape of a non-repressive reality principle, Norman O. Brown clearly implicated Marcuse's work in his sweeping assessment of Freud's: 'It is one of the great romantic visions, clearly formulated by Schiller and Herder as early as 1793, and still vital in the systems of Hegel and Marx, that the history of mankind consists in a departure from a condition of undifferentiated primal unity with himself and with nature, an intermediate period in which man's powers are developed through differentiation and antagonism (alienation) with himself and with nature, and a final return to a unity on a higher level or harmony.'[26] Marcuse and Brown, like Freud and Nietzsche, Marx and Hegel, Herder and Schiller before them, took seriously the dimensions of the eternal return of the repressed.

In the pursuit of the repressed into 'the tabooed and subterranean history of civilization', Schiller was in fact to prove an indispensable guide – no longer the Schiller of the antiquarian bookseller in Berlin, but the theorist of an aesthetic rationality 'conceived as a principle governing the entire human existence', and of the goal of 'a remaking of civilization by virtue of the liberating force of the aesthetic function'.[27] At the height of the later eighteenth-century ascendancy of rationalism in European philosophy and liberalism in politics, Schiller had undertaken to redress the imbalances of modernity. Following Kant in the idealist tradition, he had sought to restore the 'instinct' of sensuousness (*der sinnliche Trieb*) to its existential and epistemological rights within an enriched structure of rationality; the free play of the imagination was assigned this task of anticipating the reconciliation (remembrance) of the severed unity of nature and freedom, sense and intellect; and resonating with the last of the themes of Marcuse's thought over the past three decades, a standard of critical judge-

---

26. Norman O. Brown, *Life Against Death,* Middletown 1969, p. 86, and his remark that *Eros and Civilization* is 'the first book, after Wilhelm Reich's ill-fated adventures, to reopen the possibility of the abolition of repression'. (p. xii). Cf. also M. H. Abrams, *Natural Supernaturalism,* New York 1971, passim.

27. *Eros and Civilization,* ch. 9, passim.

ment was to be raised, transcending the fractured conditions of psychic and social existence in the present and immune to its integrative forces. For Schiller this standard was *beauty*, and its science *aesthetics*.

'By means of beauty', Schiller had written, 'sensuous man is led to form and thought: by means of beauty spiritual man is brought back to matter and restored to the world of sense.'[28] Once he had reformulated it in light of the material and intellectual history of the succeeding century-and-a-half, Marcuse would be fully in accord with this pivotal conception. Schiller had proposed the aesthetic as the faculty that comprehends 'the whole complex of our sensual and spiritual powers in the greatest possible harmony', and had formulated his recognition of the political potential of beauty in his idea of the 'aesthetic state' (*Staat*);[29] with *Eros and Civilization* aesthetics – in its modern form as the theory of art and beauty – first began to emerge from latent to manifest centrality in his thought.

The work of art, more than any other embodiment of the unconscious, anticipatory memory 'of the liberation that failed, of the promise that was betrayed',[30] carries into the material plane the eternal protest that Freudian metapsychology had implicitly assigned to fantasy. Embodied in style, rhythm, metre, shape – in the ordered permanence of aesthetic form – the 'alienation' linked with the content of aesthetic ideas fortifies itself as freedom. 'Outside the language of art', however, these images 'change their meaning and merge with the connotations they received under the repressive reality principle'.[31] The opposition to social reality ends in reconciliation, the indictment in acquittal, and there may be no escape from the prosaic world of labour into the poetic world of beauty.

Here again is the dialectical theory of the 'affirmative character of culture': aesthetic form preserves the political content of the

28. Friedrich Schiller, *Briefe über die Ästhetische Erziehung des Menschen* (1794–95), edited and translated by Elizabeth Wilkinson and L. A. Willoughby, *On the Aesthetic Education of Man in a Series of Letters*, Oxford 1967, Letter XVIII, pp. 122–3.

29. Ibid., fn. to Letter XX, ¶4, pp. 142–3. Although Marcuse awarded Schiller's theoretical writings his highest plaudit – 'These ideas represent one of the most advanced positions of thought' (p. 188) – he always maintained a somewhat reserved attitude toward Schiller's (sentimental) poetry.

30. *Eros and Civilization*, p. 144.

31. Ibid., p. 165.

Great Refusal, but confines it to the aesthetic dimension. In the 1930s, Marcuse had been concerned to refute the practices and philosophies of renunciation; adapting his earliest writings on *Künstlertum* to the requirements of a critical social theory, he tended to view aesthetic culture – precisely because of its 'alienation' from social reality – as the possible preserve of the image (memory) of gratification. Against the political backdrop of that decade, namely the violent cooptation of cultural production and its enslavement to the broader purposes of the authoritarian state, the problem of aesthetics became acute.

In the post-war decade of unprecedented affluence and – to borrow Marcuse's impressionistic language – 'advancing techno-logy', effective resistance to the administration of existence could no longer find shelter in the consciousness of the proletariat; rather, it was the aesthetic imagination in which there was retained an image of the whole individual unhindered by the reality principle of a repressive society whose gods were work and power, productivity and performance: not the labour of Prometheus and Hermes, but the enjoyment of Orpheus and Narcissus provide the archetypes of rebellion against socially steered modes of fulfilment. 'The culture of the performance principle makes its bow before the strange truths which imagination keeps alive in folklore and fairy tale, in literature and art':[32] guiltless pleasure, sustained happiness, the harmony of sensuousness and reason, subjective fantasy and objective reality, nature and civilization are preserved within and against the antagonistic world of work and power in the 'aesthetic dimension'.

II

Eros and Civilization, which brought international recognition to its author,[33] was concerned with the potentialities of human existence in advanced industrial society, with the present indicators of the direction authentic progress might take, and with the social forces of repression arrayed against them. The range of its concerns thus

32. Ibid., p. 160.
33. A measure of the immediate impact made by *Eros and Civilization* is that the other participants in the cycle of lectures in Frankfurt and Heidelberg (1956), in which Marcuse delivered the concluding addresses, included analysts of the internation-al stature of Franz Alexander, Ludwig Binswanger, and Erik Erikson.

transcends conventional political categories, but also links it with his contemporaneous study of Soviet Marxism published a few years later. As one friendly critic perceived at the time, a common 'universe of discourse' enveloped Marcuse's very different studies: 'In each case, Professor Marcuse has taken for his subject an entity no less grand than "Western culture" or "late industrial civilization". Despite the immense erudition which he has brought to his studies of Hegel, Freud, and the USSR, respectively, his real interests have been in problems transcending them in generality.'[34] This is indeed the case. While Marcuse explicitly repudiated the familiar 'convergence' thesis, he did undertake to situate the distinctive features of Soviet development within the broader political and ideological processes of mature industrial society.

This bivalent (political/industrial) approach was indicated by the presuppositions of Soviet Marxism itself, according to which 'the transition from socialism to communism' was to take place on a technical-industrial base that had been brought to maturity during the 'first phase' of socialist revolution. Following this theoretical stipulation, and confronted with the 'long-range international integration of the Western world', the early Bolshevik leadership had embarked upon a drive toward full industrialization to which socialist theory and practice were subordinated. Despite the fundamentally different ('eschatological') goals of Soviet and Western society – which in fact fix the *limits* to their possible 'convergence' – the process of 'total industrialization seemed to exact patterns of attitude and organization which cut across the essential political and ideological differences'.[35] It is on this broad level of a common technological denominator, rather than in his detailed, 'empirical' analyses of the vagaries of official Soviet self-interpretation, that *Soviet Marxism* falls within the long-range evolution of Marcuse's thought.

In this context, the pivotal issue of private ownership or nationalization no longer appears as decisive, for the process of rapid, competitive industrialization follows its own 'suprapartisan' logic: 'Both systems show the common features of late industrial civilization – centralization and regimentation supersede individual

---

34. Richard De Haan, review of *Soviet Marxism* in *Ethics*, vol. 69 (October 1958), p. 63.
35. Herbert Marcuse, *Soviet Marxism: A Critical Analysis,* New York 1958, reissued with a new Preface by the author, New York 1961, p. 179.

enterprise and autonomy; competition is organized and "rationalized"; there is joint rule of economic and political bureaucracies; the people are coordinated through the "mass media" of communication, entertainment industry, education.'[36] It is the 'supranational and even supracontinental' instrumental logic dictated by the integrated technological apparatus.

Nor does the exercise of political terror fundamentally distinguish the Soviet Union from the industrialized West, when seen in relation to broader, shared social requirements. If the struggle for freedom is in fact rooted in deep structures of the psyche, as Marcuse had argued in his psychoanalytic writings, the social forces of repression arrayed against it will be fully mobilized. Beneath the democratic forms of the United States and Europe lie the painless and comfortable techniques of mass manipulation, of an entertainment industry that effectively regulates leisure time, of a productive apparatus that stabilizes the existing order by delivering the goods. 'The democratic form', he told his Frankfurt audience in 1956, 'rejects terror because it is strong enough and rich enough to preserve and reproduce itself without terror.'[37] In the Soviet case, where the binding of the underlying population to the existing order was no less immediate a goal, the trend toward the relaxation of the obsolete terroristic controls which followed the death of Stalin marked not so much the creation of a new policy orientation as the consummation of the old one.

Unlike the Western cultures, where two centuries of enlightened absolutism and liberalism had enshrined the ethics of humanism and individualism at least on the plane of ideology, Soviet Marxism virtually acknowledged the totalitarian structure in its claim that the October Revolution had created a 'conformity' between base and superstructure, the expanding productive apparatus and the social relations of production. The contradiction between individual and social interest, private and public existence was prematurely resolved by fiat, and thus the antagonism that had historically guaranteed to bourgeois society a protected, critical vantage-point within its borders was being systematically reduced.

36. Ibid., p. 66.
37. Marcuse, 'Trieblehre und Freiheit', p. 4. For further reflections on Soviet terror and the Marxian theory of history, cf. his review of Popper's *The Poverty of Historicism:* 'Notes on the Problem of Historical Laws', in *Partisan Review,* vol. 36, no. 1 (winter 1959), pp. 117–29, reprinted in *Studies in Critical Philosophy.*

A conception of this long-range historical tendency, equally visible in the Ussr and beneath the pluralist surface of the democratic West, formed the very core of Marcuse's thought – his contribution to the philosophy of history expounded in the *Dialectic of Enlightenment*. For Horkheimer and Adorno, however, the 'therapeutic' impulse had begun to recede before the 'diagnostic', accompanied by a settling temper of philosophical resignation and political withdrawal. Marcuse, on the other side, never relaxed his search for alternatives and escapes, and in this the Soviet case only confirmed his earlier search for political transcendence.

The substance of Marcuse's study suggested that the development of the Ussr (and of Soviet Marxism) had been largely regulated by the requirements of competitive industrialization. In strict Marxist language, 'the functional differences between base and superstructure therefore tended to be obliterated'[38] as the ideological superstructure was systematically assimilated to the patterns imposed by the total productive apparatus: 'The more the base encroaches upon the ideology, manipulating and coordinating it with the established order, the more the ideological sphere which is remotest from the reality (art, philosophy) precisely because of its remoteness, becomes the last refuge for the opposition to this order.'[39] The notion of an intrinsic cultural protest, however, denied the most fundamental tenets of Soviet Marxism as well as the official claim that the new Soviet society embodied the objective interests of the population: 'The fight against ideological transcendence thus becomes a life-and-death struggle for the regime.'[40] The political requirement of substantively and stylistically 'accepting the established social reality as the final framework for the artistic content'[41] which passes under the name of 'Realism' seemed especially critical for, as Marcuse had maintained throughout his life, it is the very principle of the work of art to embody a protest on behalf of 'a sphere of fulfilment'. Prior to the ultimate reconciliation of Reason and History, reality and ideology, 'art retains its critical cognitive function: to represent the still transcendental truth, to sustain the image of freedom against a denying reality'.[42] When

38. *Soviet Marxism,* p. 104. The technical base is always understood broadly as 'the machine process as ensemble of institutions, functions, and attitudes'. (p. xi).
39. Ibid., p. 110.
40. Ibid., p. 114.
41. Ibid., p. 112.
42. Ibid., p. 115.

Soviet aesthetics attacked 'Formalism' and 'Romanticism', as well as the even more abstract forms of atonality and surrealism, it attacked 'the ideological reflex of freedom' in a repressive society. This was surely disastrous for humanity, but was also disastrous for art: 'through the reinstatement of harmony by administrative decree, the banning of dissonance, discord, and atonality, the cognitive function of art is "brought in line", and conformity is enforced in the *per se* non-conformistic artistic imagination.'[43] Soviet aesthetics wants art that is not art, he concludes, 'and it gets what it asks for'.[44]

In the modern, industrial world, then, the Actual was being forcibly brought into line with the Rational against the background of an all-embracing technical apparatus that left ever-narrower regions of life free of control. All sectors of cultural and political life were geared to the productive apparatus, to such an extent that even opposition tended to take place on the terms of this technological totality.

A striking ambiguity ran through Marcuse's interpretation, however, and he himself declared his dissatisfaction with his formulation. While seeking to avoid the pitfalls of the simplistic 'convergence' theory of capitalist and socialist economies, he had nonetheless been driven to recognize that technological rationalization was a factor in some ways transcending political institutions: the autonomy of 'technological rationality', 'industrial civilization', 'the requirements of competitive total industrialization', and other such manifestly unpolitical constructs is implicitly recognized, though explicitly their political neutrality is maintained.[45]

Marcuse recognized the ambiguous status of capitalism and industrialism in his analysis, and the significance of the problematic upon which this ambiguity rested. He confronted it directly in the coming decade, concentrating his work on the analysis of politics and technology in a fully integrated, 'one-dimensional society', and on the embattled theoretical and practical escape routes from it.

43. Ibid., p. 119.
44. Ibid., p. 116.
45. Ibid., for example p. 169, but cf. also hints of the inherent political tendencies of a large-scale industrial apparatus on pp. 69, 236, 239–40, 244.

5
YEARS OF CHEERFUL PESSIMISM (1959–1969)

In the late phase of his career, that of the thesis of 'one-dimensionality', Herbert Marcuse withstood attacks from the Kremlin and the Vatican, the Minutemen and the Weathermen, the American Legion and the Progressive Labor Party, and parents, pundits, and professors of every shade. Reviewing his controversial work in the midst of the uprisings of 1968, the French Marxist Henri Lefebvre concluded: 'The debate is open.'[1] In fact, in this period of unsolicited international attention, Marcuse added almost nothing to the theoretical framework he had already constructed. His influence and notoriety came rather from his strategy of returning his abstract formulations to the concrete ground and underground of everyday life in the 1960s: speech, television, and sex, the shopping centre, the home, and the workplace, the restiveness of students, women, and minorities. If the achievement of *Eros and Civilization* had been to anticipate the libertarian impulses of the 1960s, the achievement of *One-Dimensional Man* was to resonate perfectly with them.

During the preceding two decades, Marcuse had pursued a scholarly career that ran parallel to but outside of the academic establishment. Aside from incidental lectures delivered at Columbia, Harvard, and the American University in Washington, he had done virtually no teaching, and he had had no sustained contact with university students since his own studies in Freiburg. He rose to his new calling, however, and soon after accepting his appointment in Philosophy and Politics at Brandeis, he became one of the

1. Henri Lefebvre, review of *One-Dimensional Man* in *Le Monde,* 16–17 juin 1968.

commanding figures in the university community, drawing unprecedented audiences to his lecture courses on 'European Political
Thought', 'Greek Philosophy', 'Marxian Theory and Communism',
and above all, his special course on 'The Welfare and Warfare
State'. One of his students, not prone to hero-worship, recalls his
effect: 'When Marcuse walked onto the platform . . . his presence
dominated everything. There was something imposing about him
that evoked total silence and attention when he appeared, without
his having to pronounce a single word. The students had a rare
respect for him. Their concentration was not only total during the
entire hour as he paced back and forth while he lectured, but if at
the sound of the bell Marcuse had not finished, the rattling of
papers would not begin until he had formally closed the lecture.'[2]
With his frequent denunciations of the trivial or fashionable
products of a sterile climate of 'academic boredom' and his
insistence that genuine thought is normative, negative, and 'transcendent', students found him a uniquely provocative teacher; and in
his outspoken positions on the Cuban Missile Crisis, the Civil Rights
drive in the South, US support of the Brazilian military coup of
1964, and the growing intervention in South-east Asia, the emerging
political movement of the early 1960s found him an ally and – let it
be said – an inspiration.[3]

Several distinctive themes ran through the courses Marcuse
taught at Brandeis, among which the compatibility of liberalism
and totalitarianism is central: 'The most urgent concern of today',
he said in introducing his undergraduate lectures in political theory,
'is the redefinition of totalitarianism. It is currently restricted to a
type of society quite obviously totalitarian. We have failed to discuss
democratic totalitarianism.' The historical examination of representative ideologies and institutions which followed revealed that 'there

2. Angela Davis, *An Autobiography,* New York 1974, pp. 133–4. As Chairman of the
   Graduate Programme in the History of Ideas, Marcuse also taught advanced
   seminars on Plato, Kant, Hegel, and Husserl.
3. Several statements from Marcuse's students may be compared: 'Marcuse as
   Teacher', by William Leiss, John David Ober, and Erica Sherover in K. Wolff
   and B. Moore, eds., *The Critical Spirit,* Boston 1968, pp. 421–5, and 'Dear Herbert'
   by Ronald Aronson in G. Fischer, ed., *The Revival of American Socialism,* New York
   1971, pp. 257–80. It has occasionally been noted – by Irving Howe (*Harpers,* July
   1969, p. 84) and the rightist pseudo-philosopher Eric Hoffer (*Los Angeles Times,* 6
   July 1969) – that Marcuse did not unequivocally support the Hungarian uprising
   of 1956; both imply that he therefore endorsed the Soviet invasion, which is not
   only untrue but dishonest.

is no intrinsic contradiction between liberalism and dictatorship, provided that the dictatorship meets the preconditions of liberalism, namely space for the expression of individual needs and aspirations'. In the present period, however, 'it is manifestly clear that men may be manipulated. Individual needs and needs imposed by society are indistinguishable.'[4]

The first real development of the heretical notion of a comfortable, smoothly functioning 'democratic totalitarianism' had actually taken place before a European audience, however. In 1958 Marcuse had accepted an invitation to become director of studies in the influential 'sixth section' of the Ecole Pratique des Hautes Etudes in Paris – an invitation sponsored by Lucien Goldmann and others – where he lectured in French on 'Les tendances de la société industrielle'.[5] The theme of his lectures was the integration of all spheres of life under the technological imperative of advanced industrial society: 'A new monism has appeared, but a monism without substance. The tension between subject and object, the dualistic and antagonistic character of reality tends to disappear, and with it the "two-dimensionality" of human existence, the capacity to envisage another mode of existence in the reality . . . In the technological world, the capacity to understand and to live this historical transcendence is dangerously atrophied; man is no longer able to live according to two dimensions; he has become a one-dimensional being.'[6] By the time he returned to his position in Paris two years later, the (as yet unnamed) thesis of one-dimensionality had been expanded to include the adaptation of language to the operational needs of the pervasive technological apparatus, and the neutralization of critical reason by a 'technological rationality [that] renders the transcendental dimension unreal or unrealistic'. The analysis of the social and political integration of advanced industrial society was gradually being supplemented by

4. I am grateful to Professor Victoria Bonnell, University of California at Berkeley, for allowing me the extended use of her undergraduate lecture notes from Marcuse's courses of fall 1962 through winter 1964. The passages quoted are from his lectures of 25 September and 2 October 1962.

5. The ideas developed in the course were summarized in his essay, 'De l'ontologie à la technologie: les tendances de la société industrielle', *Arguments* IV 18, 1960 (unless otherwise noted, all translations from the French and German in this chapter are my own). Marcuse's colleagues that year also included André Gorz and Raymond Aron.

6. Ibid., p. 55. It may be recalled that the language of 'two-dimensionality' had appeared in Marcuse's writing at least since *Hegels Ontologie* (1932).

the identification of tendencies toward integration in the realms of thought and culture.[7]

At Brandeis Marcuse had now begun to offer a regular course on 'The Welfare State and the Warfare State', in which the historical roots and dominant tendencies of the new industrial society were examined. The analysis of economic, political, and social trends revealed that since around 1910, the extension of the productive apparatus had begun the process of integrating all spheres of society within a repressive and increasingly destructive whole. He nevertheless concluded his lectures in the spring of 1964 with 'an admittedly utopian and romantic projection of the new society which would appear with the passing of the welfare/warfare state'. The tone of his lectures thus contrasted sharply with the tone of the book that had appeared at the beginning of the term.

In fact, the categories of 'optimism' and 'pessimism' are irrelevant to Marcuse's now classic *One-Dimensional Man* – he once dismissed an interviewer's question with his characteristic good-natured impatience: 'Alright, so I'm a cheerful pessimist!' A more substantial (but equally unsuccessful) attempt to deflect such questions introduces the book: '*One-Dimensional Man* will vacillate throughout between two contradictory hypotheses: (1) that advanced industrial society is capable of containing qualitative change for the foreseeable future; (2) that forces and tendencies exist which may break this containment and explode the society. I do not think that a clear answer can be given. Both tendencies are there, side by side – and even the one in the other.'[8] The first tendency, however, is dominant, and this political imbalance is reflected in the oppressive weight of the analysis.

Manifestly, *One-Dimensional Man* studies the assimilation of public and private, inner and outer, through the extension of the realm of necessity (work, economic productivity) into the realm traditionally reserved by the ideologies of the bourgeois era for the free development of the self. Not only is the free time of the individual now invaded by total mass mobilization for consumption and

7. Marcuse, 'The Problem of Social Change in the Technological Society', lecture presented to UNESCO symposium on '*Le développement social*', Paris, 28 April 1961; printed for limited distribution under the auspices of Raymond Aron and Bert Hoselitz (Paris 1965, p. 157).

8. Marcuse, *One-Dimensional Man: Studies in the Ideology of Advanced Industrial Society*, Boston 1964, p. xv. This characteristic bivalence (which is not ambivalence) is for Marcuse an essential component of dialectical, two-dimensional thought.

defence, but the radical opposition historically preserved in art, science, and philosophy has been effectively neutralized. Previously, they had represented the inherently critical 'consciousness of the discrepancy between the real and the possible, between the apparent and the authentic truth, and the effort to comprehend and master this discrepancy'.[9] In the present, late, phase of industrial civilization, however, under the dual imperatives of capitalist profitability and competitive international coexistence, even these outposts of transcendence have been absorbed by the totalitarian organization of the technological base.

Science, once an acknowledged weapon in the fight against irrationality, has in modern times developed within an 'instrumentalist horizon' by which it is assimilated to the overarching historical 'project' of the existing society. The very process through which science emancipated itself from external determinations (theological, metaphysical) and achieved an objective value freedom, has delivered it over to the ends prevailing in the society as a whole. In an argument that draws its elements from Husserl, Sartre, and Horkheimer and Adorno, Marcuse linked theoretical and practical reason, the abstract and functional character of scientific concepts with their technological 'application'. But since politics and culture, business and the military are fused within this technological apparatus, a new concreteness is smuggled into the supposedly abstract formulations of scientific theory – the very concrete social forms of domination.[10]

Philosophy has likewise succumbed to the one-dimensional technological rationality, relinquishing its historical commitment to the hidden dimension of unexperienced reality (potentiality) in favour of the language, truth, and logic of the establishment. In its prevailing, neo-positivist forms, contemporary philosophy repudiates all transgression beyond empirical facts and rejects as 'metaphysical' those modes of thought which negate and transcend the established universe of discourse: 'Philosophical thought turns into affirmative thought; the philosophic critique criticizes *within*

9. *One-Dimensional Man*, p. 229.
10. The major sources of Marcuse's argument are *Dialektik der Aufklärung*, Sartre's *L'Etre et le Néant*, and Husserl's *Die Krisis der Europäischen Wissenschaften und die transzendentale Phänomenologie;* the critique of the hidden substance of formal logic and the *de facto* partisanship of supposedly 'objective' modes of thought is also the main theme of Horkheimer's lectures delivered at Columbia University in 1946, and published as *Eclipse of Reason* (reissued New York 1974).

the societal framework and stigmatizes non-positive notions as mere speculation, dreams, or fantasies.'[11] Again, the avowed 'purity' of thought reveals itself to be illusory, for even the abstract formulations of formal logic and linguistic analysis absorb both the historical process by which relationships are constituted, and the reified social totality within which phrases are uttered. The logical only reflects the ontological, and philosophy is social theory whether it wants to be or not.

Even *art*, which Marcuse had from the beginning valued as the final refuge of irreconcilable opposition and indictment, is losing its defining quality of being alien to the alienated existence: 'Today's novel feature is the flattening out of the antagonism between culture and social reality through the obliteration of the oppositional, alien, and transcendent elements in the higher culture by virtue of which it constituted *another dimension* of reality.'[12] The coordination (*Gleichschaltung?*) of culture with politics and society which had been carried out by totalitarian terror in the 1930s was now being accomplished – democratically and efficiently – by the totalitarian organization of technology. Industrial civilization, with its immense capacity to integrate art into the business and pleasure of daily life, to desublimate the ideals expressed in the content and embodied in the form of the *oeuvre* within a still-repressive whole, has invalidated the higher truth value of art, which depended precisely upon its estrangement from the established society. The power of art to evoke 'an uncomprehended and unconquered dimension of man and nature' resisting integration has been annulled as this dimension has yielded to technological mastery, and the critical contradiction between art and life has been resolved – prematurely.

This mobilization against conceptual and aesthetic transcendence of one-dimensional thought is the ideological reflex of the mobilization against political transcendence of one-dimensional society.[13] Accordingly, Marcuse turned his attention – and this is the new development in his writings of this period – to the social and political forces arrayed against the opposition. What he diagnosed

11. *One-Dimensional Man,* p. 172.
12. Ibid., p. 57 (emphasis in original).
13. It might be noted that the analysis of the critical functions of science, philosophy, and art, Marcuse builds upon ideas developed in his earlier essays, but does not advance theoretically beyond them: 'Some Social Implications of Modern Technology', (*SPSS,* 1941), 'Philosophie und kritische Theorie', (*ZfS,* 1937), and 'Uber den affirmativen Charakter der Kultur' (*ZfS,* 1937).

was a society of unimaginable productive capacities which, driven by the imperatives of capitalist profitability, spread waste, destruction, and misery across the globe while controlling the thoughts, needs, and actions of its own members in accord with the rationality of the productive apparatus. At the same time, the very real accomplishments of the system seemed to render protest irrational: for most of its members, the affluent society 'delivers the goods', and opposition to the irrationality of the whole must seek higher ground.[14]

In this analysis, which had been evolving throughout his whole career, Marcuse struck a resonant chord in the generation of the 1960s. Under profoundly different political and economic conditions, Marx had written that theory, the first weapon in the fight against the existing organization of power, 'is capable of gripping the masses when it demonstrates *ad hominem*, and it demonstrates *ad hominem* as soon as it becomes radical'.[15] *One-Dimensional Man*, whether despite or because of the severity of its analysis, met this requirement: it contained an analysis of the objective transformation of the capitalist mode of production in the era of high technology, but also identified the subjective feeling of poverty that prevailed within the affluent society. Within five years, Marcuse's 'Studies in the Ideology of Advanced Industrial Society' had sold over 100,000 copies in the United States, and had been translated into sixteen languages.

As he is often criticized for having cultivated a haughty philosophical disdain for analysis of 'the facts', it is interesting to note that Marcuse included far more empirical and historical material in his course on 'The Warfare State and the Welfare State' than is reflected in *One-Dimensional Man*.[16] He surveyed nineteenth- and twentieth-century trends, and had his students conduct investi-

14. In one of the most revealing moments in the reception of *One-Dimensional Man,* a conservative reviewer felt that he must point out to the readers of *Fortune* Magazine that Marcuse's portrayal of the material saturation of life in the affluent society was meant to be *critical*: Irving Kristol, 'Improbable Guru of Surrealistic Politics', *Fortune,* July 1969, p. 191. Several notable critiques of the book will be encountered further on.

15. Karl Marx, 'Critique of Hegel's *Philosophy of Right*. Introduction', in *Early Writings,* p. 251.

16. Apart from the familiar charge that he is 'too abstract', cf. the critiques of Peter Clecak, *Radical Paradoxes,* New York 1974, pp. 175–229, and 'Karl Miller' (pseud.), 'The Point is Still to Change It', *Monthly Review,* June 1967, pp. 49–57 (but also Marcuse's reply, October 1967, pp. 42–8).

gations into particular cases of the interpenetration of business, government, and the university within the modern defence economy. His sources often included *Business Week*, the *Wall Street Journal*, and the *New York Times*, which on 12–13 April 1964, carried a front-page report on the military basis of the economy of metropolitan San Diego to which he called his students' attention: fully 81.8% of total manufacturing employment was reported to be in the missile and aircraft industries. More could have been said: these plants produce over $640 million in military products annually; the Naval and Marine payroll injects $1.2 million into the San Diego economy every day; $12 thousand million in military ships and planes and 130,000 people are based in the twenty-one airfields, harbours, and military bases spread throughout the country; and ultra-conservative interests are supported by an unholy alliance ranging from newspaper magnates, business leaders, and the highest concentration of retired admirals in the country, to the John Birch Society, the Minutemen, and an array of heavily armed right-wing paramilitary groups.[17] It is surely a choice irony, then, that when, shortly thereafter, Marcuse learned of the administration's decision to allow his teaching contract at Brandeis to lapse, out of many offers he accepted a position in the Philosophy Department of the University of California at San Diego.[18] He was able to keep a rather low profile in the community for about two years, which he devoted to his teaching and to the clarification of his theoretical position before an international audience of scholars and activists; his strategy rested upon a series of calculated intellectual counter-offensives against the establishment.

Most immediately conspicuous among these was a frontal attack against the majority of his colleagues in philosophy and the social (and natural) sciences. Against the avowed methodological insularity of the disciplines, he had argued that even the most rigorous particular judgements can be corrupted by the irrationality of the whole: formal logic absorbs the substance of the status quo, value

17. Cf., for example, The *New York Times*, 12–13 April 1964; *The Nation*, 28 October 1968; the *Los Angeles Times*, 27 July 1969; the *New York Times*, 6 October 1968.
18. Although he was given no explanation for his termination, in view of his eminence and scholarly record there can be little doubt that his age (67) was not the determining factor and that political considerations were involved. The UCSD appointment was arranged by his friend, the philosopher Richard Popkin.

freedom actually serves the values of the prevailing (unfree) society, and objective science – in the very structure of its concepts – surreptitiously takes up a partisan stance toward the objectively posited order. As Husserl had demonstrated in his critique of post-Galilean science (applicable also to contemporary schools of scientific philosophy), the concrete qualities of empirical reality remain operative in the scientific abstraction from them (the *'lebensweltliche* a priori'); in this way, 'the pre-scientific, pre-given empirical reality enters the scientific enterprise and makes it a project within the pre-established general project of the empirical reality'.[19] The characteristic modern liberation of science from superimposed norms and values (whether humanistic or inhumane) has reduced it to an instrument of the totalitarian technological apparatus. No more appropriate forum for a critique of the false objectivity of the empiricist programme could have been offered to Marcuse than the 1964 Heidelberg conference marking the centenary of Max Weber's birth, where he flatly stated, 'neutrality is real only where it has the power to resist interference'.[20]

The epistemological critique of the existing internal organization of science and the humanities ('a treacherous designation: as if the sciences did not partake of humanity!')[21] carried with it a political challenge as well. For if reason is intrinsically *historical* reason, then the only true 'objectivity' would be actively partisan on the side of a rational society; it would include responsibility for the social context within which knowledge is produced, as well as for its impact upon

19. Marcuse, 'On Science and Phenomenology', paper delivered to the Boston Colloquium on the Philosophy of Science, 13 February 1964, published in *Boston Studies in the Philosophy of Science,* II, R.S. Cohen and Marx Wartofsky, eds., New York 1965, p. 286. To a less specialized audience at UCLA in July, 1966: 'to put it another way, whereas the idea of pure science once had a progressive function, it now serves, against the intention of the scientist, the repressive powers that dominate society'; 'The Responsibility of Science', in L. Krieger and F. Stern, eds., *The Responsibility of Power,* New York 1967, p. 440: the dialectic of enlightenment.

20. Marcuse, 'Industrialisierung und Kapitalismus', address to the Deutsche Gesellschaft für Soziologie, April 1964, published in O. Stammer, ed., *Max Weber und die Soziologie Heute,* Tübingen 1964; lecture and discussion trans. Kathleen Morris, *Max Weber and Sociology Today,* New York 1971, also by J. Shapiro in *Negations,* p. 215. It may be compared with Goethe's remark: 'As in the moral sphere, so we need a categorical imperative in the natural sciences'.

21. Marcuse, 'The Individual in the Great Society', *Alternatives,* vol. I, nos. 1, 2 (March-April, summer 1966), also in Bertram Gross, ed., *A Great Society?,* New York 1966, p. 74. The New Left journal *Alternatives* was founded by members of Marcuse's graduate philosophy seminar at San Diego.

society and human life. *One-Dimensional Man* had already proffered a concise formulation of the critical theory of knowledge: 'Epistemology is in itself ethics, and ethics is epistemology.'[22]

For this, Marcuse was accused of attempting to politicize the university, although, consistent with the line of his reasoning for many years, he insisted that the opposite was the case. 'The university is already a political institution', he told a student audience at the Free University of Berlin, and what is at stake is 'an attempt at the anti-politicization of the university.'[23] Knowledge of the facts must provide for the critique of them in so far as they are factors of a repressive whole, and this theoretical critique commands a political practice. For Marcuse this meant exposing academic complicity in the expanding Indochina war, endorsement of alternative educational projects, proposals, and publications, revision of existing academic curricula to include serious treatment of dissident currents of theory and practice (the 'body' of the unwritten *Corpus Hereticorum*), and an ongoing polemical attempt to clarify the tasks of philosophy and the responsibilities of the intellectual.

In this attempt, Marcuse was consistent with the dialectical programme implied or expressed in his writings over decades: philosophy must look beyond ideal concepts to the actual conditions of their possible materialization, and 'it is the task and duty of the intellectual to recall and preserve historical possibilities which seem to have become utopian possibilities'.[24] The complementary themes of 'anticipation' and 'memory' which had guided so much of his previous work thus survived into this period, and were plainly operative in the notorious 1965 essay on 'Repressive Tolerance' from which this passage is drawn.

Marcuse had argued that tolerance is not an abstract notion but a weapon in the fight for a practical and rationally discernible goal – the creation of a society that would permit the fullest realization of the objective, historical possibilities of freedom and happiness. Detached from its moorings in the concrete facts of social life, what passes for tolerance may in fact be intolerance toward ideas and

22. *One-Dimensional Man,* p. 125.
23. Marcuse, 'Das Problem der Gewalt in der Opposition', lecture at the Free University of Berlin, July 1967, published in *Das Ende der Utopie,* Berlin 1967, trans. J. Shapiro and S. Weber, *Five Lectures,* Boston 1970, p. 88.
24. Marcuse, 'Repressive Tolerance', in Robert Paul Wolff, Barrington Moore, Jr., and Marcuse, *A Critique of Pure Tolerance,* Boston 1965, p. 82.

actions that fall outside the status quo.[25] Recalling, as he often did, the self-destruction of the liberal and tolerant Weimar Republic, which he had himself witnessed, Marcuse proposed rational criteria for the determination of tolerance and concluded that where a society promoted violence, destruction, and misery, 'the realization of the objective of tolerance would call for intolerance toward prevailing policies, attitudes, and opinions which are outlawed and suppressed'.[26] Fully aware of the danger involved in his position, Marcuse ventured an 'affirmative action' theory of tolerance, weighted on the side of those heretical groups and individuals to whom it has historically been denied, and in the service of a future society in which tolerance may regain its liberating and humanizing function. 'I believe that we have discriminating tolerance here already', he told a BBC audience, 'and what I want to do is redress the balance.'[27]

The essay 'Repressive Tolerance' had been Marcuse's contribution to a collective attempt to analyse the nature and limits of tolerance 'in the prevailing political climate', and although it contained little that had not appeared elsewhere in his work, the response to it suggested that the political climate itself was changing: as his students – to whom the essay was dedicated – were beginning to shift their energies from the tactics of black voter registration in the south to the larger mobilization of an anti-war resistance, the question of the limits of tolerance had become immediate.

Even before the challenges from the ghettoes, the streets, and the occupied universities, members of the liberal intelligentsia had already been put on the defensive by the impieties of *One-Dimensional Man*, which had contested the identity of progress with technological development, challenging modern society precisely at the level of its most celebrated accomplishments: not poverty, but wasteful affluence, not the weakness of its institutions, but rather their

25. In a related essay on 'Ethics and Revolution', Marcuse developed the notion of 'rational standards and criteria for judging the given possibilities of human freedom and happiness', in R. DeGeorge, ed., *Ethics and Society,* New York 1966, pp. 133–47. The theme of the historical objectivity of reason and ethics is taken up again in his 'Thoughts on the Defence of Gracchus Babeuf', in J. A. Scott, ed., *The Defence of Gracchus Babeuf,* Amherst 1967, pp. 96–105.
26. 'Repressive Tolerance', p. 82.
27. Marcuse, interview with Robert McKenzie, published in *The Listener,* 17 October 1968, p. 499.

overwhelming power; not the repudiation of the ideals of the Enlightenment, but their transformation into vacuous or repressive ideologies in the course of their realization. Now 'academic freedom' itself seemed to be at stake, and the notion of 'discriminating tolerance' became a rallying point for its righteous defenders.[28]

Rightist defenders also were put on the alert. The consternation caused by this and related positions drifted from the scholarly journals to the mass media and into the public focus during the latter half of the decade, with inevitable distortion. It was claimed that Marcuse's work served 'as an action manifesto for street brawlers', or was 'a neo-Sorelian exhortation to violence'; he allegedly advocated tyrannical rule by 'a small elite of individuals who have learned to think rationally', and who would then withdraw toleration from all who 'oppose what the new ruling class regards as progressive'. From St Paul's, Pope Paul VI struck a different note, denouncing 'the theory that opens the way to licence cloaked as liberty, and the aberration of instinct called liberation', while *Pravda* was no less ardent in defending its faith against the 'false prophet'.[29]

Already by the beginning of 1967, Marcuse's star had begun to rise, and his name began to acquire the mystical aura of familiarity that the media have the power to create through mass circulation

28. Another crusader: A few years later, Marcuse challenged – on *academic*, not political grounds – the qualifications of a certain Fred Schwarz, leader of a 'Christian Anti-Communism Crusade', to offer an accredited course on 'Conservative and Traditional Views of Contemporary Issues' in the university Extension; Marcuse submitted dissenting materials to the administration calling the proposed lectures 'a mockery of genuine education and a mockery of conservative thought'. A public outcry followed Marcuse's statement, in which irresponsible charges were made that 'intolerance is consistent with his political philosophy . . . His essay on "Repressive Tolerance" makes this clear'. Cf. the intellectually lopsided exchange between Marcuse and William Banowsky, then Chancellor of Pepperdine College, Malibu, in the Los Angeles *Times* of 5 April (Banowsky) and 12 (Marcuse), 1970. Among serious defenders of universal tolerance, cf. Maurice Cranston, 'Herbert Marcuse' in Cranston, ed., *The New Left*, New York 1971, pp. 85–116; George Kateb, 'The Political Thought of Herbert Marcuse', *Commentary* (January 1970) and Walter Kaufmann, 'Black and White' in *Survey*, 73 (Autumn 1969).

29. Passages in this section are drawn from Kurt Glaser, 'Marcuse and the German New Left', *National Review*, 2 July 1968; Ernest Conine, 'Right, Left, and Scared Silly', Los Angeles *Times*, 14 July 1968; *Vatican Bulletin*, 1 October 1969 (reported in New York *Times* of 2 October 1969), Yuri Zhukov in *Pravda*, 30 May 1968 (trans. *Atlas*, September 1968); Eliseo Vivas, *Contra Marcuse*, New Rochelle 1971.

and compulsive repetition: 'I'm very much worried about this', he said. 'At the same time it is a beautiful verification of my philosophy, which is that in this society everything can be coopted, everything can be digested.'[30] A neatly packaged and readily digested image was conferred upon him, that of the 'white-maned, craggy-faced, cigar-puffing septuagenarian' (*Time* magazine, of course), usually depicted in genteel surroundings and speaking through a thick German accent, and it was this contrived image, rather than his books, that drew public attention.[31] Accordingly, the attacks against him became more numerous, but also more ignorant and more dangerous: he was the new 'apostle of chaos', 'a splenetic old man sputtering hatred', who 'comes close to preaching anarchy and urging destruction of our form of democracy'. And although one might have dared to hope that certain accusations would have by now lost their power to indict any but their unfortunate authors, he was charged with corrupting the minds of the young.

The new Meletus was one Harry L. Foster, judge-advocate of the San Diego county organization of the American Legion; from among many contenders, the roles of Anytus and Lycon may be assigned to California State Senator Jack Schrade and Assembly Representative John Stull, in whose (Republican) district Ucsd is located. Legionnaire Foster, who had never heard of Herbert Marcuse before May 1968, demanded 'a full-scale investigation of Dr Marcuse'; a campaign was launched, and Legion Post 6 was soon able to make a much-publicized offer of $20,000 to buy up Marcuse's contract from the University. 'The Marcuse matter', Foster said ominously, 'was brought to my attention by certain members of the community here whom I'm not privileged to name, who hoped that the Legion would move because otherwise there might be considerable trouble on the campus here.' At a more official level, Governor Ronald Reagan told the Regents of the University of California that Marcuse was not qualified to teach, while the two right-wing legislators demanded that the university cancel the contract of the rabble-rousing communist. It may not prejudice the defence to note that Mr Foster's interpretation of Marcuse's theoretical position was based upon one hostile and

30. 'Varieties of Humanism. Herbert Marcuse talks with Harvey Wheeler', *The Center Magazine*, vol. I, no. 5 (July 1968), p. 19.
31. For Marcuse's own analysis of the functional and manipulative language of the 'hyphenated abridgement' cf. *One-Dimensional Man*, pp. 92–4.

inaccurate editorial in the San Diego *Union*, Senator Schrade's critical analysis was derived from 'opinions I have received', and Assemblyman Stull's studies of Marcuse's work extended no further than reports of 'his public statements'.[32]

For the most part, Marcuse remained aloof from the growing controversy surrounding his name, leaving Chancellor William McGill to reassure the public that its safety was not imperilled. In interviews, Marcuse repeated that he had never endorsed violence or the destruction of universities, nor advocated any specific tactics in his role as a teacher ('But neither is it the role of the educator to prevent action'). He could not believe that his rightist critics had read his books, attended his lectures, or acquainted themselves with the context of his public statements; since they were without serious foundations, he said, 'I shall do with these charges what they deserve: nothing'.[33]

Marcuse's complacency turned to irritation only when the tactics of the right were escalated. In July 1968, he returned to California from several tumultuous months in Europe. Awaiting him was a hand-printed letter, dated 1 July, which spoke of the necessary unity of theory and practice: 'Marcuse you are a very dirty Communist dog. You have 72 hours to live [*sic*] the United States, 72 hours, Marcuse, and then we will kill you.' Three weeks later, by which time he had reluctantly yielded to his wife's gathering alarm and gone into 'hiding' at Leo Löwenthal's summer house near Carmel, his stepson Michael Neumann began to receive telephone calls from an unidentified woman, telling him, 'The first time he [Marcuse] gets back [for the fall semester] there will be a bombing at the philosophy department and also at his home'. By this time Marcuse was back in Europe, telling three interviewers in the south of France that he was 'certainly not in favour of authorizing free expression to racist, anti-semitic, or neo-Nazi movements, because the distance between the word and the deed is too brief today, too short'.[34] Returning to La Jolla in September, after a further series of lectures and conferences across Europe and a brief visit to Venice, he found a letter from Florence (Kentucky) deferentially addressed to: 'Filthy Communist Anti-American Professor Herbert Marcuse / c/o

---

32. Foster, quoted in the New York *Times*, 6 October 1968, and *The Nation*, 28 October 1968; Schrade and Stull, quoted in the Los Angeles *Times*, 19 July 1968.
33. Herbert Marcuse to Roger Rapoport of the Los Angeles *Times*, 27 July 1969.
34. 'Entretien avec Herbert Marcuse', *L'Express*, 23–29 September 1968, p. 56.

Department of Philosophy / University of California at San Diego'. Marcuse did not answer his correspondence from the Ku Klux Klan (1 July) or the Minutemen (10 September), or return the calling cards left by the local 'Phantom Cells', only commenting, 'If somebody really believes that my opinions can seriously endanger society then he and society must be very badly off indeed'. His family, friends, and students were less philosophical: Michael Neumann notified the FBI, Inge Marcuse forced the interviewer from the *Saturday Evening Post* to empty his pockets before entering the house, and his graduate teaching assistants took on the serious added duty of standing guard over his house through the night.[35]

Marcuse rarely responded to his academic critics who generally dismissed him as a marginal figure in contemporary philosophy, for he tended to dismiss most contemporary philosophy as a marginal phenomenon in the larger history of Western thought; correspondingly, he was not deeply distressed by the massive critical publicity that began to envelop him from about 1967, when the *New York Times* first characterized him as 'the idol of American leftists'. To a third audience, however, he was inordinately sensitive and responsive: the New Left, especially the student movement as it had begun to take shape in the United States, France, and West Germany.

During precisely the five years in which Marcuse had been writing about 'the closing of the political universe' characteristic of one-dimensional society, an unprecedented confluence of political forces was maturing that would enable him to move the analysis to a higher stage. He had already been well aware of the numbers of his students who had been making the hazardous journey from Waltham to the southern states to join in the struggle for desegregation and civil rights; the first political confrontations at Berkeley had taken place in 1964, and the SDS had called the first national protest march against the Vietnam war at the end of his last semester of teaching at Brandeis. Marcuse began to take a serious theoretical and practical interest in these emergent, still

35. Sources for these reports include discussions with Marcuse and his students, also the Los Angeles *Times*, 12 July and 26 July 1968, the New York *Times*, 29 September 1968. Did the FBI have to be informed? At least one paid FBI informant was a member of the Phantom Cells, a right-wing 'survival . . . and guerrilla group associated with the Minutemen' which operated in the San Diego area in this period, and had targeted Marcuse, Angela Davis, and other radical leftists: 'Terror From the Right: An FBI Informant Talks', Chicago *Sun-Times*, 7 March 1976.

marginal forces, and they in him.[36]

It is a disagreeable but demonstrable fact that Marcuse's theoretical work suffered in the period of his most active political engagement – he himself often admitted that 'grandiose ideas about the unity of theory and practice do injustice to the feeble beginnings of such a union'.[37] No real breakthroughs followed *One-Dimensional Man*, but far from dismissing his subsequent work on that account, the obligation is to readjust the framework within which it is to be interpreted – a framework outlined by the war, the resistance, and his abiding conception of the responsibilities of intellectuals. At a stage in his life when any scholar might deservedly have retired to his study and a valedictory opus, Marcuse, nearly seventy, threw his energies to an astonishing degree behind the tasks the movement had set for itself.

Marcuse's interpretation of the Marxian theory of the 'revolutionary subject' had undergone a significant evolution in his attempt to preserve its organic connection to the events of the twentieth century. At the end of the First World War, he had seemingly accepted the 'orthodox' designation of the proletariat of the industrialized nations as the agent of socialist revolution, in an unspecified alliance with radical members of the middle-class intelligentsia. The failure of the German revolution dealt the first blow to this conception, and with the advent of Nazism in Germany, he concluded that the revolutionary role of the working class in the industrialized West had been (forcibly) suspended for the foreseeable future. Revolutionary conditions, he wrote of the Marxian theory, imply acute class struggle and 'a self-conscious and organized working class on an international scale',[38] conditions that did not obtain in the capitalist world.

After 1945, the question of the agent of socialist revolution lay dormant in his work – except for his critique of the official Soviet position – until the revival of American socialism in the New Left. During this period he re-examined Marx's analysis and concluded

---

36. On Marcuse and the New Left in 'the 1964–65 juncture' cf. especially Paul Breines's excellent analysis in Habermas, ed., *Antworten auf Herbert Marcuse*, Frankfurt 1969, pp. 133–51; for the French perspective, Jean-Michel Palmier's *Herbert Marcuse et la nouvelle gauche*, Paris 1973, pp. 476–618.

37. Marcuse, 'Political Preface, 1966' to *Eros and Civilization*, p. xvi.

38. Marcuse, *Reason and Revolution*, p. 318.

that loyalty to Marxian dialectics meant abandoning the 'classical' Marxist theory of the revolutionary proletariat. Although Marcuse's link – both theoretical and practical – to 'the contemporary successor of the proletariat' had always been tenuous ('our *Salonkommunist*', his sister called him), he now took this last step.[39]

Marx had departed from earlier forms of socialist theory by starting not from a romanticization of the working class but from an analysis of its structural role in capitalist society; 'the proletariat', in Marcuse's rendering of the original conception, 'constituting the majority of the population, is revolutionary by virtue of its needs, the satisfaction of which is beyond the reaches of capitalist capabilities.'[40] Although he had not yet formally rejected Marx's stipulation that the blue-collar labour force, by virtue of its strategic position, remained the only class capable of arresting the process of production, he denied both its preponderant numerical weight and that it still represented the 'determinate negation' of capitalist oppression, 'a sphere which has a universal character because of its universal suffering, and which lays claim to no *particular right* because the wrong it suffers is not a *particular wrong* but *wrong in general*'.[41] The analysis of the absorption of the American working class into the economic, cultural, and instinctual life of one-dimensional capitalist society indicated that this final but decisive condition had not been met.

Far from deviating along a 'third way' between socialist and bourgeois theory,[42] Marcuse was therefore following the Marxian conception rather closely when he told an audience at the first international socialist 'Summer School' in Korčula in 1964, 'What we have in the highly developed industrialized countries *is* a class society: there is no doubt that all idle talk about "popular capitalism" or an equalization of classes is pure ideology – but it is a class society in which the working class no longer represents the negation of the established order.' The allegedly 'pessimistic' conclusions of his analysis of the suspended class struggle characteristic of one-dimensional society enabled him to emancipate the Marxian critique from nineteenth-century conditions, and to

39. Marcuse, *Counterrevolution and Revolt*, pp. 38–9.
40. Ibid., p. 38.
41. Karl Marx, 'Critique of Hegel's *Philosophy of Right*: Introduction', *Early Writings*, p. 256.
42. This is the charge of R. Steigerwald, *Herbert Marcuses Dritter Weg*, Berlin 1969.

reorient it toward *actual* points of negation.[43] Since this impulse
would have to come – as Marx had insisted – from a force that had
developed *outside* of the administered system of needs, Marcuse was
clearly looking not for an alternative, but for a catalyst to the
long-range formation of a socialist working class, however little this
would resemble the traditional proletariat of Marxist theory; this
seemed to him to be the promise and the significance of the New
Left.

The most conspicuously 'new' feature of the New Left was its
composition. It was, of course, not an organization but a radical
'movement' of politics and culture centred among anti-war university students, but which also addressed dissident religious groups,
cultural types, and the specifically radical constituencies of women
and underprivileged minorities – groups who were, as Marx had
stipulated, *in* civil society but not *of* it. From its origins in the Civil
Rights movements and rebellious cultural phenomena of the late
1950s, the New Left grew in proportion to deepening US involvement in Vietnam, and in its evolution tended to politicize the
conditions – psychological, cultural, educational, sexual – of its own
existence.[44]

The multi-dimensional character the New Left had begun to
acquire in the mid 1960s – in its demands, its tactics, and its
symbolism – suggested to Marcuse the 'juncture between the erotic
and political dimension' which had been thematic for him perhaps
as early as Eisner's ill-fated Bavarian Socialist Republic of 1918–19,
and which had been rising to the surface of his writings in the

43. Marcuse, 'Perspektiven des Sozialismus in der entwickelten Industriegesell-
    schaft', lecture, Korčula, August 1964, published in *Praxis: Revue Philosophique*,
    1965, p. 261. The highly regarded Korčula Summer School was an annual
    conference organized by a group of Yugoslav Marxists associated with the
    journal *Praxis*. In 1966 Marcuse became a member of the Advisory Council of the
    embattled journal, and he returned to Korčula in the eventful summer of 1968.
    For a full analysis of the Praxis group and its fate, cf. Gerson S. Sher, *Praxis,*
    Bloomington 1977; also the report by Rudi Supek, 'Dix ans de l'école de Korčula
    (1963–1973)', in *Praxis,* 1–2, 1974, pp. 3–15. Returning to Boston he claimed to
    his friend Marx Wartofsky that Yugoslavia proves the possibility of a peaceful
    transition from socialism to capitalism.
44. For a sensitive study of the ideals and the reality of New Left theory and practice,
    cf. Greg Calvert and Carol Neiman, *A Disrupted History: The New Left and the New
    Capitalism,* New York 1971, an analysis with which Marcuse identified strongly.
    Two studies of the cultural radicalism of the 1960s which are relevant to Marcuse
    are Theodor Roszak, *The Making of a Counter Culture,* New York 1969, esp. pp.
    84–120, and Morris Dickstein, *Gates of Eden,* New York 1977, pp. 51–88.

decades prior to its explicit formulation in *Eros and Civilization*. One of the first indications of Marcuse's positively charged reappraisal of the prospects for liberation appeared early in 1967, in the context of a review of the current book by his old friend Norman O. Brown: the author of *Eros and Civilization*, who had become the author of *One-Dimensional Man*, took on the author of *Life Against Death*, who had become the author of *Love's Body*, in a battle of world-views that must be regarded as one of the outstanding documents of the period.[45] In essence, Marcuse wondered if Brown was not ascending toward heaven just at the historical moment which called most urgently for a return to earth.

The polemical and poetic precision of their exchange has obscured the fact that although their gazes were fixed in opposite directions, the two were standing on much the same ground (underground?). To be sure, it was impossible for Marcuse to accept the strains of Christian mysticism that sounded throughout *Love's Body*, and, more severely, Brown's militant metaphysics – his refusal to return from imagery to reality, from symbolism to what is symbolized. But only more profoundly, then, do the affinities show through: both philosophers sought to restore 'the right of the imagination as cognitive power', and both saw that the reified world of liberalism and literalism is a false and repressive one, and must not be permitted to have the last word.

Norman Brown said in his reply, 'This is no joke', but Marcuse had not joined in the chorus of denunciations of Brown's attempt to put an end to politics ('literature', 'prophecy', 'nonsense'), and did not have to be told. He surely saw that *Love's Body* was in itself a 'Corpus Hereticorum' and he knew well many of the landmarks of the strange country through which Brown was then travelling almost unaccompanied: Platonic *eros*, officially proscribed currents of heretical, mystical, and utopian thought, Romanticism, Marxism, and psychoanalysis, the art of surrealism and the theatre of the absurd. For fifty years Marcuse had been rehabilitating such movements precisely because of their transcendental function – as the embattled (and often terroristic) guardians of an integrated, pre-technological rationality in which ethics and aesthetics were

---

45. Herbert Marcuse, 'Love Mystified: A Critique of Norman O. Brown', *Commentary,* February 1967, and Norman O. Brown, 'A Reply to Herbert Marcuse', *Commentary,* March 1967. The entire exchange has been conveniently reprinted in Marcuse's collection *Negations,* pp. 227–47.

more than mere reflexes of the domination of nature.

By the latter half of the 1960s, however, this critical, transcendent dimension seemed to have been rendered suspect, for there were signs that an immanent agent was finally emerging from the margins of the affluent society and taking shape as a political force. More conclusively than any of his contemporaries, Brown had achieved the conceptual demolition of the reified universe of thought and action – but his break with '*la prose du monde*' had been irrevocable. He had indeed found a 'way out', but now, when conditions seemed to permit it, could find no 'way back' to the ground of possible political action. To Marcuse, on the other hand, the war and the emergence of a radical opposition that seemed to *embody* the Great Refusal called for a descent from the transcendent dimension which had resisted the integrative powers of an oppressive and overwhelming reality. The 'recapture of reality and reason' formed the larger context of Marcuse's philosophical and political work throughout the remainder of the decade, and may explain much of the enthusiastic reception of it.[46]

The war – Marcuse's fourth – had entered a decisive phase early in 1965 when Lyndon Johnson finally ordered the long-contemplated bombing of North Vietnamese targets; by the end of that year the relatively small number of American 'advisers' in Vietnam (23,000) had increased to a military force of nearly 200,000 ground troops, a figure which had doubled by the end of 1966. In that year Marcuse developed an analysis based on insights into American foreign policy acquired during his years in the State Department coupled with the theoretical position he had constructed. His analysis of the situation, which he began to present in lectures, teach-ins, and articles, always included an evolving commentary on academic complicity in the war, and student opposition to it.

Dispensing with the official histories, pronouncements, and ideologies, Marcuse argued that in fact the United States was not fighting 'Communism' *per se*, but a very specific form of communism in very specific areas, namely the underdeveloped countries in which

46. More literal interpretations of this important episode may be found in Roszak, pp. 84–120; Paul Robinson, *The Freudian Left,* New York 1969, pp. 223–33, Richard King, *The Party of Eros,* New York 1972, pp. 116–56, and Dickstein, pp. 51–88.

no independent bourgeoisie existed to organize the processes of political and agrarian reform, industrialization, and modernization that were necessary prerequisites of liberation: 'Under these circumstances, the indigenous reform movement must from the beginning take on a radical and undemocratic form. One cannot build a democracy out of thin air; if the social basis for it is not present, it simply cannot come about. Evidently, there is only the choice between a communist dictatorship and a military dictatorship of the ruling classes in these countries, and when only these two choices exist, it is clear on which side American policy falls.'[47]

American foreign policy is not built upon abstract or moralistic preferences, however, but upon realistic assessments of threats to specific American interests. At one of the early teach-ins on the war, held at UCLA in spring 1966, Marcuse went into detail.[48] First, considered not as an isolated phenomenon but in global terms, the defeat of the Saigon government and expropriation of foreign capital by a successful revolutionary movement in Vietnam could undermine 'friendly' neo-colonial regimes throughout the world, substantially contracting the international capitalist economy. Second, a reduction of the massive US defence establishment would necessitate sweeping political and economic changes at home. And third, 'the affluent society is in need of an Enemy against whom its people can be kept in a state of constant psycho-social mobilization' – the potential for the conquest of necessity and 'the pacification of the struggle for existence' were now too great and too threatening to guarantee the protection and reproduction of social institutions built upon the necessity of labour, discipline, and renunciation.

Just as the theory of one-dimensional society had contributed to advancing the Western Marxist critique beyond the limitations of a purely economic analysis, Marcuse now opened up the analysis of the war to its social and psychological dimensions. It was not, in this view, an unfortunate but isolated quagmire in South-east Asia, but the consequence of a global policy dictated by the innermost dynamic of advanced industrial society. Accordingly, the one-

47. Marcuse, 'Die Analyse eines Exempels', lecture, published in *Neue Kritik,* 36–37, June–August 1966, p. 32.
48. Marcuse, 'The Inner Logic of American Policy in Vietnam', statement delivered at UCLA Teach-In, 25 March 1966, published in L. Menashe, ed., *Teach-Ins: USA,* New York 1967, pp. 64–7. Cf. also his 'Comment' on the 'Statement on Vietnam and the Dominican Republic' by the editors of *Partisan Review,* fall 1965, 32, §4, pp. 647–9.

dimensional society moved to suppress domestic resistance with the same determination that it battled 'Communist aggression' abroad; both signified the potentially catalytic threat that 'an elemental rebellion of human beings can be successful against the most powerful technological apparatus of repression of all time'.[49]

As in the 1930s, the prospects for such a victory were 'clouded with uncertainty': the actions and antics of the New Left may very well have anticipated (or recalled) 'the realm of freedom within the realm of necessity', but the Movement nevertheless was a small and heterogeneous force, cut off from any serious working-class base and lacking the vital synchronization with liberation movements abroad. As the overwhelming imbalance of forces showed its first signs of shifting, however, philosophy retained its right to guide tactics. As late as autumn 1966, Marcuse declined a central role at the politically oriented Socialist Scholars Conference in New York to attend the annual Hegel Congress in Prague, where the analysis was pressed to a deeper level: 'The present period', he said, 'seems to be characterized by a stalemate in the dialectic of negativity . . . Today [the] development of negativity within the antagonistic whole is barely demonstrable.'[50] This suggested that the negation could develop only *outside* of the tightly integrated, one-dimensional system of needs and satisfactions, and it was the existence of such an opposition, however embattled and disorganized, that was now giving him that ultimate hope 'for the sake of the hopeless ones' which had sustained Benjamin during the fascist period. This hopeful sentiment was now clearly ascendant in his writing and lecturing, and from the summer of 1967, when his influence really became manifest within the left, his positive appraisal became a factor in its own fulfilment.

Marcuse spent the month of July in Europe, conferring with groups of leftist students and intellectuals in a variety of contexts, the most significant of which occurred during his widely publicized 'return to Berlin'.[51] His concern here, as in the address which he delivered shortly thereafter at the London Congress on the Dialec-

49. Herbert Marcuse, 'Die Analyse eines Exempels', p. 33. Cf. also 'The Problem of Violence and the Radical Opposition' in *Five Lectures,* Boston 1970, pp. 86–7.

50. Herbert Marcuse, 'Zum Begriff der Negation in der Dialektik', address, Prague, September 1966, first published in *Filosoficky Casopis* (Prague), no. 3, 1967, pp. 375–80, trans. Karl Boger in *Telos,* 8 (summer 1971), pp. 130–2.

51. He later told a colleague that his meetings with militantly anti-fascist students in

tics of Liberation, was to encourage the New Left in precisely those of its tendencies which seemed most suspect from the point of view of Marxian orthodoxy.[52] In its unorthodox composition, its spokespersons ('such suspect figures as poets, writers, and intellectuals'), its spontaneous and anarchic forms, and in the aesthetic, erotic, and 'utopian' dimensions that permeated its politics and its culture, the radical opposition represented the only embodiment of 'the scandal of the qualitative difference', without which the vital break with the repressive continuum of needs would be unimaginable.

The lectures at the Free University of Berlin, more than the star-studded spectacle in London, were a political forum and the discussions that followed were topical and tactical. Only once does Marcuse appear really to have faltered, in response to a question about whether the transformation of needs is the condition of the transformation of society, or presupposes it. Marcuse's response: 'You have defined what is unfortunately the greatest difficulty in the matter. Your objection is that, for new, revolutionary needs to develop, the mechanisms that reproduce the old needs must be abolished. In order for the mechanisms to be abolished, there must first be a need to abolish them. That is the circle in which we are placed, and I do not know how to get out of it.'[53] He did not evade the dilemma of liberation, however; upon his return he began work on a major essay – provisionally entitled 'Beyond One-Dimensional Man' – in which he assembled the reciprocal influences of these intense exchanges.

The *Essay on Liberation*, as it was finally published, offered the radical hypothesis that the moral, political, and aesthetic privations of the affluent society have generated what is literally a *biological* need for liberation. In a minority of its members (and in its victims

Berlin 'meant some sort of a reconciliation with Germany' for him. Reinhard Lettau, 'Herbert Marcuse and the Vulgarity of Death', in *New German Critique,* 18 (fall 1979), p. 19.

52. Herbert Marcuse, 'Das Ende der Utopie' and 'Das Problem der Gewalt in der Opposition', lectures and discussions at the Free University of Berlin, July 1967, published in *Das Ende der Utopie,* Berlin 1967, also in *Psychoanalyse und Politik,* Frankfurt 1968; trans. J. Shapiro and S. Weber, *Five Lectures,* Boston 1970, pp. 62–108. 'Liberation From the Affluent Society', address at the London Roundhouse, July 1967, published in David Cooper, ed., *The Dialectics of Liberation,* Harmondsworth 1968, pp. 175–92.

53. Marcuse, 'The End of Utopia, discussion', p. 80; also 'Liberation from the Affluent Society', pp. 178–9.

in the Third World), the contradiction between the immense productive resources of the technological society and their destructive and repressive application has liberated the instinctual basis of revolt (though not the social basis of revolution); the technological transformation of the work process itself has suggested the unimagined alliance of industrial productivity (the realm of necessity) with creative receptivity (the realm of freedom); and Marcuse ventured to suggest that on the margins of the 'apparently impregnable fortress of corporate capitalism', subverting forces were at work, driven by the vital needs for peace, quiet, happiness, and beauty.[54] He was still working on this most unrestrained of his writings when the *Essay on Liberation* was overtaken by events.

These were to become known as 'the May events'. Marcuse had been invited to Paris to participate in a UNESCO symposium on 'The Role of Karl Marx in the Development of Contemporary Scientific Thought' on the 150th anniversary of his birth,[55] and was present when the wave of student strikes and factory struggles began which were to paralyse the country for much of the summer. He was again pressed into action, as he had been exactly fifty years earlier in revolutionary Berlin – and as in the German revolution, it was the confluence of the political and the aesthetic dimensions that seemed to him to represent the most progressive tendencies of the May rebellion.[56]

That month saw his participation in innumerable highly charged political debates, extemporaneous speeches delivered to packed

54. Elsewhere: 'And even I, I don't have any choice. Because I literally couldn't stand it any longer if nothing would change. Even I am suffocating.' The *Essay* is not Marcuse's attempt to work his way out of the theoretical impasse supposedly created by *One-Dimensional Man*, as a common, linear and hermetic interpretation states. In a broader and more historical perspective, the *Essay on Liberation* is not a hasty retreat from a dogmatic position but a stage in an ongoing attempt to render theory accountable to history – and vice versa.

55. Marcuse's address, 'Re-examination of the Concept of Revolution', has been published in the proceedings of the symposium, *Marx and Contemporary Scientific Thought,* The Hague 1969, pp. 476–82.

56. A few sources on Marcuse and the May–June events in France: Serge Mallet, 'L'idole des étudiants rebelles: Herbert Marcuse' in *Le Nouvel Observateur,* 8–14 May 1968, pp. 5–11; interview with Pierre Viansson-Ponté in *Le Monde,* 11 May 1968; Christian Descamps, 'Le mouvement de mai' in *Le Nef,* no. 36, January – March 1969, pp. 175–81; for a photograph, well worth the proverbial thousand words, cf. *Paris-Match,* 30 March 1974 (centrefold, n.p.). It may be noted that *L'homme unidimensionnel* did not appear in Paris bookstores until mid May, from which time, however, it was reported to have been widely discussed on the barricades.

auditoriums at the Sorbonne and the Ecole des Beaux Arts, and the organization of a *'journée marcusienne'* at occupied Nanterre. The immediate situation usually determined the direction of his statements, but three stipulations consistently recurred:

1. students and militant intellectuals should not provoke confrontations in situations where the odds are hopeless: active, ongoing political work cannot be sustained from jail or the hospital;

2. abstention from all acts of violence directed against individuals must be observed, even against 'representatives' of the system, both for reasons of revolutionary politics (they do not contribute to the weakening of capitalism) and revolutionary morality ('our goals, our values, our own and new morality . . . must be visible already in our actions.');

3. the educational means of the universities must at all costs be preserved (though certainly not in their present form), for to cut off the branch upon which the revolutionary intelligentsia is sitting, *'c'est commettre un suicide!'*

The months of May and June also included a meeting with Nguyen Than Le, chief of the North Vietnamese delegation to the Paris peace talks, a widely publicized visit to the hospital bed of the wounded Sᴅs leader Rudi Dutschke in Berlin, and some stormy sessions with audiences of militants at the Free University where, speaking on the basis of his recent experiences in France, he delivered an analysis of the obsolescence of the traditional model of a centralized, mass-based revolutionary movement: 'I don't like it and you don't like it but it is a fact.' In August and September there were further lectures in Oslo, Amsterdam, Salzburg, and Korčula, while in that summer the first placards had begun to appear in the streets of Rome carrying the extraordinary slogan, 'Mᴀʀx Mᴀo Mᴀʀᴄᴜsᴇ'.

Marcuse sustained his theoretical and practical energy at almost the same level throughout this period, for the conditions which had previously imparted to his thought its 'utopian', 'transcendental', or 'idealist' cast were now calling for its materialization. It was in this sense that the coincidence of the *Essay on Liberation* with the explosive events that continued in Europe and America throughout 1968 appeared to signify the convergence of the dimension which had survived throughout his whole intellectual career with concrete political forces, the liberation of the 'counter-trends' that had been sheltered in the ideals of philosophy and the forms of art. The heretical, 'utopian' Marxist Ernst Bloch perceived this when he said, in his emotional reception of Marcuse's paper in Korčula, '*Er ist wirklich rechtzeitig gekommen*' – he has truly arrived on time.[57]

At the end of the year Marcuse made a strong speech in New York at a fund-raising rally for the independent Marxist newspaper *The Guardian*, in which his frank discussion of the possible strategy of a disunited and vastly outnumbered opposition brought a renewed public outcry (in San Diego the Legion offered the Regents an additional $5,000 for his contract and redoubled its pressure on the administration to get rid of him).[58] The following summer, lecturing in Italy, he again drew international attention for his role in a tumultuous evening in the Teatro Eliseo in Rome where his lecture on the student movement was disrupted by the theatricals of Cohn-Bendit and assorted ultra-leftists;[59] and in the autumn, the 'ideological leader of the New Left' began to acquire the additional title of 'mentor of Angela Davis', whom he actively supported despite his unhappiness over her affiliation with the Communist Party, throughout the two years of her most serious battles with the University of California, the FBI, and the Justice Department.[60]

57. Ernst Bloch, 'Diskussion mit Herbert Marcuse', Korčula, August 1968, lecture and discussion published in *Praxis*, 12, 1969, pp. 20–5 and pp. 323–9; cf. also Michael Landmann, 'Talking with Ernst Bloch: Korčula, 1968', trans. David Parent in *Telos*, 25, fall 1975, pp. 170–3.

58. Marcuse, 'On the New Left', talk at the twentieth anniversary programme of *The Guardian*, New York, 4 December 1968; transcription of tape published in Massimo Teodori, ed., *The New Left: A Documentary History*, New York 1969, pp. 468–73.

59. In the course of the lecture he shouted back, 'I like the interruptions here. It reminds me of 1918 and 1919 and 1930. It makes me feel more alive', but afterwards he admitted (perhaps with some exaggeration), 'Es war die stürmischste Nacht meines Lebens'. The spectacle was widely publicized; cf. *Der Spiegel*, 27 (1969), pp. 108–9, and the Los Angeles *Times*, 29 June 1969. Also his fierce protest against the claim that he would now retreat from public life: *Neues Forum* (Wien), XVII, 196, I (April 1970), p. 353.

60. Angela Davis, William Leiss, and Erica Sherover were among the former Brandeis students who joined Marcuse in California. Although he said that 'the Communist Party has become and is becoming a party of order', his support for his embattled student was not merely verbal: he contributed a substantial amount to her bail in 1969, challenged her dismissal from UCLA in correspondence and public statements at demonstrations, and after her arrest (December 1970) in connection with the 'Soledad Brothers' shoot-out at the Marin County courthouse that August, he and Inge visited her several times in jail in San Rafael and he submitted legal affidavits on her behalf. Cf. Angela Davis, p. 307; New York *Times*, 21 March 1971; Los Angeles *Times*, 27 January 1971; letter to François Perroux, 22 September 1969, published in *François Perroux interroge Herbert Marcuse . . . qui répond*, Paris 1969, p. 200, and an open letter to Angela Davis in prison, published in *Ramparts*, 9, 7, (February 1971), p. 22.

The reaction of the right to Marcuse's massive influence among students of the New Left has already been described, but from the summer of 1968 the 'Old Left' mounted an intellectually feeble counter-offensive of its own: he was denounced by Yuri Zhukov in *Pravda* (May), the Italian Communist Giorgio Amendola (June), Gus Hall of the American Communist Party (July), and – most scurrilous of all – the iron-clad Progressive Labor faction of SDS.[61]

There is no paradox here, for Marcuse had appreciated that where the *mouvement de mai* broke with the authoritarian structures of the established society, it broke also with those of the established opposition whose leadership had withheld its official sanction until it was swept up in the current of protest. The insurgents' 'faith in the rationality of the imagination' now seemed to Marcuse to symbolize the vital rupture with the repressive continuum of needs which had become the central obstacle to radical change in the era of one-dimensional affluence. He drew upon insights derived in equal measure from his long-term theoretical work and recent practical experience when he wrote: 'The graffiti of the *"jeunesse en colère"* joined Karl Marx and André Breton; the slogan *"l'imagination au pouvoir"* went well with *"les comités (soviets) partout"*; the piano with the jazz player stood well between the barricades; the red flag well fitted the statue of the author of *Les Misérables*; and striking students

---

61. The quasi-official Soviet statement is translated in *Atlas,* September 1968, pp. 33–5 as 'Taking Marcuse to the Woodshed' (it was widely excerpted in the established press); for fuller documentation of Soviet criticism of Marcuse, cf. Klaus Mehnert, *Moscow and the New Left,* trans. Helmut Fischer, Berkeley and Los Angeles, 1975, ch. 6. The 1968 statements of Amendola and Hall are reported in the New York *Times,* 7 June, p. 11, and 5 July, p. 14 respectively. The PLP's notorious and contemptible articles are by Jared Israel and William Russel, 'Herbert Marcuse and his Philosophy of Cop-Out', *Progressive Labor,* October 1968, pp. 59–72, and anon. (prudently) 'Marcuse: Cop-out or Cop?' Feb. 1969, pp. 61–6. Shortly after the latter article appeared,the PLP was expelled from SDS for positions which were 'objectively racist, anti-communist, and reaction-ary'. Although the substance of their accusation – resting upon an unbelievable confusion of the anti-fascist work of the OSS and the anti-communist work of the CIA – does not merit serious consideration, the phenomenon is significant as a stage in the self-immolation of the New Left in America: cf. Paul Breines, 'From Guru to Spectre', in Breines, ed., *Critical Interruptions,* New York 1972, pp. 1–21; Ronald Aronson, 'Dear Herbert', in Fischer, ed., *The Revival of American Socialism,* pp. 257–80; also the statement of support by sixteen prominent West German leftists in response to the comparably groundless charges of one L. L. Matthias, in *Der Spiegel* 31, July 28, 1969, pp. 13–4. Marcuse himself said acidly: 'It's the exact pattern of the Stalinist purge, mixing facts with lies so it's impossible to separate them'. (Quoted in Los Angeles *Times,* 27 July 1969).

in Toulouse demanded the revival of the language of the Trouba-
dours, the Albigensians. The new sensibility has become a political
force.'[62]

To be sure, Marcuse did not allow the concrete meaning of the
events of 1968 to be submerged in their post-utopian symbolism,
and his frequent criticisms of the Movement indicate that he was
well enough aware of its limitations as well as its promises. Still, the
May revolt revealed the extent to which the tensions in the
established society 'can loosen the grip of capitalist trade union
integration and promote the alliance between working-class groups
and the militant intelligentsia',[63] and, in the larger view, the
extravagant demands of the New Left in Europe and America
appeared to herald the collective subject of a 'new sensibility' that
must be the condition and goal of a genuinely transformative
praxis.[64]

The New Sensibility is an aesthetic sensibility that has become a
political sensibility. 'Aesthetics', it will be recalled, always carried
with it a double connotation for Marcuse, referring to the foundations of art as well as to the domain of the senses, and invokes both
rationality and sensuality, the Reality Principle and the Pleasure
Principle.[65] In this crucial, bivalent sense, the gratification of
aesthetic needs and goals would not be a private affair taking place
within the museum, the concert hall, or the theatre, but would
imply the existence of an aesthetically ordered social world, or a
society in which the creative imagination has taken its place as a
productive force alongside technical reason in shaping the mental
and material conditions of human life. This distant revolution is
being prepared in the minds and bodies of those who have thrown
themselves into the fight against violence and exploitation, but also
against the control of sensuous gratification. From this perspective,
such modest, 'aesthetic' proposals as the prohibition of transistor
radios in public places or of billboards in the countryside are
directly linked to the need for the total reconstruction of cities and

62. *Essay on Liberation*, p. 22.
63. Marcuse, 'Re-examination of the Concept of Revolution', p. 23.
64. It may be worth noting that the 'new sensibility' bears no serious relation to
Charles Reich's unpolitical impressions in *The Greening of America*, which Marcuse
ridiculed as 'sentimental sublimation . . . the Establishment version of the great
rebellion'. He reviewed it in the *New York Times*, 6 November 1970.
65. Cf., for example, *Eros and Civilization*, pp. 180–3; *Essay on Liberation*, p. 24.

the restoration of commercialized nature, and thus to large-scale political change.

In his radical conception of the common denominator of the aesthetic and the political, of the practical and the poetical transformation of the given reality, Marcuse placed himself at the end of a tradition which had for nearly two centuries remained a romantic curiosity of German letters (as the German *Künstlerroman*) or been dismissed as irresponsible utopia when it was paraded as social theory (Schiller, Fourier) – and with reason. But he had also argued for decades that the very concept of utopia was on the verge of obsolescence, because ideas lose their utopian character when the means to realize them are at hand. His assessment of the technological capabilities of advanced industrial society – starting with the present trend towards the automated transformation of the work process and of work itself[66] – therefore enabled him to incorporate the concept of the 'aesthetic ethos' into his critical theory, and to issue the romantic vision of an aesthetically ordered universe as a concrete political demand.[67]

The new sensibility was thus operative in many of the demands of the radical opposition which could not be realized within the existing patterns of social and psychological life. And if it is the task of philosophy to recall and project the fullest possibilities of liberation, it is the nature of art to embody them as a form of reality. The emancipatory function of art was seen by Marcuse to lie above all in its capacity to represent the image of a transcendent, antagonistic reality, to provide 'an Archimedean point from which to view it in a different light, comprehend it in different concepts, discover tabooed images and possibilities'.[68] Genuine art, like

66. This is the theme of his important lecture at Korčula, August 1968, 'The Realm of Freedom and the Realm of Necessity: A Reconsideration', published in *Praxis* 1, 2, 1969, pp. 20–5.

67. In one of the most curious of the New Left appraisals of Marcuse's work, Peter Clecak believes that he has detected the 'conflation of aesthetic and historical/ political categories' as the worst of the 'radical paradoxes' that run through his work. Since the synthesis of the aesthetic and political dimensions was manifestly the central point of Marcuse's work during the last sixty or so years of his life, Clecak's discovery may not be so striking; cf. his *Radical Paradoxes* pp. 175–229. More importantly, Clecak's interpretation does raise the spectre of the 'aestheti-cization of politics' by which Benjamin had characterized the fascist period. Marcuse's theory, however, permits no such premature resolution of the tension between the aesthetic and the political dimensions for their reconciliation is permanently – and this is crucial – transferred to the *future*.

68. 'Remarks on a Redefinition of Culture', *Daedalus*, winter 1965, IV, 1, p. 195.

genuine philosophy, is inherently critical of the repressive status quo: it projects the harmonious union of sensuousness, reason, and the imagination, and as such 'the aesthetic dimension can serve as a sort of gauge for a free society'.[69]

The analysis of one-dimensional society, however, had exposed its enormous capacity to neutralize the opposition, to integrate the values of intellectual and aesthetic culture into the life-forms of industrial society, thus cancelling their alienation from that society – the 'technological corrosion' of their transcendent substance. It thus appeared to Marcuse that the traditional forms of art and literature were actually losing that element of estrangement which he had viewed as their defining quality: as art was increasingly reduced to mere entertainment or ornament, its images overtaken by the technological apparatus, it forfeited its intrinsic capacity to evoke a qualitatively different cognitive order. The aesthetic dimension, the most reliable contradiction of the contradictory reality, was losing its semblance of independence; the union of the aesthetic and the political, of art and technique, the Beautiful and the (empirically) True was taking place on the terms of the establishment.

Accordingly, the artistic imperative in one-dimensional society must be to *restore* the alienation of aesthetic culture from established patterns of industrial civilization, to discover new forms, a new 'meta-language of total negation'[70] capable of communicating the experience and projecting the possibilities of people and things under the changed historical conditions of the present. The centre of Marcuse's attention shifted now to that art which is most estranged not just from the established social reality (for that tension appeared increasingly to have been cancelled, 'suppressed by the systematic, organized incorporation of culture into daily life and work',),[71] but from the established limits of art itself.

Marcuse thus began in this period to elaborate the theoretical significance of the truly avant-garde works of art and literature – dadaism, surrealism, epic theatre, atonality – which have since the thirties expressed the intensified search for a poetic language *as* a political language: 'I believe that the authentic avant-garde of

---

69. *Essay on Liberation,* p. 27.
70. Marcuse, 'Art in One-Dimensional Society', lecture given at the School of Visual Arts, New York, 8 March 1967, published in *Arts Magazine,* 41, 7, p. 28 (May 1967).
71. 'Remarks on a Redefinition of Culture', p. 192.

today are not those who try desperately to produce the absence of Form and the union with real life, but rather those who do not recoil from the exigencies of Form, who find the new word, image, and sound which are capable of "comprehending" reality as only Art can comprehend – and negate it.'[72] But this revolutionary break with the existing order implies that the artistic commitment to aesthetic form is maintained; for it is in its autonomous Form that art most uncompromisingly negates and transcends the given reality, no matter how 'realistic' its content: 'the novel is not a newspaper story, the still life is not alive, and even in pop art the real tin can is not in the supermarket. The very Form of art contradicts the effort to do away with the segregation of art to a "second reality", to translate the truth of the productive imagination into the first reality.'[73] 'Living Art', guerrilla theatre, or the political 'happenings' of the 1960s betrayed rather than served the revolutionary goals of art (though not necessarily of politics), for Marcuse was adamant in his insistence that art survives only where it preserves its autonomy, and that the radical autonomy of art (including the new art) is a function of aesthetic form itself: 'In other words, art can fulfil its inner revolutionary function only if it does not itself become part of any Establishment, even the revolutionary Establishment.'[74] To collapse art into politics – even avant-garde art and vanguard politics – would be to *identify* them prematurely (precisely the historical achievement of one-dimensional society) and thus to destroy the critical, revolutionary power of art to liberate the power of the negative, to guide *praxis* as a regulative idea. The call for revolutionary art is thus supplanted by a far more radical demand for artistic revolution. The aesthetic dimension could supply the impulse, the perception, and the sensibility for the radical transformation of society envisioned in *Eros and Civilization*, but emphatically, 'the rest is not up to the artist!'[75]

---

72. Marcuse, 'Art as a Form of Reality', lecture sponsored by Guggenheim Museum, New York 1969, published in Arnold Toynbee, *et al.*, *On the Future of Art*, New York 1970, p. 132.

73. *An Essay on Liberation*, p. 42.

74. 'Art in One-Dimensional Society', p. 28.

75. Ibid., p. 28.

6
THE PERMANENCE OF ART
(1970–1979)

The final turn – or return – to the 'aesthetic dimension', the transcendental domain of beauty, form, and sensuousness, guided Marcuse's thought to its conclusion. Although the aesthetic theory had gained immeasurably in clarity, consistency, and historical concreteness since its first articulation in his analysis of the *Künstlerroman*, it was to remain somewhat fragmentary even in its final presentation – an extended essay of 1977, rather than the sort of comprehensive 'aesthetic synthesis' undertaken at the close of the long careers of Adorno or Lukács.[1] From the larger perspective, however, which views the evolution of his thought in its totality, Marcuse's writing, teaching, and lecturing in the last years of his life may indeed be interpreted as a final settling of intellectual accounts. This is the proper way to analyse his accomplishment.

Compared to his meteoric ascent during the sixties, Marcuse's last decade in La Jolla had to be more sedate. Nobody has improved upon the 'hermeneutic' description offered by his former colleague Fredric Jameson, the latter pleased by the contemplation of 'the philosopher in the exile of that immense housing development which is the state of California, remembering, reawakening, reinventing – from the rows of products in the supermarkets, from the roar of the freeways and the ominous shape of the helmets of traffic policemen, from the incessant overhead traffic of the fleets of military transport planes, and, as it were from beyond them, in the future – the almost extinct form of the Utopian idea.'[2]

1. Marcuse, *Die Permanenz der Kunst. Wider eine bestimmte marxistische Ästhetik,* Munich 1977; trans. Herbert Marcuse and Erica Sherover, *The Aesthetic Dimension,* Boston 1978; the latter is in fact a substantially Americanized version. The book has received little critical attention, most of it unfavourable.
2. *Marxism and Form,* Princeton 1971, p. 116.

I

At the end of the 1960s, the unrestrained projections of the *Essay on Liberation* were still dominant in Marcuse's thought. Already by the opening of the next decade, however, the deeply rooted scepticism that had occasionally surfaced in his criticisms of the 'extra-parliamentary opposition' had regained the ascendancy. That it was not Marcuse, but the representatives of the radical movement who had retreated before the image of liberation is confirmed by the lectures he delivered throughout the 1970s: while issuing a stern rebuke to the excesses as well as the shortcomings of the New Left, he reiterated with undiminished force the most far-reaching of his political ideas.

There were, to be sure, shifts in Marcuse's positions in the last decade of his life; far from indicating a retreat from the Marxian critique, however, they corresponded to his distinctive contribution to the attempt to prevent Marxism from petrifying into a closed system of verbal rituals long since overtaken by events. An ongoing elaboration of dialectical materialism characterized both his own method and his critique of the failure of the radical opposition to engage in a similar self-appraisal. 'The petrification of Marxian theory', he wrote, recalling Marx's own theoretical resiliency before the evolving realities of capitalism, 'violates the very principle which the New Left proclaims: the *unity of theory and practice*. A theory which has not caught up with the practice of capitalism cannot possibly guide the practice aiming at the abolition of capitalism.'[3] Marcuse's political statements in the 1970s reflected his analysis of changes within the capitalist infrastructure, as well as the enhanced capability of the state to disarm the opposition. Corresponding to 'the neo-imperialist global reorganization of capitalism' is a 'preventive counter-revolution', and against such odds, 'the heroic period of beautiful spontaneity, of personal anti-authoritarianism, of hippie rock and shock, is over'.[4]

3. Marcuse, *Counter-revolution and Revolt,* Boston 1972, p. 34 (emphasis in original). The chapter on 'the left and the counter-revolution', from which this passage is drawn, is based on lectures delivered in 1970 at Princeton University and the New School for Social Research in New York City.

4. Marcuse, 'The Movement in a New Era of Repression: An Assessment', speech delivered at the University of California, Berkeley, on 3 February 1971, published in the *Berkeley Journal of Sociology,* XVI (1971–72), p. 11.

For Marcuse, the structural changes in industrial society that have taken place since the Second World War produced two major consequences for revolutionary theory and practice, which could now be specified with a concreteness he had not thus far attempted. The first of the tendencies Marcuse identified ominously recalls the analytical framework he had taken over from Pollock at the opening of the fascist period: the economy has become increasingly dependent upon the intervention of the state – the political and military power structure – for its smooth functioning, and thus, 'what we witness is that monopoly capitalism tends toward state capitalism'.[5]

The correlate of this trend is that ever larger sectors of society are brought into a situation of dependence upon the coordinated system of 'capitalism as a whole', creating a new, vastly expanded 'technostructure of exploitation'. The philosophical interpretation of this process, which Marcuse had already achieved in *One-Dimensional Man*, was now given a firmer sociological foundation, but this entailed substantial theoretical modifications as well. By including in the 'new working class' strata of the formerly independent middle class, salaried employees of the service industries, and the educated professionals and members of the functional intelligentsia necessary to maintain the increasingly scientific and technological production apparatus, he displaced the 'classical' Marxist theory of proletarian revolution. The fact that the industrial, blue-collar labour force has not come to constitute the majority of the population does not mean that the 'working class' has shrunk, but rather that it has expanded. The working population may be divided, internally hierarchical, and comparatively affluent, but its members share the objective condition of separation from society's means of production, that is, of exploitation within the system of state-supported monopoly capitalism.[6]

From these observations Marcuse drew important conclusions for the radical movement in the 1970s, which he presented over the years to student and activist audiences across the country. Principally, the changed composition of the working class meant to him that any doctrinaire identification of the blue-collar labour force as the exclusive revolutionary subject was hopelessly antiquated, an irre-

5. Ibid., p. 3.
6. Statistical support for this position was provided in his lecture, 'Theorie und Praxis' (Frankfurt, 28 June 1974), published in Marcuse, *Zeit-Messungen,* Frankfurt 1975, p. 36, n. 3.

sponsible 'romantic nostalgia' for a defunct stage of capitalist development: 'as if the working class of the second half of the twentieth century were still that of the middle nineteenth century, as if the 1920s and 1930s were still our own eras'.[7] Accordingly, the left must not expend its energies seeking to identify with a revolutionary subject at some pre-designated position in the class structure, but must recognize *itself* as one component of that potential agent.

The second, related conclusion derived from the familiar fact that except at the margins of industrial society, needs well beyond those of bare subsistence were being satisfied. The 'impoverishment' of the working class that Marx had depicted in the pages of *Capital* had changed in nature no less than the class and capitalism itself, and must now be interpreted in terms of the actual and potential material wealth of industrial society. It followed that the modern revolutionary impulse would derive from non-material motives: 'The revolution involves a radical transformation of the needs and aspirations themselves, cultural as well as material . . . Moral and aesthetic needs become basic, vital needs, and drive toward new relationships between the sexes, between the generations, between men and women and nature. Freedom is understood as rooted in these needs, which are sensuous, ethical, and rational in one.'[8] The demands of the radical movement itself were only the most articulate expression of the 'deep malaise prevalent among the population at large', a malaise rooted in the fact that at the present stage of development, 'the satisfaction of basic needs creates needs which transcend the state capitalist and state socialist society'.[9] Where the inner dynamic of the consumer society itself demanded the perpetual augmentation of goods and services *beyond* the satisfaction of vital material needs, the attendant images of a life of peace, leisure, enjoyment, and beauty acquire the status of revolutionary demands, for their fulfilment lies qualitatively beyond this society and its capabilities. The dialectic of the present era revealed that 'capitalism has opened up a new dimension, which is at one and the same time the living space of capitalism and its negation'.[10]

Although his analysis was now finding more solid, socio-

7. Marcuse, ['Letters on Surrealism'], unpublished (October 1972), second letter; in the private collection of Herbert Marcuse, cited with permission of the author.
8. *Counter-revolution and Revolt,* p. 17.
9. Ibid., p. 18.
10. Ibid., p. 19.

economic ground than that which had supported the imprecise speculations of the *Essay on Liberation,* Marcuse clung to the most radical positions he had achieved by the end of the sixties. He had often stressed the 'total' character that revolution must assume at the stage at which capitalism is integrated and stabilized on a global scale, but he did not mean this as a merely geographical extension of the socialist vision. Rather, he sought to generalize the latent tendency of the radical opposition to draw its force 'from its roots in the whole *individual* and his need for a way of life in association with other free individuals, and in a new relation with nature – his own as well as external nature'.[11] Here, in its final formulation, is Marx's early conception of the essential human 'species-being', an ontology from which Marcuse never departed.

Throughout his writings, Marcuse had held to the central idea of the fragmentation of human life in modern (industrial capitalist) society: in this light the idealization of the artistic existence in his 1922 doctoral dissertation can be seen as only his first attempt to recover that dimension of a possible human existence that had been lost, while the ontological underpinnings of the thought of Heidegger, though they would prove inadequate, provided him with the first systematic basis for this quest. His writings as an architect of the Frankfurt School's Critical Theory, informed by his interpretation of the *Economic and Philosophical Manuscripts*, remained fully within the scope of his search for the total, social individual – no longer prior to the accomplishments of industrialism, but rather presupposing them, and the debased Nazi theories of a new 'human type' did not deter him from the great project – in *Eros and Civilization* – of harnessing the biologically based theory of the instincts to a radical social theory and political critique. In a sense, an implicit concept of 'nature' had always served him as a reference point that exposed the dismemberment of human faculties, and the promise of 're-membrance'. But only in the 1970s did he really confront the idea of 'the liberation of nature as a vehicle of the liberation of man'.[12]

'Liberated nature', in Marcuse's usage, refers to human nature as well as to the natural environment, but in a sense very different from the naturalism of romanticist thought (he nonetheless found it

11. Ibid., p. 48; also *Zeit-Messungen,* pp. 38, 44, 45.
12. Marcuse, 'Nature and Revolution', in *Counter-revolution and Revolt,* p. 59.

significant that in capitalist society such ideas are banished to the fringes of the poetic imagination). As Marx had written in the first of his *Theses on Feuerbach*, the reality we encounter is already the product of 'sensuous human activity', a notion reflected in Marcuse's view that both the subject and object of perception are historical entities, transformed and to be transformed: 'Nature is a part of history, an object of history; therefore "liberation of nature" cannot mean returning to a pre-technological stage, but advancing to the use of the achievements of technological civilization for freeing man and nature from the destructive abuse of science and technology in the service of exploitation.'[13] But even with this necessary qualification, the radical conception of 'nature as a dimension of social change' survives: 'History is also grounded in nature', he wrote in his last book, 'and Marxist theory has the least justification to ignore the metabolism between the human being and nature and to denounce the insistence on this natural soil of society as a regressive ideological conception'.[14] Above and beyond Marx's 'mature' concern with transformed social institutions, Marcuse returned once again to the fundamental instinctual and physiological level of existence, 'where individuals most directly and profoundly experience their world and themselves: in their sensibility'.[15] A 'radical sensibility', he conjectured, that draws its images and experiences from 'the life-enhancing, sensuous, aesthetic qualities inherent in nature', would necessarily partake of the qualitative break with the repressive continuum of needs that is the condition but also the substance of the next revolution. This conception was already operative in the most advanced demands of the radical opposition; movements for ecological harmony, cultural revolution, and the liberation of women envisioned not merely a social and political upheaval, but an end to the exploitative domination of (human and external) nature, the restoration of the fractured totality of existence.

This notion of a new sensibility – 'this outrageously unscientific, metaphysical notion', as he himself acknowledged – was an *aesthetic*

13. Ibid., p. 60. An outstanding study of this problem is found in Alfred Schmidt, *The Concept of Nature in Marx*, London 1971; cf. also Trent Schroyer, *The Critique of Domination*, New York 1973, esp. ch. 3, and William Leiss, *The Domination of Nature*, New York 1972, part 2.

14. *The Aesthetic Dimension*, p. 16.

15. *Counter-revolution and Revolt*, p. 62.

conception, for, as has been seen, he followed the German idealist tradition in his understanding of the aesthetic as pertaining not only to art and beauty, but to the senses themselves. Although the term appears for the first time only in *Eros and Civilization*, the concept of an 'aesthetic dimension' as the ground of a free and integral humanity can be detected as far back as Marcuse's studies in Freiburg: in the concept of *Künstlertum*, to be sure, but also perhaps, in his work with Heidegger in the period of the latter's demonstration of 'the central role of the aesthetic function in Kant's system'.[16] At every stage, although with varying degrees of rigour, Marcuse had interpreted the domain of the aesthetic as the non-repressive meeting-ground of reason and sensuousness, creativity and receptivity, subjective (human) freedom and objective (natural) necessity.

II

Marcuse had argued that only through a fundamental break with the reified universe of needs, of consciousness, and of the perceiving senses themselves could life be *'opened to a new dimension of history'*[17] – thus his long-standing quest for a higher ground from which to stage the revolt against the alienated society. Unquestionably, the most profound expression of this requisite negation resided in the work of art: the beauty of aesthetic form embodied for Marcuse, as it had for Schiller, 'the sensuous appearance of the idea of freedom'.[18]

The 'aesthetic dimension', the transcendent realm of art and sensuousness in which are enforced none but the non-repressive 'laws of beauty' (Marx), represented to Marcuse the only medium in which a critique of the prevailing reality could find concrete sensuous embodiment in the image of a qualitatively different and better one. It is the inherently subversive capacity of the authentic art-work 'to break the monopoly of the established reality (i.e. of those who established it) to *define* what is *real*',[19] by presenting another dimension, subject to a different causality and answerable

16. *Eros and Civilization,* p. 176, n. 3, referring to Heidegger's *Kant und das Problem der Metaphysik* (1929), trans. James Churchill, *Kant and the Problem of Metaphysics,* Bloomington 1962, pp. 39ff and 141ff.
17. *Counter-revolution and Revolt,* p. 72 (emphasis in original).
18. Ibid., p. 116.
19. *The Aesthetic Dimension,* p. 9.

to different laws. The transfigurative repose of the great *oeuvre*, its embodiment of the perfect harmony of sensibility, imagination, and reason, is in itself an expression of the divorce between the laws governing the repressive order, on the one hand, and the law and order of the repressive reality on the other. This intrinsically antagonistic quality of the aesthetic form is ultimately more subversive than any particular artistic content or style (realism, for instance, or partisan *Tendenzliteratur*), for what could be more disturbing than the discovery that 'we live under the law of another repressed causality: metaphysical, spiritual, but altogether *of this world* . . . a different order of things which interferes with the established one without abolishing it?'[20]

This critical capacity pertains to the aesthetic dimension only because (and in so far as) it preserves a fundamental estrangement from the given reality, and here Marcuse's theory meets what is perhaps the most distinctive theme running through his intellectual career: the search for a transcendent, Archimedean standpoint, removed from the practice as well as the truncated, instrumental rationality of the material world, capable of grasping it without being grasped by it. Against the social and political alienation of the repressive Establishment, the 'illusory universe of art' commands a 'second alienation':[21] negation of the negation.

In so far as the content of aesthetic culture is at a permanent remove from that of material culture, the work of art preserves its negative character even where it affirms, decorates, or advertises the status quo. This concept of the simultaneously negative and 'affirmative character of culture' had first appeared in 1937, in Marcuse's essay by that title, but there is a new development at the present stage, one which links it historically with the wide-ranging essays of the 1930s, the unpublished post-war study of surrealism, and the systematic theoretical analyses in *Eros and Civilization* and *One-Dimensional Man*. In each of these phases he had clung to the central idea of the necessary autonomy of art, but his evaluation of the potency and the possibility of this autonomy was a direct reflex of the magnitude of the apparent threat to it – emblematic of his sensitivity to the shifting balance of historical forces, but also, it seems, of a measure of theoretical uncertainty.

By the time of the 1964 thesis of 'one-dimensionality', the happy

20. ['Letters on Surrealism'], first letter.
21. *The Aesthetic Dimension*, pp. 72, 79.

and erotic anticipation of the 'aesthetic dimension' which had given *Eros and Civilization* its utopian cast seemed to have been darkened by the closure of the system and its apparent capacity to absorb every alternative: the vision of the reconciliation of sensuousness and reason within an aesthetic *ordre de la beauté* (the aestheticization of politics) had faded into the spectre of a one-dimensional totalitarian order, capable of subjugating even the artistic imagination (the politicization of art). In either case, aesthetic culture and material civilization could be conceived as merging within a single, 'unalienated' totality. Whether or not the ultimate identity – liberating or repressive – of the aesthetic and the political dimensions had been fully intended in his earlier works, in his writings of the 1970s Marcuse explicitly denied any such possibility.

On the contrary, the contradiction between aesthetics and politics was now moved to the centre of his theory. The realization of art in life, he argued, the reconstruction of social reality on the ground of beauty and sensuousness, remains in the *telos* of both art and politics, 'but the goal is a permanent one; that is to say, no matter in what form, art can never eliminate the tension between art and reality. Elimination of this tension would be the impossible final unity of subject and object: the materialist version of absolute idealism.'[22] It is in the essential nature of art, he finally claimed, to activate a 'depth dimension' of human subjectivity that is in a permanent state of rupture with the reality principle (*any* reality principle).[23] It exposes conflicts that cannot conceivably be resolved or dissolved by altering social institutions or expanding the mastery over nature – the misery of love and the inexorability of death, the conflict between freedom and necessity, the rivalries of the generations, the ultimate recalcitrance of nature: 'Art remains committed to the Idea . . . and since the tension between idea and reality, between the universal and the particular, is likely to persist until the millennium which will never be, art remains *alienation*.'[24] With its

---

22. *Counter-revolution and Revolt,* p. 108. Cf. also *The Aesthetic Dimension:* 'In all its ideality, art bears witness to the truth of dialectical materialism – the permanent non-identity between subject and object, individual and individual'. (p. 29).

23. In a severe but profoundly insightful judgement on Marcuse, Lucio Colletti calls this Hegelian inheritance 'a fight against objects and things . . . The old spiritualist contempt for the finite and terrestrial world . . .', *From Rousseau to Lenin,* London 1972, p. 130. On this subject, cf. also Herbert Schneidau, *Sacred Discontent,* Baton Rouge 1976, ch. 1.

24. *Counter-revolution and Revolt,* p. 103.

built-in '*Verfremdungs-Effekt*', its intrinsic estrangement from reality, art will always preserve in sensuous representation the supra-historical themes of life, the image of unactualized potentialities, the 'natural' limits of liberation: 'The very permanence of art indicates these limits. Art is essentially tragic. Not everything is the fault of class society, exploitation, the exchange economy; and the proletariat is no Saviour.'[25]

But if the unique qualities of aesthetic form indicate the limits of possible liberation from the prevailing reality, they also determine the limits of integration into it. With this optimistic note Marcuse's final challenge begins, in the form of a critique of a determinist (*bestimmte*) Marxist aesthetics, and of the engaged artistic practice that would seem to correspond to it: 'I shall submit the following thesis: the radical qualities of art, that is to say, its indictment of the established reality and its invocation of the "beautiful image" of liberation are grounded precisely in the dimensions where art *transcends* its social determination and emancipates itself from the given universe of discourse and behaviour while preserving its overwhelming presence.'[26] This radical reformulation of the notion of the autonomy of art (and, as a corollary, of the artist) has profound consequences for Marxian aesthetics, that is to say, for the aesthetic theory that might logically be derived from the fragmentary opinions of Marx and Engels on questions of literature and art.[27]

The most fundamental consequence to be drawn from Marcuse's thesis is that any crude attempt to reduce art to an ideological reflex of socio-economic forces misunderstands both the nature of art and of politics, and is doomed to failure. Although the *content* of an art-work may indeed tell the story, depict the image, or convey the perceptions of a particular historical class, the aesthetic *form* – the totality of qualities that make the work a self-contained whole set off

25. ['Letters on Surrealism'].

26. *The Aesthetic Dimension*, p. 6.

27. An attempt to collect the primary sources of a 'Marxist Aesthetics', which reveals the difficulties of such an undertaking is *Marx and Engels on Literature and Art*, ed. Lee Baxandall and Stefan Morowski, St Louis 1973. Several useful anthologies exist, esp. Maynard Soloman, ed., *Marxism and Art*, New York 1973 and Fritz J. Raddatz (hrsg.), *Marxismus und Literatur*, Hamburg 1969, 3 Bd. For an excellent discussion of the controversies of the 1920s and 1930s, central to Marcuse's ideas, cf. Helga Gallas, *Marxistische Literaturtheorie*, Neuwied u. Berlin 1971.

from the external reality – universalizes and thereby transforms and transcends this content: 'The universality of art cannot be grounded in the world and world outlook of a particular class, for art envisions a concrete, universal humanity which no particular class can incorporate . . . The inexorable entanglement of joy and sorrow, celebration and despair, Eros and Thanatos cannot be dissolved into problems of class struggle.'[28] If the notion of a 'class art' has in fact been rendered meaningless, then Marcuse has accomplished, with a stroke of the pen, what Stalin's promulgations and police could not: the abolition of 'bourgeois' art!

But a final severing of the link between an art form and the interests of the class which produced it (or is represented in it) also subverts the determinist conception of revolutionary art as that which expresses the consciousness and interests of the ascending social class – in capitalism, the proletariat. Having seen, in the successive phases of his life, the Western proletariat misled, terrorized, or bribed into complicity, Marcuse was by this time fully prepared to denounce the impossible claim that a proletarian world-view exists which represents a qualitative break with the prevailing order, and to which a revolutionary art would have to respond and correspond. A truly revolutionary art is so only inasmuch as it expresses goals that are universal and transcendent, and it does this through the transfiguration of any specific class content according to the internal laws of aesthetic form.

Only indirectly, then, is art to be considered a revolutionary force: as implicit critique of the given Reality Principle, as contribution to the liberation of subjectivity, as sensuous embodiment of a transcendent order of beauty and harmony – the form of freedom in the realm of appearance. If it is to preserve its essential quality of negation, of 'uncompromising estrangement' (Adorno), in short, of autonomy, the tension between the aesthetic and the political must not be abolished but actively *cultivated*, for it is precisely in this tension that art has its truth. Thus Marcuse goes to war against all those attempts to make art a direct expression of life: socialist realism, living theatre, people's art, and the various contemporary movements of 'anti-art', all of which strive for a premature – and thereby one-dimensional – reconciliation of the perfect standards of aesthetic form with those of the miserable

28. *The Aesthetic Dimension,* p. 16.

reality whose perpetual negation it is. Once again – as in the mid 1940s – he drew most heavily upon the surrealist project for his conceptual armament, for in no other movement could the competing claims of the political and the poetical be traced with greater precision.

Late in 1972, provoked by an activist collective in Chicago, he began a series of 'Letters on Surrealism' in which he sought to demonstrate the 'irreconcilable contradiction between art and politics, due to the transcendence of art beyond all political goals (including those of the revolution!)'.[29] It is hardly surprising that Marcuse was drawn to the surrealist programme, for its founders – André Breton, Louis Aragon, Paul Eluard, Benjamin Péret, Philippe Soupault – were all his exact contemporaries in a generation with which he had always identified strongly. As young men in their twenties, they had emerged from the transfiguring experience of the First World War determined to overthrow the conventional logic and rationality (not to say the ruling classes) that had made such a catastrophe possible, and 'to undo the mutilation of our faculties' that perpetuated it.[30] It is more than a coincidence, then, if the theorist of the 'Great Refusal' repeatedly found points of intersection with 'the unlimited capacity for refusal' with which Breton launched his movement.[31]

More substantively, Marcuse still found in the successes and the failures of the surrealist project the clearest corroboration of his critique of a determinist Marxist aesthetics, for nowhere could the insoluble contradiction between the necessary autonomy of art and the demands of revolutionary politics be more precisely followed than in the history of that movement. Juxtaposing the various manifestos and proclamations of the surrealists with their stormy political course through the inter-war years, he found only verification of his thesis that the condition of '*un art révolutionnaire*' is '*un art indépendant*', that 'authentic art is in its very substance revolutionary

29. ['Letters on Surrealism']; some minor editorial changes have been made in citations. Fredric Jameson's excellent essay on 'Marcuse and Schiller' perceptively detected the internal link between the idealist aesthetics of the German Enlightenment, twentieth-century French surrealism, and Marcuse's own theoretical intentions; cf. his *Marxism and Form,* pp. 83–116.

30. ['Letters on Surrealism'], first letter.

31. André Breton in 1924, quoted by Susan Buck-Morss, *The Origin of Negative Dialectics,* p. 125.

and, precisely for this reason, free from the requirements of any specific revolutionary *praxis*'.[32]

III

Marcuse's response to the cultural revolutionaries of the 1970s recalls the rebuke delivered by Horkheimer in 1937, when he chastened those activist intellectuals who 'cannot bear the thought that the kind of thinking which is most topical, which has the deepest grasp of the historical situation, and is most pregnant with the future, must at certain times isolate its subject and throw him back on himself.'[33] The revival of this fundamental tenet of Critical Theory (its fundamental problem, some would say) was no more arbitrary than Marcuse's return to the inspiration of the surrealist programme. Indeed, he believed that the assault on aesthetic form that underlay the attempt to create a people's art could only turn into the attack on art itself, just as the attack on 'bourgeois-capitalist' rationality was degenerating into yet another revolt against Reason *per se*. 'Anti-art' was the reflex in the sphere of aesthetics of the *anti-intellectualism* that had come to pervade the New Left generally.

Corresponding to the inherent qualities of the form of the authentic art-work, which transcend the brutalized conditions of the working class in a direction that is 'universally human – above all classes', theory is likewise abstract and anticipatory in its character. He frequently reminded leftist audiences, in his last years, that mindless 'action for action's sake' had proven to be a valuable component of fascism, and sought to reconcile them to the dialectical principle that 'theory and practice *never* stand in an immediate unity . . . The tension, indeed the conflict with *praxis* belongs to the essence of theory, and is grounded in its very structure'.[34] If the necessarily 'anticipatory consciousness' of the New Left had conferred upon the movement an 'elitist' character, this fact must not promote a false and self-destructive denial, for this

32. ['Letters on Surrealism'], second letter (referring undoubtedly to the 1928 Surrealist Manifesto, 'Pour un art révolutionnaire indépendant').
33. Max Horkheimer, 'Traditionelle und kritische Theorie', trans. James O'Connell *et al.* in Horkheimer, *Critical Theory,* New York 1972, p. 214.
34. Marcuse, 'Theorie und Praxis', p. 21.

isolation, far from being fortuitous, 'has its roots in the social structure of advanced monopoly capitalism, a structure that has long since integrated large portions of the working class into the system'.[35] Vanguard politics, no less than avant-garde art, derives its authenticity precisely from its rupture with the repressive totality and the mutilated consciousness that corresponds to and reproduces it.

Writing in the 1970s, in the wake of the killings of students at Kent and Jackson State Universities, the militarization of urban police forces, and the brutalization and continued imprisonment of leftist militants, Marcuse did not hold the New Left overly accountable in assessing its success or failure. The media, police, and judicial apparatus of the preventive counter-revolution (still in its 'democratic-constitutionalist' phase) had grown accustomed to dealing with demonstrations, occupations, and even the privatized expressions of anti-bourgeois morality; but 'something that the Establishment is increasingly incapable of tolerating, namely independent thinking and feeling',[36] was being systematically undermined by ascendant tendencies in the radical opposition itself. This capitulation – which he denounced as 'a hand-out to the establishment, one of the fifth columns of the establishment in the New Left',[37] was evident in its ritualized language, its ascetic puritanism, its propensity to engage in desperate acts of terrorism or 'revolutionary suicide', and above all, its masochistic, self-destructive anti-intellectualism.

The battle to preserve the genuine accomplishments of the New Left – its extension of the concept of revolution to embrace aspects of sensibility traditionally displaced to the realm of 'aesthetics' – and to counteract its own disintegrative tendencies formed the boundaries of Marcuse's politics in the last years of his life. As timely and topical as his statements appear, however, they were formulated in a manner inextricably bound up with who he was and what he had seen. It was less as a strategist, perhaps, than as a philosopher, trained and cultivated in the German humanistic tradition, that he

35. Marcuse, 'Scheitern der Neuen Linken?', lecture, University of California, Irvine, April 1975, enlarged version first published in *Zeit-Messungen*, pp. 37–48; trans. Biddy Martin, 'Failure of the New Left?' in *New German Critique*, 18 (fall 1979), p. 5.

36. *Counter-revolution and Revolt*, p. 129.

37. Marcuse, 'The Movement in a New Era of Repression: An Assessment', p. 12.

diagnosed 'the pest' of anti-intellectualism 'that infests the New Left';[38] he spoke not only as a political analyst but as a refugee from Hitler's Germany when he cut short a critic's repudiation of his defence of supposedly 'bourgeois' civil liberties with the words: '*You* have not yet experienced a fascist regime';[39] as a scholar and educator, and not merely a tactician, he repeatedly defended the importance of the university;[40] and on an even more intimate plane, the 'revolutionary morality' upon which so many of his personal friends have commented balanced the 'revolutionary pragmatism' that informed his positions on political events.[41]

Indeed, perhaps even his silences were eloquent testimonies: was it precisely as a characteristically 'non-Jewish Jew',[42] a living vehicle of the historical, cultural, and moral tradition of Judaism in spite of himself, that Marcuse fixed his gaze on the liberation of what is 'universally human', following an earlier radical social theorist of the German-Jewish middle class in resolving 'the Jewish Question' into 'the "general question of the age"'?[43] In a debate with Rudi Dutschke and Wolfgang Lefevre in Berlin, a few weeks after the Six-Day War, Marcuse permitted himself an unusual digression: 'I feel in solidarity and identify myself with Israel for personal reasons . . .' – only to qualify it immediately by returning his remarks to the universal plane: '. . . but not solely for these reasons. I who have always asserted the complete legitimacy of emotions, moral concepts, and feelings in politics and even in science, who always supported the impossibility of realizing science and politics without a human component, I am compelled to see in this solidarity more

38. Ibid., cf. also 'Theorie und Praxis', p. 34.

39. Marcuse, lecture delivered at the Centre of the Study of Epic Theatre (Epic West), Berkeley, 12 June 1977 (unpublished).

40. Cf., for instance, his remarks in an interview skillfully conducted by Pierre Dommergues and Jean-Michel Palmier, published in *Le Monde* (10 mai 1974), pp. 22–3.

41. This balance is finely struck in his brief statement on terrorism within the German 'extra-parliamentary opposition' and the official government reaction to it: 'Murder is not a Political Weapon', in *Die Zeit* 23 September 1977, trans. Jeffrey Herf in *New German Critique*, 12 (fall 1977), pp. 7–8.

42. This is the phrase applied by Isaac Deutscher to Spinoza, Heine, Marx, Trotsky, Luxemburg, and Freud in his beautiful essay by that title; cf. *The Non-Jewish Jew and Other Essays*, New York 1968, pp. 25–41.

43. Karl Marx, 'On the Jewish Question' (1843), in *Early Writings*, p. 215. A tendentious but scholarly analysis of this problem is carried out by Julius Carlebach, *Karl Marx and the Radical Critique of Judaism*, London 1978.

than a mere personal prejudice.'[44] He proceeded to expound on the complexity of the issues but did not 'personally' re-enter the debate.[45] Nowhere in his writings does Marcuse seriously discuss either Judaism or anti-semitism, even where such discussion might have significantly illuminated his work.

IV

Thus, even its uncritical hostility toward Israel came within Marcuse's wavering verdict on 'the failure of the New Left' since the 1960s: along with its anti-intellectualism, its reactionary aesthetics, the humourless *esprit de sérieux* with which its strategists intoned the gospels of liberation, its misplaced anarchism, its flight into the transcendental escapism of drugs, 'therapies', and guru-mongering, and all the rest. Of the important *positive* legacies that survived into the seventies, one figured of paramount importance in Marcuse's final reckoning: the theory and practice of the total, liberated human being represented by 'feminism'. In fact, he believed the women's liberation movement to be the most important component of the opposition, and potentially the most radical. He was pressed to this conclusion by considerations that were philosophical, political, and perhaps even personal.

Philosophically, Marcuse had for decades drawn much of his inspiration from the victims of historical progress, not so much out of a romantic solidarity with 'the outcast' (though there is a conspicuous measure of that) as out of the belief that many of the positive human resources and potentialities that had been sacrificed to the progress of industrial society found refuge on its fringes. This

---

44. Remarks made in Berlin in July 1967, in *Conditions and Prospects of Peace in the Middle East,* Paris, n.d. The episode is confirmed by Marek Halter, 'Déchirement et solidarité face à Israël', *Le Monde* (3 août 1979), p. 13.
45. Likewise, in his 'Introduction' to the Hebrew edition of *One-Dimensional Man* and the *Essay on Liberation* (October 1969), the defence of Israeli security was counterbalanced with the implied critique of Israeli society: 'one of the themes which I proposed in my books states that the goals of liberation must be present *prior* to liberation – present in the behaviour, actions, and values of men and women struggling for liberation. They must be free from the repressive and aggressive needs of a society based on the exploitation and domination of man by man . . . Freedom is that of *all* men, *all* races, *all* civilizations – or it is in itself repressive'. (trans. in *Israel Horizons,* June–July 1976, p. 17). Cf. also the account of Herbert and Inge Marcuse's visit (December 1971) to the '*salon littéraire et politique*' in the West Bank city of Nablus, in Raymonda Hawa Tawil, *My Home, My Prison,* New York 1979–80, p. 231f.

sensitivity is far from a sentimental exaltation of madness, criminality, or poverty, for it was always rooted in the fully materialist notion that a truly revolutionary break with the given society presupposed the cultivation of elements of a qualitatively different sensibility, and these could develop only outside of the integrated, 'one-dimensional' productive apparatus. Without supposing the prevailing images of woman as mother, wife, and mistress to be anything short of repressive, he had nonetheless maintained that the isolation of the woman from the alienated productive process in favour of these domestic roles 'enabled the woman to remain less brutalized by the Performance Principle, to remain closer to her sensibility: more human than men'.[46]

Marcuse was also well aware of the consolidation of the women's liberation movement as a political force – his attention followed logically enough from his work with the Frankfurt School on the breakdown of patriarchal authority within the family, although it began to be registered concretely in his writings only from the mid 1960s.[47] A Movement which adds the growing number of politically organized women to its base of intelligentsia, militants in the professions, minorities, and radicalized sectors of the working class could yet become a powerful oppositional force: 'If this is an "elite" ', he once remarked, 'it is a mighty big elite'.

But Herbert Marcuse may have also had a *personal* access to the 'feminist dimension' which had become an integral and formally articulated component of his theoretical position, for he had shared his entire adult life with three particular women whose contributions to his life and thought are reflected in more than the simple but moving dedications to his books.

Sophie Marcuse, his first wife, in whose company he had begun his intellectual career and who accompanied him in the difficult years of emigration and exile, was a competent mathematician, whose practical sense compensated well for her husband's lack of it. The twenty-five years of their marriage, however, spanned the period of his most 'technical' philosophical work, and one cannot

46. *Counter-revolution and Revolt,* p. 77; cf. also his similar but much earlier and less well formulated remarks on the 'Emanzipation der Frau in der repressiven Gesellschaft', *Das Argument,* 23 (October 1972), pp. 4–11.
47. Marcuse, 'Vietnam: Analyse eines Exempels', in *Neue Kritik,* no. 36–37 (June–August 1966), esp. p. 36, contains his first discussion of the women's movement as an actual political force.

really speak of intellectual collaboration in a strict sense, except, perhaps, during their exceptional wartime work in the American intelligence agencies (she had served as a statistician in Naval Intelligence while he worked as an analyst in the Oss).

His life with Inge Marcuse, however, seems to have been as different from his first marriage as the decades that separated them. Indeed, there is good reason to suppose that she bears a substantial measure of responsibility for his dramatic rise to prominence, for she served as an indispensable critic, stimulus, and ally.[48] Inge came from a cultural background that complemented Marcuse's: she was born in 1914 into the wealthy upper-middle-class Jewish society of Magdeburg, the youngest of four daughters, but from her family she absorbed much of the cultural richness and progressive ideas that Marcuse had to struggle to attain. Her father was a well-connected but radical attorney, a pacifist and inveterate anti-monarchist who defended Social Democrats and was himself in and out of jail (and duels!) for his outspokenly 'unpatriotic' ideas; her mother was active in humanitarian causes and a great patron of the arts, and her oldest sister, a radical law student at Heidelberg, nourished her with the heresies of psychoanalysis, atheism, and reports from the seminars of Jaspers and Mannheim.

Inge herself passed her *Abitur* in 1932, with ambitions of becoming an interpreter at the League of Nations; shortly thereafter, a fortuitous skiing mishap kept her hospitalized in Grenoble at the time of the Nazi seizure of power. Rather than return to uncertain conditions in Germany, she moved to England and enrolled in the London School of Economics, where she first met Franz Neumann; they were married in America in 1937.

With Marcuse, a fuller intellectual rapport was established. While pursuing studies of French literature and history, and ultimately a teaching career of her own, Inge read and discussed with him everything he wrote and commanded the revisions and reformulations that would make his convoluted German style (more or less) accessible to an American audience. Many of their friends have testified that it was also Inge who first pressured him to become more actively allied to the political movements taking shape in the 1960s. She died of cancer in 1973, a year in which Marcuse

48. I am indebted, for the following, to Inge Marcuse's sister, Ms Harriet Henze, and to her son, Osha Neumann.

published nothing of substance and cancelled or declined all speaking engagements. When he finally broke his brooding silence in March 1974, it was to deliver an original paper entitled 'Marxism and Feminism', which has been widely discussed within the women's movement: it is the opinion of her sister that their intellectual and political alliance had liberated both of them.

The probing of the possible ground of reconciliation between Marxism and feminism which occupied Marcuse in much of his subsequent work went beyond a political endorsement of women's liberation and beyond the superficially Marxist notion that the alleviation of sexual oppression would be 'the mere by-product of new social institutions'.[49] In its positive aspects, the thesis he developed bears evidence of Marcuse's last critic and collaborator, Erica Sherover-Marcuse, who had been one of a handful of graduate students to join him in San Diego. She became his research assistant in 1965, from which time she read and discussed with him all of his writing, and they were married in summer 1976. In particular, the new emphasis on the personal dimension of social liberation which began to show up in Marcuse's last statements, and his concern with the concrete political conditions of the women's movement, reflect his contact with a younger and more immediately engaged generation.

Nevertheless, in its final formulation Marcuse's ideas were his own, most evidently perhaps in his central proposition that at its most advanced positions, 'women's liberation' is all but a misnomer, for the movement raised issues leading 'beneath and beyond the male-female dichotomy' to 'the human being whose liberation, whose realization is still at stake'.[50] Paradoxically, it is precisely by reason of the universality of these issues that he insisted that a separate women's movement 'is not only justified but necessary'.

The reasons follow from Marcuse's whole cast of mind. Only a change in *sensibility*, he had maintained, in the very structure of

---

49. Herbert Marcuse, 'Marxism and Feminism', lecture at Stanford University, 7 March 1974; published in *Women's Studies*, vol. 2, no. 3 (1974), p. 281; also in *North Star*, 4, 15 (1–15 April 1974), pp. 34–41, and in *Zeit-Messungen*, pp. 9–20. For a response to Marcuse's essay and an appraisal of its impact among women, cf. Joan B. Landes, 'Marcuse's Feminist Dimension', *Telos*, 41 (fall 1979), pp. 158–65, and esp. Nancy Vedder-Shults, 'Hearts Starve as Well as Bodies', *New German Critique*, 13 (winter 1978), pp. 5–17.

50. Marcuse, 'Marxism and Feminism', p. 289.

consciousness, could open the possible way to a higher stage of personal and social life; and short of that we do little but further democratize the prevailing repression of our best potentialities. The difficulty of the elusive concept of a 'new sensibility' may be precisely what validates it, for only elements of it exist, and these are dispersed to the fringes of modern society: in the synthetic world of art; in alienated intellectuals, students, and minorities who are marginal to the one-dimensional productive apparatus and may for that reason be less damaged by it; and in women.

Marcuse's analysis indicated to him that the historical evolution of patriarchal capitalism had in large measure removed women from the sphere of productivity to that of the home. In the history of civilization, the human characteristics irrelevant or antagonistic to the domination of nature and the instrumental rationality that sustains it have likewise been removed to the private (domestic) sphere and thereby designated as feminine: receptivity, sensitivity, pacification, tenderness, 'characteristics which, in the long history of patriarchal civilization, have been attributed to the female rather than the male'.[51] Obviously, Marcuse is *not* identifying these as 'feminine' qualities, but the opposite – arguing that their designation as such is the ideological product of a specific historical development.

In so far as these *culturally* distributed needs stand opposed to those prevailing in the male-dominated world of competitive commodity production, they could develop into a force of negation, the first moment of liberation: 'What has been considered the *feminine* antithesis to masculine qualities in patriarchy, in reality a repressed social, historical alternative, would be the socialist alternative: in order to create those conditions under which people are able to enjoy their sensuality and their intellect, and trust their emotions.'[52] Marcuse had more of an affinity with Schiller's 'aesthetic' quest for the internal equilibrium of the sensuous and rational faculties than with those who call for equal opportunity within the institutions of either capitalist or patriarchal domination, within the established hierarchy of needs: 'equality', he said, 'which is the absolute prerequisite of liberation . . . is not yet freedom'.[53]

51. Ibid., p. 283.
52. Marcuse, 'Failure of the New Left?', p. 11.
53. Marcuse, 'Marxism and Feminism', p. 285.

Indeed, although he had made his home in America, it was obvious that he had never entirely emigrated from Europe – 'l'Europe de ma jeunesse . . . celle des grands penseurs';[54] he returned nearly every year (usually flying first class, allegedly because of his long legs). The passive, graceful landscape of southern France and the Alpine resort at Pontresina were especially favoured, but he was at least equally drawn to the public life of the cultural capitals, where he never stopped writing, lecturing, and conferring with an international group of friends and followers. After last-minute consultations with his biographer, he had returned to Europe in the spring of 1979, where he spoke out in more concrete terms than ever on feminism, the ecology movement, and other flourishing survivors of the allegedly moribund New Left, whose practices still held open new dimensions of social change. But there were no signs of one-dimensional optimism: he continued his denunciation of terrorism on the left, of the repressive bureaucratic regimes of Eastern Europe, and of the fascist tendencies that coexisted with constitutional democracy – a deep and personal fear he had harboured for decades; he referred with increasing frequency to Auschwitz.[55]

Herbert Marcuse had been welcomed that spring at the Max Planck Institute in Starnberg, near Munich, a guest of Jürgen Habermas, its director and the most prominent successor to the Frankfurt tradition of Critical Theory.[56] He was visited there by another member of his international network of colleagues and comrades, the French philosopher Jean Marabini, whose recollection of their last conversation conveys a most exceptional note of quietism. Marcuse: 'We must resume our discussions of the new right, and of the "new *philosophes*" – whom I consider to be snobs, as comical as characters out of Molière. Of course I would love to see Venice again, and Padua, and to inquire into Negri and the Red Brigades: all this violence, all this cruelty – it must be analysed,

---

54. Marcuse to Jean Marabini, 'Un Pyromane à la retraite', *Le Monde* (19 novembre 1978).

55. On Marcuse's intellectual preoccupations during this trip, cf. the remarks of his friend Reinhard Lettau, 'Herbert Marcuse and the Vulgarity of Death', *New German Critique,* 18 (fall 1979), pp. 19–20, and Jeffrey Herf, 'The Critical Spirit of Herbert Marcuse', ibid., pp. 24–7.

56. Habermas's relation to Marcuse is reflected in the discussions they held in Starnberg in July 1977, published on the occasion of the latter's eightieth birthday, in Jürgen Habermas, et al., *Gespräche mit Herbert Marcuse,* pp. 9–62.

explained, exposed, and transcended. But I have, in spite of myself, some fear that I would die in Venice of the heat, like the character in Thomas Mann. If I must go, I would rather stay in my Germany . . . I believe that the hour of my final *rendez-vous* with death has arrived, but I am reconciled to it.'[57]

57. Herbert Marcuse, quoted by Jean Marabini, 'Derniers désirs', in *Le Monde* (3 août 1979), p. 12.

CONCLUSION

THE PHILOSOPHICAL DIMENSION

> And if you want biographies,
> do not look for those with the legend:
> 'Mr So-and-So and his times',
> but for those whose title page might be inscribed,
> 'A fighter against his times'.
>
> NIETZSCHE
> *The Use and Abuse of History*

Consistent with every phase of his career, Herbert Marcuse spent the summer of 1979 waging a two-dimensional 'battle against his times': on the historical plane was a political struggle for the release of the East German dissident economist Rudolf Bahro, imprisoned in the DDR for having written the book *Die Alternative*, the critique of '*realexistierende*' socialism which Marcuse called 'the most important contribution to Marxist theory and practice to have appeared in the last decade';[1] there was also a struggle on the 'essential' ontological plane. He won only the first: Bahro was released in August, a few days after Marcuse's death, in Starnberg, on July 29.

To the very end of his life, Marcuse maintained that he was still a Marxist – even an 'orthodox' Marxist – although he had, over a period of more than fifty years, come to reject some of the most central conclusions drawn by Marx and subsequent generations of Marxists: he had asserted the non-identity of the modern blue-collar

---

1. Herbert Marcuse, 'Protosozialismus und Spätkapitalismus. Versuch einer revolutionstheoretischen Synthese von Bahros Ansatz', *Zeitschrift für Sozial Diskussion,* 19 (1978), p. 5 (a translation of this essay is found in Ulf Wolter, ed., *Rudolf Bahro: Critical Responses,* White Plains 1980, pp. 25–48. Bahro's book has been translated as *The Alternative in Eastern Europe,* London 1979.

labour force with the nineteenth-century proletariat and thus called the whole theory of the revolutionary subject into question; he had adapted the original theory of class struggle to the realities of one-dimensional society; he had diffused the concept of revolutionary class-consciousness throughout representatives of all levels of society, and had called special attention to the new role of the intelligentsia, and much else. In addition, there had been some major borrowings from 'non-revolutionary' traditions of thought: his fundamental stance of negation derives primarily from Hegel, ontological concepts survived in his thought even after his break with Heidegger, psychoanalysis provided him with a theory of the instinctual basis – and limits – of revolution to which he always adhered, he drew freely upon the ideals of liberal humanism, on surrealist poetics, and raised such categories as art, nature, and feminism to positions of priority in his critical social theory. If this ongoing reformulation can truly be interpreted as his attempt to compensate for the inadequacies of an analysis based purely on the writings of Marx, what sense is to be made of his claim to 'orthodox Marxism'?

A comprehensive answer will ultimately have to confront the whole issue of what is Marxism and what has been its course in the twentieth century, and then determine Marcuse's relation to it – hopefully, the materials that have been collected here will contribute to this analysis. The main conclusion to be drawn from Marcuse's work is that Marxism is not a body of empirical propositions, nor even a 'method', as Lukács had proposed in his own attempt to prevent radical thought from being overtaken by historical developments. For Marcuse, Marxism was rather a theory of the 'universal individual', but one which surpasses simple humanism because it speaks both to the material forces which obstruct its realization, and to the existing emancipatory forces that may yet achieve it.[2] Thus he consistently rejected the distinction between the young, allegedly 'humanistic' Marx and the author of the mature critique of political economy, for the concepts of exploitation, surplus-value, profit, and abstract labour reveal the fragmentation of human life in capitalist society and thus contain – in negative form – the substance of a genuine humanism.

2. 'Das ist orthodoxer Marxismus: das "allgemeine Individuum" als Ziel des Sozialismus'. ('Protokolsozialismus und Spätkapitalismus', p. 13).

Marcuse could reassert his claim to be a Marxist even at the end of a lifetime during which the class that was to have ushered humanity into its next historical stage had either sold out or bought in to the present one, for it was Marx's reasoning, not his *zeitgebunden* conclusions, that was essential. Historical materialism required a revolutionary subject whose needs were universal and whose interests were identical to those of all humanity, a condition which may have been imputed to sectors of the militant proletariat of the later nineteenth century, but which now applies to no particular class – either within 'socialism as it actually exists' or in contemporary 'late capitalism'. Marcuse believed that Bahro's formulation of 'the subject of the impending transformation' in Eastern Europe could be applied, *mutatis mutandis*, to the West as well: 'From a purely empirical standpoint, this subject consists of the energetic and creative elements in all strata and areas of society, of all people in whose individuality the emancipatory interests predominate, or at least play a major part in influencing their behaviour.'[3] There was no one-dimensional optimism in Marcuse's contribution to this analysis, and his references to 'the revolution of the twenty-first century' or to the vaguely cheering fact that 'no social system has ever lasted forever' testify to the sobriety that was forced upon him by history; 'Not summer's bloom lies ahead of us', Max Weber had similarly prophesied in 1918, 'but a polar night of icy hardness and darkness'.

In the interim, however, there was work to be done, actions to be carried out immediately, positions to be achieved and defended with deadly earnest. And there were some significant beacons to illuminate the icy darkness: the eternal protest emanating from the Aesthetic Dimension, the struggle of the ecology movement to defend Nature against the violence of the establishment, the resistance from the Feminist Dimension to the integrative powers of the one-dimensional society, and the ongoing work of numerous other 'catalyst groups', as he called them. In the last analysis, however, Marcuse seems to have taken his own stand on the 'Philosophical Dimension' – which he named only once, to assign it

3. Rudolf Bahro, 'The Alternative in Eastern Europe', trans. David Fernbach and Ben Fowkes, *New Left Review* 106 (November–December 1977), p. 19.

the monumental historical task of the 'dissolution and even subversion of given facts'.[4]

'The concrete conditions for realizing the truth may vary', Marcuse wrote at the outset of the Second World War, 'but the truth remains the same and theory remains its ultimate guardian. Theory will preserve the truth even if revolutionary practice deviates from its proper path. Practice follows the truth, not vice versa.' From this attitude, Marcuse had never wavered; no revolutionary was ever more militant a defender of the intellectual life. One of his favourite anecdotes was of the painter Victor Neep, challenged by a student to define the alleged element of protest in a *Still Life with Apples* by Cézanne: ' *"Gegen nachlässiges Denken"*, *antwortete Neep*' – it is a protest 'against sloppy thinking'.[6] Likewise Marcuse.

Exactly as Marx had concluded of the revolution in Paris 120 years earlier, in the aftermath of the challenge to the established order of summer 1968, Marcuse observed, 'Historically it is again a period of Enlightenment prior to material change – a period of education, but education which turns into *praxis*'.[7] The function of theory – the political emissary of the 'philosophical dimension' – is thus central in the present struggle for life, Eros, survival. Like the epistemological function he had identified in art, the instincts, the feminist drive toward 'the legendary idea of androgynism', theory itself held for Marcuse, 'a thinker in a time of need', the position once assigned by Marx to the proletariat: a force *in* bourgeois society, but not *of* bourgeois society. In the measure that it preserves its 'alienation' from the facts of the oppressive reality, a critical theory can become a force within it to stimulate change in the direction of unactualized potentialities.

Marcuse cultivated this distance, in his person, in the substance of his analysis, even in the 'aesthetic form' of its presentation: like the epic theatre which he admired, Marcuse had his own 'alienation-effect'. If his sometimes oracular, always dialectical prose shifts the burden of understanding onto the reader, has the latter really been cheated? It was to protect the autonomy of radical theory that he pleaded in his last years with the New Left to purge

4. *One-Dimensional Man,* p. 185.
5. *Reason and Revolution,* p. 322.
6. *Die Permanenz der Kunst,* p. 10n.
7. *Essay on Liberation,* p. 53.

its language of the encrustations of a ritualized Marxism. A brittle fabric of slogans could be absorbed, accommodated, integrated in the way a critical theory could not: The truth of theory, Marcuse had written in 1937, unlike the beauty of art, is incompatible with the bad present.[8]

Herbert Marcuse, 1898–1979: *Der Geist, der stets verneint.*

8. 'Uber den affirmativen Charakter der Kultur', *Zeitschrift für Sozialforschung,* Bd. VI, 1 (1937), p. 79.

BIBLIOGRAPHY
OF THE WRITINGS OF
HERBERT MARCUSE

Books

Schiller=Bibliography unter Benutzung der Trömelschen Schiller=Bibliothek, Berlin 1925.

Hegels Ontologie und die Grundlegung einer Theorie der Geschichtlichkeit, Frankfurt-am-Main 1932.

Reason and Revolution: Hegel and the Rise of Social Theory, New York 1941. Second edition with 'Supplementary Epilogue', New York 1954. Paperbound edition with new preface, 'A Note on Dialectic', Boston 1960.

Eros and Civilization: A Philosophical Inquiry into Freud, Boston 1955. Paperbound edition with new preface, New York 1962. 2nd ed. with 'Political Preface 1966'.

Soviet Marxism: A Critical Analysis, New York 1958. Paperbound edition with new preface, New York 1962.

One-Dimensional Man: Studies in the Ideology of Advanced Industrial Society, Boston 1964.

Kultur und Gesellschaft, I, Frankfurt-am-Main 1965, republication of entries 18, 22, 23, 24.

Kultur und Gesellschaft, II, Frankfurt-am-Main 1965, republication of entries 15, 29, 51, 54, 56, 67.

Das Ende der Utopie, lectures and discussion at the Free University, Berlin, July 1967, Berlin 1967.

Negations: Essays in Critical Theory, Boston 1968, republication in English of entries 18, 21, 22, 23, 24, 54, 71, 77.

Psychoanalyse und Politik, Frankfurt-am-Main 1968, republication of entries 40, 41, 51, 1967 (above). (*Five Lectures,* Boston 1970).

An Essay on Liberation, Boston 1969.

Revolution oder Reform? (with Karl Popper), München 1971. (*Revolution or Reform: A Confrontation,* A. T. Ferguson, ed., Chicago 1976).

Counter-revolution and Revolt, Boston 1972.

Studies in Critical Philosophy, London 1972, republication of entries 14, 19, 29, 43, 89.

Zeit-Messungen, Frankfurt-am-Main 1975, republication of entries 102, 103, 104.

Die Permanenz der Kunst: Wider eine bestimmte marxistische Aesthetik, Munich 1977. (*The Aesthetic Dimension,* Boston 1978).

NOTE: Suhrkamp Verlag, Frankfurt-am-Main, is in the process of issuing a nearly complete edition of the writings of Herbert Marcuse. At the time of this writing, the following volumes are available:

Schriften, 1: Der deutsche Künstlerroman. Frühe Aufsätze, 1978; republication of entries 1, 2, 3, 6, 7, 9, 11, 12, 14, 15.
Schriften, 3: Aufsätze aus der Zeitschrift für Sozialforschung, 1934–1941, 1979; republication of entries 18, 19, 21, 22, 23, 24, 26.
Schriften 5: Triebstruktur und Gesellschaft: Ein philosophischer Beitrag zu Sigmund Freud, 1979; republication of *Eros and Civilization,* trans. Marianne von Eckhardt-Jaffe.

Books Edited

Franz Neumann, *The Democratic and the Authoritarian State,* Glencoe, Illinois 1957.

Essays, Articles, Book Reviews, Published Lectures

1. 'Der deutsche Künstlerroman', phil. diss. University of Frieburg-im-Breisgau, 1922.
2. 'Beiträge zu einer Phänomenologie des historischen Materialismus', in *Philosophische Hefte,* (Berlin 1928), no. 1, pp. 45–60 (translated in *Telos* 4, 1969).
3. 'Uber konkrete Philosophie', in *Archiv für Sozialwissenschaft und Sozialpolitik* (Tübingen 1929), vol. 62, pp. 111–20.
4. 'Besprechung von Karl Vorländer: *Karl Marx, sein Leben und sein Werk*', in *Die Gesellschaft* (Berlin 1929), vol. VI, part II, pp. 186–9.
5. 'Zur Wahrheitsproblematik der soziologischen Methode', in *Die Gesellschaft* (Berlin 1929), vol. VI, part II, pp. 356–69.
6. 'Zum Problem der Dialektik I', in *Die Gesellschaft* (Berlin 1930), vol. VII, part I, pp. 15–30 (translated in *Telos* 27, spring 1976).
7. 'Transzendentaler Marxismus?' in *Die Gesellschaft* (Berlin 1930), vol. VII, part I, pp. 304–26.
8. 'Besprechung von H. Noack: *Geschichte und Systeme der Philosophie*', in *Philosophische Hefte* (Berlin 1930), vol. II, pp. 91–6.
9. 'Das Problem der geschichtlichen Wirklichkeit: Wilhelm Dilthey', in *Die Gesellschaft* (Berlin 1931), vol. I, pp. 350–67.
10. 'Zur Kritik der Soziologie', in *Die Gesellschaft* (Berlin 1931), vol. VII, part II, pp. 270–80.
11. 'Zum Problem der Dialektik II', in *Die Gesellschaft* (Berlin 1931), vol. VII, part II, pp. 541–57 (translated in *Telos* 27, spring 1976).
12. 'Zur Auseinandersetzung mit Hans Freyers *Soziologie als Wirklichkeitswissenschaft*', in *Philosophische Hefte* (Berlin 1931), vol. III, nos. 1 and 2, pp. 83–9.
13. 'Besprechung von Heinz Heimsoeth: *Die Errungschaften des deutschen Idealismus*', in *Deutsche Literaturzeitung* (Berlin 1932), vol. 53, no. 43, pp. 2024–9.
14. 'Neue Quellen zur Grundlegung des historischen Materialismus', in *Die Gesellschaft* (Berlin 1932), vol. II, pp. 136–74 (translated in *Studies in Critical Philosophy*).

15. 'Uber die philosophischen Grundlagen des wirtschaftwissenschaftlichen Arbeitsbegriff', in *Archiv für Sozialwissenschaft und Sozialpolitik* (Tübingen 1933), vol. 69, pp. 257–92. (translated in *Telos* 16, summer 1973).

16. 'Philosophie des Scheiterns: Karl Jaspers Werk', in *Unterhaltungsblatt der Vossischen Zeitung*, no. 339 (14 December 1933).

17. 'Besprechung von Herbert Wacker: *Das Verhältnis des jungen Hegel zu Kant*', in *Deutsche Literaturzeitung* (Berlin 1934), vol. 55, no. 14, pp. 629–30.

18. 'Der Kampf gegen den Liberalismus in der totalitären Staatsauffassung', in *Zeitschrift für Sozialforschung*, vol. III, no. 1 (1934), pp. 161–95 (translated in *Negations*).

19. 'Theoretische Entwürfe über Autorität und Familie: Ideengeschichtlicher Teil', in *Studien über Autorität und Familie*, Paris 1936, pp. 136–228. (translated in *Studies in Critical Philosophy*).

20. '*Autorität und Familie in der deutschen Soziologie bis 1933*', in *Studien über Autoritat und Familie*.

21. 'Zum Begriff des Wesens', in *Zeitschrift für Sozialforschung*, vol. V, no. 1 (1936), pp. 1–39 (translated in *Negations*).

22. 'Uber den affirmativen Charakter der Kultur', in *Zeitschrift für Sozialforschung*, vol. VI, no. 1 (1937), pp. 54–94 (translated in *Negations*).

23. 'Philosophie und kritische Theorie', in *Zeitschrift für Sozialforschung*, vol. VI, no. 3 (1937), pp. 631–47 (translated in *Negations*).

24. 'Zur Kritik des Hedonismus', in *Zeitschrift für Sozialforschung*, vol. VII, nos. 1/2 (1938), pp. 55–89 (translated in *Negations*).

25. 'An Introduction to Hegel's Philosophy', in *Studies in Philosophy and Social Science*, vol. VIII, pp. 394–412.

26. 'Some Social Implications of Modern Technology', in *Studies in Philosophy and Social Science*, vol. IX, pp. 414–39.

[NOTE: Between 1933 and 1941, Herbert Marcuse was a regular book reviewer for the *Zeitschrift für Sozialforschung* and its American successor, *Studies in Philosophy and Social Science*. His reviews are found in the following issues:

ZfS II, 2 (1933), pp. 269–73.
ZfS II, 3 (1933), pp. 424–8.
ZfS III, 1 (1934), pp. 87–9 and 102–3.
ZfS III, 2 (1934), pp. 263–5.
ZfS III, 3 (1934), pp. 416–8 and 437–40.
ZfS IV, 2 (1935), pp. 269–73.
ZfS IV, 3 (1935), pp. 437–40.
ZfS V, 1 (1936), pp. 107–11.
ZfS V, 3 (1936), pp. 411–5.
ZfS VII, 1/2 (1938), pp. 219–22, 225–7, 229–30, and 233.
ZfS VII, 3 (1938), pp. 404–10.
ZfS VIII, 1/2 (1939), pp. 221–32.
SPSS IX, 1 (1941), pp. 144–8.
SPSS IX, 3 (1941), pp. 483–90, 500–1, 512–4, 531.]

27. 'A Rejoinder to Karl Löwith's review of *Reason and Revolution*', in *Journal of Philosophy and Phenomenological Research* (Buffalo 1941–42), vol. II, pp. 560–3.

28. 'Some Remarks on Aragon: Art and Politics in the Totalitarian Era', (unpublished, Washington DC, September 1945).

29. 'Existentialism: Remarks on Jean-Paul Sartre's *L'Etre et le Néant*', in *Journal of Philosophy and Phenomenological Research* (Buffalo, March 1948), vol. VIII, pp. 309–36.

30. 'Lord Acton: *Essays on Freedom and Power*', in *American Historical Review* (Richmond, Virginia, April 1949), vol. 54, no. 3, pp. 557–9.

31. 'Review of Georg Lukács: *Goethe und seine Zeit*', in *Journal of Philosophy and Phenomenological Research* (Buffalo 1949), vol. XI, pp. 142–4.

32. 'Anti-Democratic Popular Movements', in H. Morganthau, ed., *Germany and the Future of Europe*, Chicago 1951, pp. 108–13.

33. 'Recent Literature on Communism', in *World Politics* (New York, July 1954), vol. VI, no. 4, pp. 515–25.

34. 'Dialectic and Logic Since the War', in Ernest J. Simmons, ed., *Continuity and Change in Russian and Soviet Thought*, Cambridge, Mass. 1955, pp. 347–58.

35. 'Eros and Culture', in *I.E., The Cambridge Review* (Cambridge, Mass., spring 1955), vol. I, no. 3, pp. 107–23.

36. 'The Social Implications of Freudian "Revisionism" ', *Dissent* (New York, summer 1955), vol. II, no. 3, pp. 221–40 (reprinted as the epilogue to *Eros and Civilization* and also in *Voices of Dissent*, New York 1958).

37. 'A Reply to Erich Fromm', in *Dissent* (New York, winter 1956), vol. III, no. 1, pp. 79–81.

38. 'La théorie des instincts et la socialisation', in *La Table Ronde* (Paris 1956), no. 108, pp. 97–110.

39. 'Theory and Therapy in Freud', in the *Nation* (New York, 28 September 1957), pp. 200–2.

40. 'Trieblehre und Freiheit', in *Freud in der Gegenwart: Ein Vortragszyklus der Universitäten Frankfurt und Heidelberg zum hundertsten Geburtstag*, Frankfurt-am-Main 1957; *Frankfurter Beiträge zur Soziologie*, vol. VI, pp. 401–24 (translated in *Five Lectures*).

41. 'Die Idee des Fortschritts im Lichte der Psychoanalyse', in ibid., pp. 425–41 (translated in *Five Lectures*).

42. 'Preface' to Raya Dunayevskaya, *Marxism and Freedom*, New York 1958, pp. 15–20.

43. 'Notes on the Problem of Historical Laws', in *Partisan Review* (New York, winter 1959), vol. 26, pp. 117–29.

44. 'The Ideology of Death', in Herman Feifel, ed., *The Meaning of Death*, New York 1959, pp. 64–76.

45. 'De l'ontologie à la technologie: les tendances de la société industrielle', in *Arguments* (Paris 1960), vol. IV, no. 18, pp. 56–9.

46. 'Language and Technological Society', in *Dissent* (New York, winter 1961), vol. VIII, no. 1, pp. 66–74.

47. 'The Problem of Social Change in Technological Society', lecture presented to a UNESCO Symposium on Social Development. Printed for limited distribution under the auspices of Raymond Aron and Bert Hoselitz, Paris, 28 April 1961, pp. 139–60.

48. 'Idéologie et société industrielle avancée', in *Mediations,* (Paris, summer 1962), no. 5, pp. 57–71.

49. 'Emanzipation der Frau in der repressiven Gesellschaft: Ein Gespräch mit Herbert Marcuse und Peter Furth', in *Das Argument* (Berlin, October–November 1962), no. 23, pp. 2–12.

50. 'Zur Stellung des Denkens heute', in *Festschrift: Theodor W. Adorno zum 60. Geburtstag,* Frankfurt-am-Main 1963, im Auftrag des Instituts für Sozialforschung, herausgegeben von Max Horkheimer, pp. 45–9.

51. 'Das Veralten der Psychoanalyse', lecture delivered at annual meeting of the APSA, 1963.

52. 'Dynamismes de la société industrielle', in *Annales: Economies, Sociétés, Civilisations* (Paris 1963), vol. 18, pp. 906–32.

53. 'World Without Logos', in *Bulletin of the Atomic Scientists* (Chicago, January 1964), vol. 20, pp. 25–6.

54. 'Industrialisierung und Kapitalismus', in *Max Weber und die Soziologie Heute,* Tübingen 1964, pp. 161–80 (translated in *Negations*).

55. 'Perspektiven des Sozialismus in der entwickelten Industriegesellschaft', in *Praxis* I, (Zagreb 1966), nos. 2/3, pp. 260–70 (address presented in Korčula, Yugoslavia, summer 1964), followed by 'Einige Streitfragen', exchange with Serge Mallet, pp. 377–9. Translated as 'Socialism in the Developed Countries', in *International Socialist Journal* (Rome, April 1965), vol. II, no. 8, pp. 139–52.

56. 'Remarks on a Redefinition of Culture', in *Daedalus* (Cambridge, Mass., winter 1965), vol. 94, no. 1, pp. 190–207, reprinted in Gerald Holton, ed., *Science and Culture,* Cambridge, Mass. 1965, pp. 218–35.

57. 'A Tribute to Paul A. Baran', in *Monthly Review* (New York, March 1965), vol. 16, no. 11, pp. 114–5.

58. 'Nachwort', to Walter Benjamin, *Zur Kritik der Gewalt und andere Aufsätze,* Frankfurt-am-Main 1965, pp. 95–100.

59. 'Repressive Tolerance', in *A Critique of Pure Tolerance,* Boston 1965, pp. 81–117.

60. 'Nachwort', to Karl Marx, *Der 18. Brumaire des Louis Bonaparte,* Frankfurt-am-Main 1965, pp. 143–50; translated in *Radical America* (Cambridge 1969), 3, 4, pp. 55–9.

61. 'Der Einfluss der deutschen Emigration auf das amerikanische Geistesleben: Philosophie und Soziologie', in *Jahrbuch für Amerikastudien,* Heidelberg 1965, vol. X, pp. 27–33.

62. 'Socialist Humanism?' in Erich Fromm, ed., *Socialist Humanism,* New York 1965, pp. 96–106.

63. 'Reply to M. Berman's review of *One-Dimensional Man*', in *Partisan Review* (New York, winter 1965), vol. 32, no. 1, pp. 159–60.

64. 'Statement on Vietnam', in *Partisan Review* (New York, fall 1965), vol. 32, no. 4, pp. 646–9.

65. 'On Science and Phenomenology', in Robert S. Cohen and Marx W. Wartofsky, eds., *Boston Studies in the Philosophy of Science*, II, New York 1965, pp. 279–91.

66. 'Sommes-nous déjà des hommes?' in *Partisans* (Paris, April 1966), no. 28, pp. 21–9.

67. 'Ethics and Revolution', in R. T. deGeorge, ed., *Ethics and Society*, New York 1966, pp. 133–47.

68. 'Vietnam: Analyse eines Exempels', in *Neue Kritik* (Frankfurt-am-Main, June–August 1966), no. 36/37, pp. 30–40.

69. 'Zur Geschichte der Dialektik', in *Sowjetsystem und Demokratische Gesellschaft* (Freiburg 1966), vol. I, pp. 1192–211.

70. 'The Individual in the Great Society', part 1, *Alternatives* (San Diego, March–April 1966), vol. 1, no. 1; part 2, (summer 1966), vol. I, no. 2. (Also in Bertram M. Gross, ed., *A Great Society?* New York 1966, pp. 58–80.)

71. 'Love Mystified: A review of Norman O. Brown's *Love's Body*', in *Commentary* (New York, February 1967), vol. 43, no. 2, pp. 71–6.

72. 'The Inner Logic of American Policy in Vietnam', in Louis Menashe, ed., *Teach-Ins: USA*, New York 1967, pp. 65–7.

73. 'The Obsolescence of Marxism?' in Nicholas Lobkowicz, ed., *Marx and the Western World*, Notre Dame 1967, pp. 409–17.

74. 'Art in the One-Dimensional Society', in *Arts Magazine,* (New York, May 1967), vol. 41, no. 7, pp. 26–31, lecture delivered at the School of Visual Arts, NYC, 8 March 1967; reprinted in Lee Baxandall, ed., *Radical Perspectives in the Arts,* Baltimore 1972, pp. 53–67.

75. 'Das Ende der Utopie', lecture and discussion at the Free University of Berlin, July 1967 (published in *Five Lectures*).

76. 'Thoughts on the Defence of Gracchus Babeuf', in *The Defence of Gracchus Babeuf,* Boston 1967, pp. 95–105.

77. 'Aggressivität in der gegenwärtigen Industriegesellschaft', in *Neue Rundschau,* Heft 1, 1967 (translated in *Negations*).

78. 'Zum Begriff der Negation in der Dialektik', in *Filosoficky Casopis* (Prague 1967), no. 3, pp. 375–80 (translated in *Telos*, 8, summer 1971).

79. 'On Changing the World: A Reply to Karl Miller', in *Monthly Review* (New York, October 1967), pp. 42–8.

80. 'Die Gesellschaft als Kunstwerk', in *Neues Forum* (Vienna, November–December 1967), vol. XIV, no. 167–168, pp. 863–6.

81. 'The Responsibility of Science', in *The Responsibility of Power: Historical Essays in Honor of Hajo Holborn,* Leonard Krieger and Fritz Stern, eds., New York 1967, pp. 439–44.

82. 'Ist die Idee der Revolution eine Mystifikation?' in *Kursbuch* 9 (Frankfurt-am-Main 1967), pp. 1–6 (translated as 'The Question of Revolution' in *New Left Review,* 45, London 1967, pp. 3–7).

83. 'Re-examination of the Concept of Revolution', in *Diogène* 64 (winter 1968), pp. 17–27; also in *Marx and Contemporary Scientific Thought,* The Hague 1969; and *New Left Review,* 56 (London 1969), pp. 27–34.

84. 'Liberation from the Affluent Society', in David Cooper, ed., *The*

Dialectics of Liberation, London 1968, pp. 175–92.

85. 'Friede als Utopie', in *Neues Forum,* (Vienna, November–December 1968), vol. XV, no. 179–180, pp. 705–7.

86. 'The Realm of Freedom and the Realm of Necessity', in *Praxis,* International Edition (Zagreb 1969), nos. 1/2, pp. 20–5; followed by discussion, 'Revolutionary Subject and Self-Government', pp. 326–9.

87. 'On the New Left'. Talk at the Twentieth Anniversary Programme of *The Guardian,* New York, 4 December 1968, published in Massimo Teodori, ed., *The New Left: A Documentary Study,* New York 1969, pp. 468–73.

88. 'The Relevance of Reality', Presidential Address at the annual meeting of the Pacific Division of the American Philosophical Association, published in *Proceedings and Addresses of the APA* (College Park, Md., 1969), pp. 39–50.

89. 'La liberté et les impératifs de l'histoire', in *La liberté et l'ordre social,* Rencontres Internationales de Genève, Neuchâtel 1969, pp. 129–43, English (original) in *Studies in Critical Philosophy,* pp. 211–23.

90. 'Nicht einfach zerstören', in *Neues Forum* (Vienna, August–September 1969), vol. XVI, no. 188/189, pp. 485–8.

91. 'Student Protest is Non-violent Next to the Society Itself', in *New York Times Magazine,* 4 May 1969, p. 137.

92. 'Only a Free Arab World Can Co-exist with a Free Israel', (Introduction to the Hebrew edition of *One-Dimensional Man* and *Essay on Liberation*), published in *Israel Horizons* (June–July 1970), p. 17.

93. 'Art as Form of Reality', Guggenheim Lecture, 1969, published in *On the Future of Art. Essays by Arnold Toynbee and Others,* New York 1970, pp. 123–34; also in *New Left Review,* 74, (London, July–August 1972), pp. 51–8.

94. 'Humanismus – gibt's den noch?' in *Neues Forum,* (Vienna, April 1970), vol. XVII, no. 196, pp. 349–53.

95. 'Marxism and the New Humanity: An Unfinished Revolution', in John C. Raines and Thomas Dean, eds., *Marxism and Radical Religion: Essays Toward a Revolutionary Humanism,* Philadelphia 1970, pp. 3–10.

96. 'Dear Angela', letter to Angela Davis, published in *Ramparts,* 9, (Berkeley, February 1971), p. 22.

97. 'Charles Reich as Revolutionary Ostrich', in Philip Nobile, ed., *The Con III Controversy,* New York 1971, pp. 15–7.

98. 'The Movement in a New Era of Repression: An Assessment', speech delivered at the University of California at Berkeley, 3 February 1971, published in the *Berkeley Journal of Sociology* (Berkeley 1971/72), vol. XVI, pp. 1–14.

99. [Letters to Chicago Surrealists], October 1972, untitled and unpublished, among private papers of Herbert Marcuse.

100. 'When Law and Morality Stand in the Way', *Society,* (New Brunswick, September–October 1973), vol. 10, no. 6, pp. 23–4.

101. 'Some General Remarks on Lucien Goldmann', in *Lucien Goldmann et la sociologie de la littérature,* Brussels 1973–74, pp. 51–2.

102. 'Marxism and Feminism', lecture delivered at Stanford University, 7 March 1974, published in *Women's Studies* (Old Westbury 1974), pp. 279–88; also in *North Star* (1–15 April 1974), vol. 4, no. 15, pp. 34–41; reprinted as 'Socialist Feminism: The Hard Core of the Dream', in *Eccentric* (Eugene, November 1974), pp. 7–47.

103. 'Theorie und Praxis', lecture delivered in Frankfurt, 28 June 1974, published in *Zeit-Messungen,* pp. 21–36.

104. 'Failure of the New Left?' lecture, University of California at Irvine, April 1975, first published in German ('Scheitern der Neuen Linken?') in *Zeit-Messungen,* pp. 37–48 (translated in *New German Critique,* 18, Milwaukee, fall 1979, pp. 3–11).

105. 'Un nouvel ordre', in *Le Monde Diplomatique,* juillet 1976, no. 268.

106. 'Enttäuschung', in Günther Neske, ed., *Erinnerung an Martin Heidegger,* Pfüllingen 1977, p. 162–3.

107. 'Mord darf keine Waffen der Politik sein', in *Die Zeit,* 39 (Hamburg, 23 September 1977), pp. 41–2; (translated in *New German Critique,* 12, Milwaukee, fall 1977, pp. 7–8).

108. 'Protosozialismus und Spätkapitalismus. Versuch einer revolutions-theoretischen Synthese von Bahros Ansatz', in *Zeitschrift für Sozialdiskussion* 19 (1978), pp. 5–27; ('Protosocialism and Late Capitalism: Toward a Theoretical Synthesis Based on Bahro's Analysis') in Ulf Wolter, ed., *Rudolf Bahro. Critical Responses,* White Plains 1980, pp. 25–48.

109. 'The Reification of the Proletariat', in *Canadian Journal of Political and Social Theory* (Winnipeg 1979), vol. 3, no. 1, pp. 20–3.

Selected Interviews and Discussions

'Role of Conflict in Human Evolution: Discussion', in *Conflict in Society,* Anthony de Renck and Julie Knight, eds., London 1966, pp. 36–59; participants: Marcuse, Kenneth E. Boulding, Karl W. Deutsch, Anatol Rapoport, et al.

'Professoren als Staat-Regenten? Spiegel-Gespräch mit dem Philosophen Herbert Marcuse', in *Der Spiegel* (Hamburg, 21 August 1967), pp. 112–8.

'Herbert Marcuse und die prophetische Tradition', interview with Peter Merseberger, 23 October 1967, published in Hans Eckehard Bahr, ed., *Weltfrieden und Revolution,* Hamburg 1968, pp. 291–307.

'Le philosophe Herbert Marcuse: "maître à penser" des étudiants en colère', interview with Pierre Viansson-Ponté, published in *Le Monde,* 11 mai 1968, pp. 1, 111.

'Les étudiants se révoltent contre un mode de vie', interview with Michel Bosquet, published in *Le nouvel Observateur,* 20 mai 1968.

'Varieties of Humanism', interview with Harvey Wheeler, published in *The Center Magazine,* vol. 1, no. 5 (Santa Barbara, July 1968), pp. 13–5.

'L'Express va plus loin avec Herbert Marcuse', interview published in *L'Express,* 23 septembre 1968, pp. 54–62.

' "The father of the student rebellion"?' Interview with Robert McKenzie on Bʙᴄ, published in *The Listener,* 17 October 1968, pp. 498–9.

'Marcuse Defines His New Left Line', interview published in the *New York Times Magazine,* 27 October 1968, pp. 29, 109.

'Marcuse: Turning Point in the Struggle', interview with Robert Allen, published in *The Guardian,* New York, 9, 16, and 23 November 1968.

'Revolution 1969', interview with Heinrich von Nussbaum, published in *Neues Forum,* (Vienna, January 1969), vol. XVI, no. 181, pp. 26–9.

'Revolution aus Ekel: Spiegel-Gespräch mit dem Philosophen Herbert Marcuse', published in *Der Spiegel,* 31 (Hamburg, 28 Juli 1969), pp. 103–6.

'USA: Organisationsfrage und revolutionäres Subject', interview with Hans Magnus Enzensberger, first published in *Kursbuch,* 22 (West Berlin 1970), pp. 45–60; reprinted in *Zeit-Messungen,* pp. 51–69.

'A Conversation with Herbert Marcuse', interview with Sam Keen and John Raser, published in *Psychology Today,* 4, 9 (Del Mar, February 1971), pp. 35–40, 60–66.

'Remplacer le "travail aliéné" par la création: Un entretien avec Herbert Marcuse', interview with Pierre Dommergues and Jean-Michel Palmier, published in *Le Monde,* 10 mai 1974, pp. 22–3.

'Heidegger's Politics', interview with Frederick Olafson in San Diego, 4 May 1974, published in the *Graduate Faculty Philosophy Journal* (New York, winter 1977), vol. 6, no. 1, pp. 28–40.

'Ist eine Welt ohne Angst möglich? Aus einem Streitgespräch zwischen [Cᴅᴜ-General-Sekretär Kurt H.] Bredenkopf, Marcuse, und [Psychoanalytiker Alexander] Mitscherlich', in Düsseldorf, published in *Der Spiegel* 37 (Hamburg, 6 September 1976), p. 199.

Gespräche mit Herbert Marcuse, Frankfurt-am-Main 1978; discussions with Jürgen Habermas, Silvia Bovenschen, *et al.,* held between 1975 and 1977.

'Un pyromane à la retraite', discussion with Jean Marabini, published in *Le Monde,* 19 novembre 1978.

'Marcuse and the Frankfurt School', in Brian Magee, *Men of Ideas: Some Creators of Contemporary Philosophy,* London 1978, pp. 60–73.

Nᴏᴛᴇ: Several extremely useful compilations of secondary works exist. See expecially the extensive bibliography in Morton Schoolman, *The Imaginary Witness: The Critical Theory of Herbert Marcuse,* New York 1980; François H. LaPointe, 'Bibliographic Essay', *Journal of the British Society for Phenomenology* (Manchester), 4, 1973, pp. 191–4; and François and Claire LaPointe, 'Herbert Marcuse and His Critics', *International Studies in Philosophy* (Binghamton), 7, 1975, pp. 183–96.

INDEX

231

232

234